MANAGING RETIREMENT

The Surprising Opportunities and Challenges

Howard Shank

CONTEMPORARY
BOOKS, INC.
CHICAGO

Library of Congress Cataloging in Publication Data

Shank, Howard.
    Managing retirement.

    1. Retirement—United States.   I. Title.
HQ1062.S53   1985   646.7'9   84-29223
ISBN 0-8092-5336-4

Adaptation of chart on page 222 of *Pathfinders* © 1981 by
Gail Sheehy by permission of William Morrow & Company.

Published by Contemporary Books, Inc.
180 North Michigan Avenue, Chicago, Illinois 60601
Manufactured in the United States of America
Library of Congress Catalog Card Number: 84-29223
International Standard Book Number: 0-8092-5336-4

Published simultaneously in Canada by Beaverbooks, Ltd.
195 Allstate Parkway, Valleywood Business Park
Markham, Ontario L3R 4T8 Canada

CONTENTS

PREFACE

WHAT THIS BOOK IS.
WHAT IT ISN'T.

Fair Warning to Prospective
Buyers and Readers:
You May Want to Demand Your Money Back

This is a book about retirement. But it is not what publishers call an "all about" book.

If you want information about Social Security, investments, your budget, insurance, or senior citizen discounts, I am not your man. And this is not your book.

There is no health advice here. I leave diet, exercise, and other health-related matters to you, your doctor, and your conscience. Particularly your conscience.

You will find nothing in these pages about easel painting, stamp collecting, gardening, or any other hobby, although I'll send you a list of such books if you send me a letter and a stamped return envelope.

Furthermore, this book will tell you nothing of practical value about geography, climate, or real estate.

What you have in your hand is not even sociology, history, philosophy, psychology, or psychiatry, although you will find all those subjects represented here.

The Gut Issues

Instead, the premise of the pages to follow is that the tough problems in retirement are those of the spirit, the emotions, and the attitudes. You can be rich, you can live in the ideal house in the ideal climate, you can pass every health test your doctor has in his repertoire, and you can still be miserable.

Or just the opposite can be true.

This is a ball game of the head, the heart, and the gut.

The Surmountable Opportunity

I can't put my central thesis into words without sounding like Pollyanna or Goody Two Shoes. Too bad. Here it is, nonetheless:

Retirement is one of the opportunities of your lifetime, a unique chance for satisfaction and self-fulfillment.

It is a chance to grow as a human being as you've never grown before.

It is a chance to achieve the heretofore unachievable.

It is a time to enrich your spirit, to set your own agenda, to be your own boss, to serve yourself by serving others—to name just a few things.

Unique as the opportunity is, it has one thing in common with all other opportunities: You have to work at it—and just when you thought you'd stopped working.

For one thing, you need to work at getting your facts straight. Mass retirement is so new that no one's head is free of myths and misconceptions.

You need to take inventory of what you'll lose when you leave your job. The more you understand why you feel down in the mouth, the easier it is to get yourself out of it.

You need to take a fresh look at your values and priorities. The more you depended on your job for emotional satisfaction, the more urgent this task is.

You need to take a hard, fresh look at your marriage and you need to do it in concert with your partner.

You need to rediscover how creative you are, how good you are at problem-solving. This is not as easy as it sounds but it will be one of the most rewarding parts of your work. That's a promise.

How This Book Is Designed to Help

Part I of this book looks briefly at the folklore of retirement— most of it out of date—and it tries to set the record straight. Some facts are bound to bring you up short. For example, the idea that older people are poorer than everybody else just ain't so anymore. Nor is it true that retirement kills. As you'll see.

Part II deals with what you lose when you leave your job, the idea being to get your guard up. You're in for some surprises. I don't know which of the losses will surprise you, but I guarantee that some of them will. No matter how smart, how thoughtful, how foresighted you are, you will be surprised.

Part III tells you how your retirement will affect your spouse. (Though written primarily for men, some principles apply for women as well.) You will get some insight into what *your* new life will do to *her* life—her schedule, her privacy, her freedom, her sense of her place in the world. Most of us who are now retired had never thought about that. Alas.

Part IV talks about the retirement opportunity in detail and in specifics.

In Part V, I instruct you on how to read the next three parts of this book. And I warn you that you are in for a lot of Dutch-uncle-type talk.

Part VI urges you to work in your retirement and it ventures to dispense wisdom on how to do it. Some of this is wisdom that I have earned the hard way, by making mistakes. Most of it is the wisdom of others.

Part VII comes back to the subject of your retirement, your wife, and your marriage. What do you get from being willing to change? What does she get? What do the two of you stand to gain from changing together? How can *you* change?

Part VIII is dedicated to this proposition: that your retirement will be a lot easier if you prepare your emotions beforehand. And it offers some key thoughts on how to do it.

Part IX is the longest part of the book. There are twenty-five retirement stories here, twenty-nine retired people in all. Here you will meet a retired president of the United States and a retired career secretary; an ex-astronaut and a former railroad worker; several big-wheel executives; and the first set of grandparents ever to wheel a motorcycle around the entire perimeter of the Lower Forty-Eight.

I have picked these twenty-nine people to make one transcendent point: It is not your used-to-bes that count when you retire. What does count is your gumption quotient. As you will see.

Part X—very short—tells you a little of what happened to me in my first five years of retirement—and draws an obvious moral for your consideration.

For all that I dish up a lot of wisdom here, I do so with this thought firmly in mind: wisdom is in no way the be-all and end-all at any stage of life.

I agree with Ecclesiastes: "In much wisdom is much grief."

And with Ecclesiasticus: "The joyfulness of man prolongeth his days."

I wish you joy in retirement. In the end, that's the wisest I know how to be.

ACKNOWLEDGMENTS

THANK YOUS.
A BIG BOUQUET.
A DEDICATION OF SORTS.

To fire poison "arrows" at our fellows: ah, how we relish it!

Our quiver takes up . . . *how* many pages in our unabridged dictionaries? God knows. We English-speakers have always been creative.

Try these. Out loud. *Addlepate, balloon head, cretin, dog's breakfast, egomaniac, fly-by-night, goon, hellhound, ingrate, jack-anapes, killjoy, lightweight, miasma, nice-Nellie, offal, pestilence, quitter, reprobate, self-seeker, timeserver, undercutter, virago, whiner, Xantippe, yellowbelly, zero.* See how resoundingly they roll off your tongue?

When it's time to toss bouquets, though, the vocabulary falls flat, lacks pow, wants wallop.

Yet toss I must.

I cannot send this book off to press until I pass out orchids where orchids are due.

Reader, believe it. There is *hope* for the human race.

In the three years it has taken me to bring this book into being, hundreds of people have helped me with no thought of *quid pro quo*.

Friends have egged me on, shared experiences, lavished their wisdom and good wishes on me.

Bare acquaintances have taken the time to open doors for me, recruit respondents for me.

Dinner partners have heard me out far past the point of common courtesy. And they have taught me things I badly needed to know.

Some thirty retired people have spent hours, even days, with me, talking to me and my tape machine, showing me unfailing patience and good humor. You'll find their stories all through these pages.

As a body, these men and women have shown me awesome quantities of *acuity, benevolence, courage, dedication, excellence, fairness, goodness, heart, industry, joy, kindness, love, motivation, niceness, openness, patience, quality, resilience, selflessness, tolerance, undauntability, virtue, warmness, xenophilia* (I had to make that one up, but it's apt), *youthfulness, zeal.*

They have given me a downright uplifting experience. I am grateful to them all.

I dedicate this book, therefore, to the sink-proof, shrink-proof human spirit.

May it *never* retire!

INTRODUCTION

ANSWERS TO QUESTIONS YOU OUGHT TO ASK— IF YOU HAVEN'T ALREADY

"Who, for heaven's sake, is Howard Shank?"

"What qualifies Shank to give me advice on retirement? Where does it say he's a doctor of this, that, or the other?"

"Who says I need advice anyway?"

"And what if I don't *want* to retire?"

Good questions. If you were Howard Shank and I were you, I'd be asking the same things. Retirement ought to be approached with a light heart—but ought not to be taken lightly.

I, Howard Shank, am an ex-advertising man, of all things. June 15, 1984, was the fifth anniversary of my retirement. Within those five years, I went through the following phases:

1. A honeymoon. Brief.

2. Terminal boredom. B-o-r-e-d-o-m.

3. Mindless bursts of activity. Clutching at straws.

4. A significant period of self-examination. "Who am I *now*?" "What am I?" All those momentous questions. As you read along, you'll learn more about what went on in my head.

5. A time of searching for professional experts on the psychology and philosophy of retirement. (I found none.) "Don't expect too much from psychiatry," Dr. Paul Pruyser of The Menninger Foundation said to me. "Retirement is too new. We are still learning, as is everybody else."

6. Resolution day. The day I decided to learn all I could about the problems and opportunities of retirement and to write a book about it.

7. Two years of research. Thousands of hours of reading, conversing, interviewing, poking around in my own head. A year of writing. The three happiest years of my life.

Research and writing were not new to me. In my thirty-seven years in the advertising business, I had learned more than you will ever want to know about such arcana as the following: the psychological differences among dog feeders, the emotional effects of having acne, the symbolism of sandwich-making in the lives of homemakers. I had been father, grandfather, or godfather to Charlie the Tuna, the Marlboro Man, the Man from Glad, the Keebler Elves, the Green Giant and the Little Green Sprout, Morris the Cat, Tony the Tiger, Poppin' Fresh the Pillsbury Doughboy. As president and chief creative officer of Leo Burnett Company, I daily dealt with these and some two hundred other trade characters and trade names. You might say—and you'd be right—that I earned my living all those years by being curious and asking a million questions.

I hear you: "OK, OK," you say. "So you've learned a thing or two about retirement and retired people. But you don't know a thing about *me*. What makes you think *I* have to know what you know?"

I don't say that. God forbid.

I say only that you, like all the rest of us, have a big opportunity in front of you, a once-in-a-lifetime opportunity. If you know exactly what that opportunity is, if you know exactly what problems will stand in your way, if you have your plan and program all nailed down, if you are neither starry-eyed nor unduly pessimistic about your future—if all those things are true, you certainly don't need this book. Good luck and Godspeed!

I have written this book for the following kinds of people:

1. People for whom retirement was or will be mandatory.

2. People who have retired or will retire by choice—early or otherwise.

3. People who have looked upon retirement day as the beginning of a perpetual vacation and couldn't or can't wait for it to start.

4. People who equate retirement day with the end of usefulness and fear the consequences.

5. People who think retirement may, indeed, be an opportunity and want to do everything they can not to miss the opportunity.

To these people, I promise only this: By the time you have heard me out, you will know a good deal more about yourself and retirement than you do now. That knowledge couldn't hurt. And it could, just could, help a lot.

One more thing before we get down to the business at hand. I know this book talks a lot about retirement-as-opportunity. But this does not mean that I think you should retire. You say you have the option to keep your job as long as you like and you're happy about that? Wonderful! You've got my vote. And you're excused from further reading.

Otherwise . . . turn the page.

I
FICTION, FOLKLORE, FANTASIES,
and Other Cultural Baggage We Bring to Retirement

YOUR MOTHER
DIDN'T RAISE
YOU TO
RETIRE

Your mother may have cried on your first day of school, but that didn't mean she wanted you to come back to the nest. Hardly. She had only one direction in mind for you.

Up.

She saw you working your way up through the grades, up the ladder of success, up the social scale. You were to work your way up to riches, up to fame. You were to present her with grandchildren and they were to follow you right on up in the world. You were, in short, to be the embodiment of the American dream.

Which did not include retirement.

If and when people retired in those days, they did so because they were too old and too sick to get their bodies to work any longer. Even the rich kept on working when they got rich and they

3

put their sons to work early (think of the Rockefellers). Sure, all work and no play were bad for you. Everyone agreed to that. That's what Sundays and vacations were for.

Don't blame your mother.

She was only doing it for your own good. She knew it was for your own good because her mother and father had said so, her husband said so, her teachers had said so. And whoever the President was, he surely thought so. (Theodore Roosevelt said, "I pity the creature who doesn't work—at whatever end of the social scale.")

Of course, Higher Authority had been in favor of work from the very beginning. The Reverend Mr. Henry Ward Beecher summed up the wisdom of the ages when he said:

"When God wanted sponges and oysters, He made them, and put one on a rock, and the other in the mud. When He made man, He did not make him to be a sponge or an oyster; He made him with feet, and hands, and head, and vital blood, and a place to use them, and said to him, 'Go, work.' "

If, for any reason, such sentiments did not provide enough ammunition to suit your mother, she had only to go to her dictionary of quotations for further reinforcement from secular authorities:

"Blessed is he who has found his work; let him ask no other blessedness. He has a life purpose."

—Thomas Carlyle

"The Russian Socialist Federated Soviet Republic declares labor the duty of all citizens of the U.S.S.R."

—Constitution of the U.S.S.R.

Retirement, on the other hand, has never inspired any quotations deemed worthy of Bartlett's or the Oxford Dictionary of Quotations. You can search all you like and you'll find nothing about moving to Florida and playing golf every day.

Indeed, among the couple of thousand novels I have read, I remember only two that presented retired men as heroes: Sinclair Lewis's *Dodsworth* and Arnold Bennett's *Mr. Prohack*. But even Sam Dodsworth and Arthur Prohack were not heroes because they retired. On the contrary. Both men suffered mightily when sudden riches—and their wives—seduced them into retiring. Their triumph was in overcoming these setbacks and in, by golly, going back to work.

Horatio Alger would have approved.

A SHORT PREHISTORY
OF THE WORK ETHIC

Actually, man's devotion to work antedates the Old Testament by a million and a half years, more or less. My theory is that it all began when we got hooked on meat.

Somewhere along the path of evolution, *Homo sapiens* had the first brainstorm. He saw that he didn't have to wait for chance to present him with a drumstick or ham or steak. He could fire away with rocks or find a hole in the ground and cover it over and hope that something would fall in. That's how hunting, trapping, and serious meat-eating got started and that's how work was invented.

We could have gone another way.

If, like the gorilla branch of the family tree, our old folks had elected to go on living in the easy, or herbivorous, way, all would have been different. When a gorilla gets hungry, he reaches up to the tree or bush he is bright enough to lie under and there it is— the original fast food. Gorillas do not retire. They have nothing to retire *from*.

Ah, well.

The next milepost for man was this: the inventor of work got a taste for rewards beyond survival.

Creature comfort entered the picture first. And status was not far behind. The truth of the following propositions became self-evident:

Some is good. More is better.
A meal is good. A feast is better.
One fur is good. Two are showier.
And so on.

What early man wanted and needed—already to want was to need—was a better rock and a deeper pit. So he invented tools, including that guided missile of the rock-throwing age, the spear.

With the creation of the sharp rock and other technologies, the rat race was on. To be sure, it took tens of thousands of years to get from the Old Stone Age through the New Stone Age and from there to the Bronze Age, but there was no turning back. The plow, the wheel, the boat, the domesticated animal, the cookpot, the bow and arrow—all came in the wink of an eye as we measure human history.

There quickly followed such giddy added motivators as the glorification of self, wealth for wealth's sake, and the ever-higher standard of living.

And era by era, the compulsion to work burrowed its way deep in the genetic coding of the species.

There you have, simply explained, a large part of the problem we retired people face today.

Is it any wonder, do you think, that we human beings need a hell of a lot of moral stamina to retire and enjoy it?

WHY WE RETIRED PEOPLE STILL FEAR THE POORHOUSE

Until a generation ago, retirement was not an option, except for a handful of the rich.

People scrimped and saved all their lives and still wound up with one—and only one—solid economic asset: a body that worked. When the body stopped working, the savings started melting and the children began getting the spare room ready.

That's what people had in mind when they used to claim, "My ambition in life is to die with my boots on."

Even the handful who did build a nice nest egg had no guarantee that it would last. George Washington had to let go of prime real estate at fire-sale prices in order to make ends meet when he left the presidency. Thomas Jefferson was worse than broke when he died—he was up to his ears in debt and his heirs had to sell Monticello to settle accounts.

You didn't have to be famous to go through the wringer, either. Plenty of ordinary people were wiped out by cyclical economic crises.

Starting in our great-great-grandparents' time, America suffered the busts of 1836–37, 1847, 1857, 1862, 1873, 1882, 1890, 1900, 1907, 1913–14, and 1920. Ancestral anecdotes about those times rang in our parents' ears when we were growing up, but they didn't need stories about the bad old days to learn how to worry. They had the Great Depression.

And worry is not yet dead. A lot of people continue to speak of retirement and the poorhouse in the same breath. For example:

Dr. Robert N. Butler, physician, researcher, psychiatrist, first director of the National Institute on Aging, was a Depression child, raised on the edge of poverty by a widowed grandmother. He wrote a book called *Why Survive?* Its dust jacket says, in part:

> To look face-to-face at what it is to grow old in this country is to look at our own futures, and this is more than we can bear. In most instances, to be old is to be poor.

Simone de Beauvoir had her full share of age paranoia. Dr. Paul Pruyser of The Menninger Foundation wrote of her:

> [She] perceived a societal conspiracy against the aged, particularly those who are forced into retirement, in which people are put on the shelves, kicked upstairs if they are lucky . . . and grossly exploited economically.

Those are true children of the Great Depression speaking and we other Depression children do not laugh at them—far from it. We *identify* with them.

One of these days, someone younger is going to speak up. He or she is going to say to you and me and all the others who grew up in the thirties, "Hey, you guys! Wake up, it's all over. There's been a *revolution!* It's OK to retire now!"

When Declaration Day does come, the speaker's blockbuster fact is going to be this:

In 1983, older people, the people sixty-five and older, became the most affluent age segment in the United States.

In fact, the speaker will add, eighty-five percent of such people were financially independent in 1983. They may not have had a lot of money, but they had enough. And they were in no danger of having to live off their children.

The speaker is going to tell us, moreover, that older people can now afford to retire from paid work in droves. Between 1972 and 1982, the percentage of people over sixty-five who still had to work for money *went down from fifty percent to twenty-five percent.*

For such things to happen, we Americans, like it or not, had to participate in a second American Revolution.

We had to take a whole new approach to the creation and distribution of wealth.

We had to adopt a hybrid economic system which we may as well call sociocapitalism.

We had to take the federal and other governments right up to the window with us on payday. Who, in Depression days, predicted all that? Not even Franklin Delano Roosevelt.

Thus the game today is very different from the one that our parents and their parents and their parents' parents played.

Like it or not, Social Security benefits are with us to stay and they keep rising with the consumer price index.

Like it or not, our employers, our labor unions, and our governments are putting money away for our retirements and they are putting it away by the bushel.

Like it or not, Washington is doing its not-so-bad best to protect us from bank failures, from predatory businesses, from hanky-panky in the stock market, from disasters either natural or man-made.

Like it or not, our national appetite for the consumption of goods and services is still looking for its upper limit.

And like it or not, you and I—all of us—are committed to a policy of peace-by-deterrent, which generates jobs, incomes, and taxes at a rate that would have rendered Franklin Roosevelt sleepless.

In spite of all this, it may be that your retirement money will run out and that mine will and that we'll go to the poorhouse together.

It may also be that hell will freeze over.

In truth, the real goblins of retirement must be lurking behind some other tree.

The health tree, perhaps?

THE KILLER MYTH:
IT'S TIME
TO RETIRE IT

The most dogged and durable of the myths about retirement is this: it will kill you.

Or, if it doesn't kill you outright, it will smite you hard and take away your physical independence.

This is not superstition, not lay ignorance speaking. Dr. Valery A. Portnoi, writing in the *Journal of the American Medical Association* (1981) said this:

> The common belief, held by the medical community and lay persons alike [is] that retirement has a profound negative effect on the health of the retired person.

Dr. George Wendel, my internist and a thoroughly modern man, said this to me: "These patients of mine, these bright, alert, active, attractive people retire and they become vegetables. Vegetables! They put on the slippers, they sit in front of the TV, they eat too much, they drink too much, they gain weight, their blood pressure goes up, they invite cardiovascular disease, they get more and more bored, and they just become vegetables! I want to get them outside and kick their asses around the block."

Royal Little, former chairman of Textron, also uses sharp words: "I don't believe in retiring," he told the *Wall Street Journal*. "I've had friends who ran big corporations. They went off to Florida or somewhere, and in four or five years they were dead. Their minds died first, then their bodies. That's not for me."

When, in the 1980s, we marshal the facts about health and retirement, our old idea is exposed for what it is—positively medieval, as out-of-date as that other medieval notion, that the earth is the center of the universe. Witness:

1. An American worker can expect to spend an average of nineteen years in retirement, a quarter of his lifetime. And that nineteen years is heading toward twenty-five in 2000 A.D. (Portnoi)

2. Among 257 people, 40 percent saw their health *improve* with retirement and another 37 percent experienced no change. (*American Journal of Public Health*)

3. We are in the middle of a longevity epidemic. Americans today are living an average of twenty-six years longer than Americans did in 1900. Indeed, the fastest-growing age segment is those eighty-five and older.

4. In 1982, eighty-five percent of all people over sixty-five were still running their own lives, still physically independent. Another

ten percent were able to stay home with some help. These numbers include *all* people over sixty-five.

5. We have won all but total victory over such diseases as influenza, pneumonia, tuberculosis, typhoid and paratyphoid fever, diphtheria, polio, and scarlet fever.

6. We are still waiting for total victory over cancer and heart disease, to be sure, but medical scientists have won dozens of less-than-total victories. Significant discoveries create headlines almost weekly.

7. Our new ability to stay physically independent is, arguably, the most heartening news of all. Doctors today can help us cope with arthritic knees and hips, with cataracts, with hearing loss, with dental disease, with high blood pressure, with coronary artery disease, and with dozens of the lesser ailments which plagued earlier generations as they aged. The odds that we will live quality lives in retirement are improving geometrically.

In the face of all this, why is retirement still regarded so widely as hazardous to our health?

One reason, I think, is that we grew up at a time when retirement and "old, sick, and poor" were synonymous. People retired when they grew too sick or feeble to work; it was a tiny minority who could afford to retire on any other basis. It is understandable that we saw cause and effect in this.

Indeed, one of the most striking facts in Dr. Portnoi's piece has to do with a confusion of cause and effect. A medical research team set out to analyze a group of people who had died of heart attacks soon after retiring. Their assumption was that retirement was the cause of these deaths. To their surprise, they discovered that the truth was exactly the other way around—these people had retired when they did because they already had heart disease!

Dr. Portnoi offers a second reason in his article. There is a medical phenomenon called "the giving up–given up" complex. Severe emotional stress, such as some people suffer when they retire, can cause feelings of helplessness and hopelessness. This, in turn, can lay the distressed person open to "activation of neurally-regulated biological processes potentially conducive to disease." Portnoi notes, however, that even this reaction can be prevented by solid preparation for retirement.

My point here has nothing to do with guarantees. No one guarantees us good health in retirement or any other time.

My point is that the odds have turned spectacularly in our favor.

We may not have nineteen years of life in retirement and we may not spend our last nineteen years at the peak of our physical powers. But the odds say that we will have the time and the physical resources to move a lot of mountains before we're through—*if* we prepare ourselves early and well—a subject we will come back to in the middle section of this book.

TOO OLD

Old is often a good thing to be, as in old pro, old master, old fox. The Old Man is a synonym for Boss. Older, wiser heads rule the world.

Too old is flatly bad. It is a putdown, always used so, always understood so.

"Retirement," in our society, is a code word for too old.

No matter how fond the farewell party, the message is clear: "Too bad you're too old. But face it. You're too old to build any plans around, too old to stand the gaff, too old to be worth your salt any more. Go in good health—but, for God's sake, go. Oh, and take it easy."

The trouble comes when we agree, "Yep, too old to work now," and use that estimation as a measuring stick for every chance that comes along thereafter. People do that. Here are two examples:

A friend told me about his father's retirement. The father was a crack accountant with a long career, a man heaped with honors. "I have a promotional brochure in my desk somewhere," my friend said, "something about La Jolla. Dad and Mother are on the cover of it, walking hand in hand down the beach, sporting big smiles. It wouldn't be worth mentioning, except for one thing. That's the only smile I saw on Dad from the day he retired until the day he died. He would get up in the morning, read the newspapers a couple of times and that was it. He never could think of another thing to do."

Leland and Martha Bradford wrote a book entitled *Retirement: Coping with Emotional Upheavals*. It cites the experience of a bus driver who retired to Florida after years of anticipation. It was honeymoon time, at first. Then the man began to miss his old route, miss his long-time customers. "He began to realize," the Bradfords say, "how important his work had been in the lives of many. He realized that he had had pride in his work. Nothing took its place for him. He didn't find situations in which he felt he had significance in other people's lives. He didn't try very hard. He lost his self-respect and was unhappy for the few remaining years he lived."

We learn young about priorities: "Eat your spinach first, then you'll get ice cream." "Do your homework first, then you'll go to the movie."

When we've been working for half a lifetime, no one has to tell us, "Finish the report first, then you can go home."

By the time we should be thinking about retirement, we have dedicated ourselves heart and soul to the proposition that everything revolves around The Job. And therein lies a major problem for us.

We have let our career become synonymous with life itself. It is not just a livelihood. It is sport, pastime, hobby, lover. It provides our friends and our social life. It sets our goals, defines our ambitions, gives us our report cards. Slowly, seductively, it comes to define the very word "important."

Then we get too old for the job and what have we left? If we retire with the conviction that we're too old to do anything new, too old to undertake anything important—what then?

A fourth of a lifetime is a lot of years to sit around in the sun, pining for the good old days. It is also the one sure way to *become* too old.

II
WHAT
YOU'LL MOURN
at the End of the Job

AFTER THE
HONEYMOON

The feeling of retirement, at first, is like the feeling of playing hooky. Naughty. Nice.

It delights our spirit to do anything the working class can't. To ignore the alarm clock, duck the rush hour, let the telephone ring, stop the paper avalanche. To play. To loaf.

Then comes the day we discover the truth that Mark Twain's Huckleberry Finn discovered before us: hooky-playing as a way of life is *boring*.

"OK," we say. "Enough." And we make our resolutions. *Now* we will get down to systematic reading or fishing or golf practice or getting things organized or to whatever other job substitutes we may have put on our lists. The time has come, we see, to get serious about retirement.

When I made my own to-do list, it seemed long enough and real enough to me. I did want to paint, to practice my tennis and golf, to learn to use a computer, to write. I yearned to get on top of my personal affairs. And there was always reading for me, reading and lots of it.

After a few days' flurry, I discovered that I still was bored. Worse, there was nothing on my list that I could not easily put off, nothing that fit my definition of the word "important."

I grew depressed and listless. In fact, I went into mourning, although the word did not occur to me then.

Where did I go wrong?

Oddly—it seemed odd to me then—it was not the job I missed so acutely. I had absolutely no urge to call up my old associates and say, "Hey, I made a mistake." Even in the trough of my depression, I never second-guessed my decision to retire.

The mistake I did make was to put first things second and second things first. When I wrote down my to-do list, I was writing possible solutions—to what I didn't yet know. It never occurred to me that I had skipped Step One: identifying the problems of no longer being a jobholder.

Those problems are what this part is all about.

I offer you this analysis not to throw cold water on your retirement honeymoon. Rather, I hope it will help you get your personal problem-solving done faster than I did and that you can get on sooner with the opportunity part of your new life.

You know the truism, "A problem well-stated is a problem half solved." Don't scorn it just because it's trite. Truisms get to be truisms because they are so damn true.

THE UNQUIET INSTINCT FOR SURVIVAL

To retire is to perform an unnatural act. It flies straight in the face of our genetic coding and our childhood training.

We know from birth that a nipple is not a faucet and that we have to work at it to make it work. We learn about hands and spoons and what they have to do with puréed spinach long before we're weaned. We learn because we want to and because our parents know we must.

Much of our preschool play is rehearsal for the work to come. We stack blocks and put pegs in holes for the same reason that cheetah cubs stalk each other and strive to surprise. They and we are pushing toward independence. We will outlive our parents. We must be able to live without them.

This imperative was a guest on all the big, teary occasions involving us: the first day of school, the first date, graduations, the wedding, anything that came under the heading of leaving the nest. Our parents mourned the diminution of our needing them but they celebrated as well. Their child was becoming free and freestanding.

Dr. Paul Pruyser of The Menninger Foundation says: ". . . In our culture, we are exhorted to be maximally independent. The ideal of maturity prescribes self-sufficiency, self-help, competence in managing one's own affairs, a display of unshakable strength in the face of adversity, the ability to seek and organize one's own pleasures and to ward off pain effectively, skill in seeking our own sources of contact and support, capacity for making friends, ability to earn one's own money. . . ."

We comply with all of that. For sixty-odd years we live by the oldest law of them all, "Them as works eats." Suddenly we stop working and all hell breaks loose.

In an ideal world, the old law would be repealed the moment we retire. A new law would say, "Them as works hard till age sixty or more may also eat—even while taking it easy."

But the world is not ideal. Our survival instinct simply refuses to retire when we do.

Inner voices yell at us. "You let them defang you, you let them declaw you. You *let* them! Now you can't do for yourself anymore. Who else will?"

If this sounds overstated, listen again to Paul Pruyser:

"If loving and working are pillars to health maintenance, as Freud said, *the reduction or stoppage of work undermines the very structure of personality.*"

The drive to keep working can find bizarre outlets. A recent Ann Landers column featured a letter from a woman whose husband was new to retirement. The lady was going bonkers. Little by little, she complained, he was taking out his need to work on all *her* jobs around the house. What had happened to send her off to write a letter? That morning, her husband had wakened her at 6:00 A.M. by running the vacuum under her side of the bed.

Sooner or later we, too, will face the question, "What will you work at when you retire?" The answer had better be good. The last one-fourth of our lives is at stake.

RETIREMENT AND
SEX APPEAL

We now enter the realm of high speculation. Be warned.

Sex appeal exists. It exists as romantic love exists, as intuition exists. We know it exists, we have a name for it and we use the name as familiarly as we use words like "money" and "power." We attribute sex appeal to people we know and to people we will meet only in the media. This person has sex appeal in spades. That person has the sex appeal of a green persimmon.

The problem is, we can't prove what we know.

Not being able to prove its existence, we get into never-never land for fair when we try to show that retirement affects sex appeal or does not.

Please note: the question here is *not* whether sex goes on after retirement. It does—there is plenty of testimony to that on my bookshelves and among my clippings. Gerontologists assure us that the practice of sexual intercourse is limited not by age but by individual interest. (Remember Strom Thurmond. Remember William O. Douglas.)

But sex *appeal* after retirement? The experts stand mute. I have found only two references to the subject:

1. Henry Kissinger is widely quoted as having said that power is "the ultimate aphrodisiac."

2. Dr. Morris Chafetz, a Washington psychiatrist, says that power is indeed an aphrodisiac: "Men who do not look attractive before they achieve power suddenly have great attractiveness for women, an appeal they lose the moment they leave power."

If Dr. Chafetz is right—and he sounds right to me—I suspect that the sex appeal of power goes straight back to the origins of our species. A million-plus years ago, there must have been an enormous premium on a hunter's strength, endurance, and stealth. The more deadly the hunter, the more meat he could put in front of his loved ones. The equation is persuasive. In nature, everything alive follows the same survival strategy: pass on the genes of the fittest.

The red deer of the island of Rhon give us an example of the way nature works, and the example is strikingly relevant. Only the biggest, strongest, most heavily antlered of red deer may command the nubile does. As long as a boss deer can face down the younger fellows, the females permit him to keep them tightly herded when they are in estrus. Their fauns-to-be depend for survival on a legacy of blue ribbon genes.

Sooner or later, however, mandatory retirement comes along in the form of stronger muscles, deadlier antlers, and steelier determination. Hello, young lover. Goodbye, old fellow.

As I write, I think of my long-ago girlfriend, Christine. A practical child of practical Paris, Christine had a computer in her head with which she classified every man she ever met.

A man was either handsome or ugly. Wise or foolish. A dancer or a nondancer. Well-spoken or badly spoken. It was all either/or with her.

It was better, of course, to rate high in as many of her categories as possible, but a man could surmount a lot of shortcomings if only he ranked high in seriousness.

Christine might say of someone, "He is as ugly as a frog and he dances like a frog and a woman might kiss him all she likes and he would never look and dance like a prince, but I tell you he is a serious man!" And she might be willing to kiss any such man just to demonstrate her approval.

If I had met Christine not when I did but rather at someone's dinner table after my retirement, it would have taken her perhaps ninety seconds to discover that I no longer worked for a living. Her computer would have whirred and, although she might have found me worthy in other respects, I would have entered her memory bank under "Not Serious."

Adieu, Howard.

If you are hell-bent on finding reasons to fear, to resent, to feel down in the mouth about retirement, this one will do nicely for openers. It is guaranteed to strike right at the heart of your self-esteem.

Never mind that Gail Sheehy did a massive survey of men and women from sixteen to seventy+ and found that the happiest years of a lifetime begin right around retirement age.

Who wants to be happy if he's worried about his sex appeal?

POWERLESSNESS

We Americans like personal power as much as anyone. We don't admit that. We feel we can't admit it to ourselves, let alone to the world at large. "Power is the taboo subject of the age, much the way sex once was," according to *New York Times* writer, Bryce Nelson.

"Taboo" may be a strong word but that doesn't mean it's an inappropriate word. Not only is power an aphrodisiac, it is a turn-on in other ways. "The holding of power compares to a heroin high," says a Washington psychiatrist. "Exercising power is the most effective short-range antidepressant in the world," says Dr. Bertram E. Brown. "The more resources you control the better you feel," says Dr. David Kipnis.

If we can't admit to liking any of that decadent-sounding stuff, how can we admit that we hate to give it up? Who wants anyone to think he is power mad? Or drunk with power? Nonetheless, the loss of power does depress, according to Dr. George H. Pollack, and our own eyes and ears confirm what he says.

Consider the politicians we've seen on television, speaking to us just as the power had eluded them.

Think of the look you saw on Adlai Stevenson's face when he said, "It hurts too much to cry."

Think of Lyndon Johnson, announcing his decision not to run again. He says he must devote his time to getting us out of Viet Nam. But he knows, and we know he knows, that he cannot win in 1968. He chooses to resign in effect rather than endure defeat. He does not put his sadness and depression into words. Of course not. But the tone of his voice and the look on his face leave no room for doubt about his feelings.

Think of Jimmy Carter on election morning, 1980. He is addressing his neighbors in Plains but the network cameras are rolling. He speaks of his long-held desire to make his fellow townsmen proud of him. His voice breaks. He puts a hand to his face and turns away for four beats before he can resume. The polling places are barely open but the word from his private pollsters is overwhelming: he has lost the office.

Anyone who wants to deny that he likes power will see an easy out at this point. All he has to do is claim he never sought power, never had much, never wanted to be president or chairman or commanding officer, never ached to be a big frog in a big puddle. How, then, may he be accused of liking power?

The answer to that question is another question: Who ever said that power has to be big to be beautiful?

Nietzsche said, "Life [itself] is will to power" and "Wherever I found a living creature, there I found the will to power."

Emerson said, "Men, such as they are, very naturally seek money or power, and power because it is as good as money."

William Hazlitt said, "To do anything, to dig a hole in the ground, to plant a cabbage, to hit the mark, to move a shuttle, to work a pattern—in a word, to attempt to produce any effect, and to succeed, has something in it that gratifies the lover of power."

If we accept what Nietzsche, Emerson, and Hazlitt say, we might as well deny that we need food, clothing, and shelter as deny that we need power. We see that power is more than the ability to send millions to Siberia or to save thousands from polio; more than the prerogative to hire and fire at will; more than the charisma it takes to walk into an arena and bring a crowd to its feet, clapping, stamping, and cheering.

Every talent, every skill, every body of knowledge confers power on its owner. Even the man who comes to take away our garbage has us in his power. Fortunately, he almost always uses that power to do good.

In time, every variety of power, malign or benign, hooks its holder. It defines him to others and to himself. It commands respect. It reassures him, says that he has some control over his own destiny. It gives any sort of work its goal, its meaning, its reward. That may have been what Emerson meant when he said, "Power is the first good."

If we get fixated on a single kind of power, if we feel in our gut that the only kind of power worth having is the kind that goes with our job, we are in trouble, like the La Jolla accountant and the Florida bus driver.

If, on the other hand, we see that we have other important powers or that there are other good places to use the powers we know best, then we are looking straight in the eye of opportunity.

The choice of viewpoint is ours.

Therefore, the fault is ours if we make the bad choice.

PURPOSELESSNESS

"I won't know what to do with myself."

Those are the words about retirement that I hear most often, but I hear others that have the same sad ring: "It will bore me silly." "I'll have too much time on my hands." "I'm not like you—I don't have a lot of interests." "My job is the only thing I know how to do." "More than a week of vacation and I'm ready to go back to work."

That is fear I'm hearing.

People who talk that way are dead right to be afraid. What they predict for themselves in retirement is a life without central point or purpose and they are sure bets to fulfill their own prophecy.

Then there are the ostrich types. They take a different road to trouble:

"Me worry about retirement? Hah! I can't wait. I'll sleep late. I'll wake up laughing at the thought of all those people still commuting. I'll hunt, fish, play golf, travel, catch up on my reading, go to ball games, have the time of my life. I've earned it. I'm gonna do it."

A former ostrich, George Stege, wrote the following about his first try at retirement.

"On December 31, 1949, I had quit my job as Director of Sales for the Pepsodent Division of Lever Brothers. Our daughter was married. I had set up a fund to provide for the completion of our son's education as a lawyer, and we had a nest egg on which to live comfortably. On January 17, 1950, free as birds, Honey and I left by car for Florida for that long-awaited-for big vacation and to look for a place to retire. We were also going to get our fill of our big love—fishing.

"After only five weeks of loafing, I became very restless. I discovered I couldn't be content with just loafing.

"Until December 31, I had been active—spending fifty of fifty-two weeks telling and showing 175 guys how to get those orders, busy fifteen to eighteen hours a day—and then I just stopped to fish. It can't be done.

"After seven weeks of inactivity, I was despondent. . . ."

In his book, Leland Bradford speaks from personal experience about the problem that is sure to afflict both these groups of people:

I didn't realize that I faced a sudden, abrupt reversal in my life from long-range goals to short-range goals, and that hidden in this reversal was the terrible danger of goallessness with its consequent apathy, boredom, and depression.

A feeling of goallessness can creep up on one little by little. Stealthily. There are days when there seems no purpose in getting up in the morning because now there is no business to be about. Sometimes it's easier to drift into nostalgic thoughts of the past when one was strong and energetic or young and beautiful, rather than think about what one might do in the present. Especially so when the present seems dark and depressing and the past bathed in a romantic glow. Without purposes, and with goals now more short-range, it becomes easy to be inactive. First excuses, then rationalizations until motivation and will weaken. Then one gradually ceases to have pride in oneself, liking for oneself, belief in one's competence. An individual can become hooked on goallessness as readily as on alcohol or drugs. Alcohol and drugs often follow goallessness because they provide a temporary way of blocking out self-dislike.

How can we be so dumb?

Who among us has never seen people with the malaise that Bradford describes? Who among us has not had the answer for them?

"Get a hobby!"

"Get a part-time job!"

"Get involved!"

"Keep busy! There's nothing wrong with you that being busy won't cure!" We are lavish with exclamation points because the answer is so clear to us.

It *is* the answer, of course, but we might as well tell people to grow younger and younger, not older and older. It fails to address the real problem. The real problem is that goal-oriented people need nonplastic reasons to keep busy. They can't make do on make-work.

Why did we get so hooked on serious goals?

Our mothers and fathers were the original villains in the piece, if we're looking for villains. No sooner could we sit up than the next goal was to stand. Then standing wasn't enough and we had to walk and talk. And on and on.

The fact is that we have dealt all our lives in goals and aims, targets and objectives, missions and standards. We have counted out our days in deadlines, schedules, and priorities. If we have had one unchanging motto, it has been "Onward!" Know it or not we all signed on early to Samuel Johnson's pronouncement, "Life, to be worthy of a rational being, must be always in progression; we must always purpose to do more and better in our lives."

I do not mean to say that we ourselves set all the goals and standards. Far from it. As the time came, teachers, coaches, Scout leaders, bosses, and organizations joined our parents in telling us what to work on and when to work on it. *They* told us whether we had succeeded or not. *They* kept control of the carrot and the stick and they kept them ever handy.

And that's a big part of the problem.

Right this minute, you may be sending me a message by thought wave: "Wait a minute! Some of us have learned to think and plan for ourselves. We know how to set our own goals."

My return message to you is: "Thank your lucky stars."

Those of us who are not so blessed are not necessarily dumb or passive or even unwilling. The problem is that we never got the training or the practice.

Nor has anyone ever told us that it is a big job, making a success of retirement.

Nor has the conventional wisdom ever looked upon retirement as a big opportunity for satisfaction, growth, and fulfillment.

That's why I'm writing this book.

LOSING A FAMILY

The most overworked half-truth in the American language is that an institution is like a family.

The untrue half of that can be harmless; it can also be cruel. Anyone who assumes that an organization that acts paternally will always act paternally is setting himself up for disillusionment or worse.

The head of a natural family may disinherit a child, may not speak to him for decades, but can't divorce the kid. The head of an organizational "family" can divorce you at his pleasure and he gets to keep all the community property besides.

The workers at Texasgulf discovered those realities soon after the 1981–1983 recession began.

"For years," said a 1982 story in the *Wall Street Journal*, "Texasgulf preached to its employees that everyone in the company was part of a family. Everyone at company headquarters ate free lunches together. Any worker could telephone the chairman on a toll-free line. And the company boasted that some families worked for Texasgulf for three generations."

Then came the layoffs and the lesser indignities.

Within a few weeks, one of every five Texasgulf workers was laid off for "general economy" reasons. Rumors that the new French owners would close Texasgulf headquarters overloaded the circuits of the company grapevine. Even the company picnics and softball leagues were canceled to help reduce costs.

"In the past, the company philosophy had been to ride out the bad times without layoffs," said one former employee. Another said, "You didn't have to worry about your job because this was a family." Yet another person, still employed, said, "Now when you say 'family' around here, people snicker."

But what about the true part of the half-truth?

We human beings are going to go right on behaving like the bosses and the workers at Texasgulf, no matter what. Our need for surrogate parents, siblings, aunts, and uncles is ancient and instinctive. In this, we are not different from elephants, gorillas, and lions, or from other species that travel in herds, troops, or prides.

Human needs for community are different only in being more varied and complex. We need to be with people who speak the same language, laugh at the same jokes, share deities and devils. We relax most when everyone in the room understands the pecking order.

We crave the feeling of being with people who understand and care about our problems, personal or corporate. We like it best when everyone plays by the same rules and aims at the same targets. We need to fight among ourselves, but when an outsider attacks we want the ranks to close *pronto*.

Most of all, we need to work with people who will give us due respect and rewards, who will encourage us, who will punish us for our own good, who will, in short, act *in loco parentis*.

Leo Burnett was the kind of person who was born to play the magisterial, parentlike boss. Very early in our relationship—I was thirty, he sixty—Leo spoiled all other bosses for me. This tough, shy man, this passionate lover of advertising he thought good, called me to a review meeting with no more than a few minutes warning and sent me into a fit of wholly justified apprehension. The subject was a new campaign for a major client who was new to me, and I had been working on it alone. Leo thus had no reason to trust me to solve the problem. As it happened, though, he did like the ads, he liked the strategy, and he liked my presentation. To express all that, he did something entirely out of character and, to the best of my knowledge, never repeated it. He got out of his chair, beamed at me, bowed (!) from the waist and said, "Howard, I *compliment* you." I have always thought that my real career at the agency began that day.

Exalting as such times are for all of us, our family feelings are mostly made of homelier stuff. Susan Edmiston, writing in the *New York Times*, quoted a friend who said it took three years to get over leaving her job. "You miss calling up so-and-so and saying I'm so-and-so of such-and-such and not being of or from anywhere," the friend said. "You get attached to the building, the office, the elevator, the guy who works the elevator, the coffee wagon, the newsstand. There's something very nice about going downstairs to the newsstand and getting *The Wall Street Journal* or a Snickers. And you know the guy who runs it, and one day the gates are down and you worry about what happened. There's all this life going on around you all the time; you're much more connected to the world."

To a point, these familial feelings are natural and healthy. We human animals are not robots.

"Beware, though," say psychologists. "Don't put all your emotional blue chips on your job. Organizations are not set up to provide emotional rewards, especially to retired people. If you look only to your job for satisfaction, you'll have nothing to retire *to*— and that can be devastating."

"Of course, of course," our heads tell us. "Any fool knows that—it's obvious."

But our hearts tell us something else: that we're different, that we're too smart to suffer from the fickleness of our organizational loved ones. We'll be fine.

Tell it to Sweeney.

The implacable fact is that when we make the sea change from working to not-working, the toughest of us is vulnerable. Our feelings will be heard from, whether we like it or not.

"Nobody's indispensable," we have always said. But we have also said, "There are exceptions to every rule." And that little "yes, but" leaves an elephant-size hole in our defenses. When our time comes, it is disconcertingly easy to listen when the voices start up in the center of the gut:

"All those years I gave them—and this is the thanks they give me?"

"They used to fight to get appointments with me—now they don't even return my calls."

"You'd think that greenhorn who got my job would *want* some good, sound advice."

"They invite me to lunch and it's shop talk, shop talk the whole darned time—stuff I never heard of."

If you wonder why your retired friends never talk to you about having such feelings, think about it.

Would *you* own up? Even in private?

DOWN THE
STATUS LADDER

There is no way to put a good face on what retirement does to our status. In our own eyes especially.

First, they ask us to surrender our sword, then they use it to cut off our epaulets. Next come feelings of rejection, rebuke, devaluation, and retreat. Never mind logic. Never mind rationality. Our brain's right lobe has a mind of its own and, when it comes to retirement, it outshouts all the cogency our left lobe can bring to bear.

As though that were not indignity enough, the culture forbids us to mourn. Especially out loud. The love of status and status symbols is taboo. Period.

The taboo is potent—people violate it only under stress or under the influence. I can recall only a few episodes of violation, but I recall those in full color.

Once I met a man at a dinner, not knowing that he was second in command in one of the great companies. He did not have his mind on where he was, he could not focus on anything or anyone there, he could not finish a sentence. In the end he apologized.

"It used to be that when I walked into the office in the morning, I could go anywhere in the world on my own say-so," he said. "If I chose to go to Saudi Arabia, I told my secretary and the wheels would turn. People would fuel up a company jet, make phone calls, set up meetings, get the documents into my briefcase, lay on limousines, have the red carpet rolled out.

"Tonight I walked out of the office and left all that clout behind. Tomorrow, I won't even have a secretary.

"I retired this morning."

At the time I wrote off the man as a boaster, a guy with crummy values. All I heard was the self-pity of a kid who'd lost his favorite toys. I did not know enough to see that what he mourned was loss of identity and self-esteem.

At another time, I saw the same naked feelings in the one man from whom I'd least have expected it—Leo Burnett.

Leo hated status consciousness. Doing good work was not everything to him. But I never knew what the other things were. In an unforgettable speech to his employees that he called, "When to Take My Name Off the Door," he urged us, among other things, never to "lose your itch to do the job well for its own sake," never to "narrow your outlook down to the number of windows in the walls of your office."

When Leo was 75, he was trying hard to turn over the company he loved to the next generation and to do it with grace. I measure the toughness of that job by two things he did.

Once during that time, he came to the office all roiled up by the question of what his new title would be. Our suggestion—chairman emeritus—suddenly was anathema. He didn't want a title that some future retiring chairman could take. He wanted a title that would always be unique. In the end, Founder Chairman was his choice and everyone was happy.

On another day, he decided that we should not move anyone into his office after he died. Was it his idea that we should make it some sort of Leo museum or Leo memorial? I don't know. I do know that it was the most un-Leo-like thing we ever saw him do.

You and I were introduced early to the American way of double-think. We knew about achievement and the status that flows from achievement long before we knew about sex.

Status came from getting the right kind of grades on our report cards and the right color stars beside our names, from being class president and getting a part in the big play, from making the first team and being an Eagle Scout.

To excel was clearly the right way to go. ("Excelling" was a nicer word than "winning," although winning was the true name of the game.) The rewards for excelling were smiles, kisses, and hugs, and they were a lot better than the alternatives.

Meanwhile, the more we "lived up to our potential" (although the phrase had yet to be invented), the more the world wanted us not to get a swelled head or to think we were better than anyone else. If we were smarter, we were to play it down. If we got As, we weren't to flaunt them—unless they were the kind of As you wear on a sweater. If we got into a better college, we were to go out of our way to be modest and democratic. This was America.

As time went by, this charade of think-one-way-and-act-another became more complex and so did we. The bigger our title, our car, our house, our name in the community—the more the gods of success smiled—the more we were supposed to act "old shoe." We were to be just one of the guys.

Finally, on retirement day, we are asked to sit up there all smiles, while a lifetime of excelling goes down the tube. We are expected to accept the gold watch with gratitude, to look unassuming during the testimonials, to look on benignly while the guy who's taking our place gets the lion's share of attention. We are *not* supposed to look as though we'd lost our best friend. We are supposed to go quietly.

Unfair and unreasonable as all of this is, I have personally proved one thing about it: it does no good to brood. Or sulk.

Retirement time may seem a little late in the game to be asked to learn a whole new set of rules about status, but that's the way it is.

Still, there are ways and ways to beat the rap if we want to. We are going to consider those ways in the middle part of this book.

A MISERY OF CHOICE

The day you go home from your job for the last time, open your ears wide. Use your imagination. In the distance, you will hear the sounds of crumbling and crashing.

What you are listening to is the demolition of the habits of a lifetime.

For a few days, you will enjoy yourself. It is childish, but it is *fun* to thumb your nose at the clock, the calendar, and the schedules that other people make. You can think of yourself as Huck Finn, Tom Sawyer, and Joe Harper all rolled into one. You can even go them one better. They were too young to know the delights of not shaving.

There will come another day, however. Sooner or later, your spirit will sag under some weight you can't see. You will find yourself wishing for you don't know what. Your spouse will give you a complicated little list of errands and you will be grateful to her for an hour.

That is the day you discover the misery of choice.

Dr. Ernest Dichter, an early practitioner of "motivational psychology," defined "misery of choice" for me. He observed that we perform hundreds of small tasks each day, most of them out of habit. We don't decide anew every day which side of our faces to shave first, which newspaper to buy, which route to take to work. To have to make such choices every time we act would make us miserable.

When we were still working, therefore, we had our habits, our routines, our schedules so well constructed that we could arise, dress, eat breakfast without ever having to think. We bragged that we could do this, that, or the other job "with our eyes shut." We agreed with Thomas B. Reed who said, "For the ordinary business of life, an ounce of habit is worth a pound of intellect."

Psychologists refer to our habitual routines as "structure" and they get serious looks on their faces when they talk about it. No doubt they are thinking about those experiments with laboratory rats. You know the ones. You teach a rat to find his way through a maze to the food or some other reward. Then you change the configuration of the maze and watch while the rat develops symptoms of a nervous breakdown. The Portuguese have a proverb that applies: "He who changes his habits will soon be dead."

The moral of all this is clear: when the time comes to put behind you the habits of a lifetime, make some new ones. Pronto.

Neat, isn't it?

The only problem is that it's hard advice to take. You don't just come home one day and say, "Well, out with the old and in with the new." Changing habits takes thought, and thinking is *work*. Making a lot of new choices can be hazardous to your health.

Still and all, the reality is compelling when retirement comes: we get to work on a new set of habits and learn about the misery of choice. Or we do nothing and suffer a worse misery—that of living in the past.

ADVENTURELESSNESS

It happens to a lot of people. They work hard. They accept the risks; they win some, they lose some. But they learn. They grow. They break new ground. They progress. And, all things considered, they have a whale of a good time.

Then they retire and that's the end of adventure.

It happens to doctors, lawyers, merchants. It happens to athletes, actors, astronauts. It happens to scientists, clerks, carpenters, to anyone and everyone who gets emotional satisfaction from his job and from very little else.

They retire and that's bad news.

Listen to Blaise Pascal (*Pensées*, 1670.) on the consequences of the carefree life. No one has said it better: "There is nothing so insupportable to man as complete repose, without passion, occupation, amusement, care. Then it is that he feels his nothingness, his isolation, his dependence, his impotence, his emptiness."

You may never have thought your job adventuresome. Our society uses the word to describe space flights, high-risk medical research, entrepreneurship, rescue missions in enemy territory, transoceanic flights in hot-air balloons, salvage operations a mile down in the ocean, and other glamorous exotica.

Don't be misled by this. Apply logic. All glamorous jobs are adventuresome. But it does not follow that all adventuresome jobs are glamorous. Adventure takes place wherever there is risk and the outcome is unknown in advance. A coal miner's job is adventuresome, every day.

The craving for adventure is like smoking. You can retire from the source of your adventures just as you can retire from smoking. But that doesn't mean the craving goes away.

When you do retire, one of two things is going to happen: you will find new ways to satisfy your craving—something we'll discuss at length in the middle part of this book, or you will conclude that no new pursuit could ever offer as much fun as your old job did—so why try, why seek, why explore? If that happens to you, and don't bet a nickel that it can't, you will settle down to bitterness and ennui as a way of life. You will dine on thin, thin gruel instead of good, red meat. You will see firsthand why Anthony Trollope said, "Men and women can endure to be ruined, to be torn from their friends, to be overwhelmed with avalanches of misfortune better than they can endure to be dull."

God forbid that you be "dull."

COMRADELESSNESS

You don't lose friends when you retire, but you do lose comrades. Friendship endures. Comradeship doesn't.

All your life up to now, you have watched classmates, teammates, neighbors, fellow workers, and other comrades-at-arms fade out of your life, and you have borne the losses with grace and hope. Callous as it sounds, you knew that such people were replaceable. As you went from school to school, situation to situation, job to job, you knew there'd be new people to share your experience, new people to speak your language.

Whether you know it or not, you have been in agreement with Samuel Johnson and Ralph Waldo Emerson all this time.

Johnson said to Boswell, "If a man does not make new acquaintance as he advances through life he will soon find himself alone. A man, sir, should keep his friendship in constant repair."

Emerson said, "A man's growth is seen in the successive choirs of his friends."

Retirement is a condition in which old comrades progress from "Call me for lunch next week" through "I can't make it the next few weeks—let me call you" to "Let's do it again. Sometime."

Retirement is a condition in which you attempt to fill the gaps by making over your wife and your wife's life. I don't say that it won't work. I do say that the odds against are 50-1. (That's a subject unto itself. More about it in Part III of this book).

Retirement is a condition in which you can easily give up and easily come to illustrate the bleaker dictionary definitions: to seek seclusion. To live in isolation. To retreat to privacy. To withdraw from circulation.

Retirement is not, however, an automatic life sentence to loneliness. It is merely (merely!) a mandate to change your habits and attitudes—or suffer the consequences. It is a mandate to grow into new relationships.

Friendship and comradeship do not grow, of course, just because you want and need them. They grow when other things grow. Friendships and comradeships form when there are common interests, common goals—even common enemies—as well as common chemistry. They form where there is shared enthusiasm, shared knowledge.

Retirement communities are powerful testimony to that.

Listen to Bess Melvin of Sun City Center, Florida, as quoted by Frances Fitzgerald in an excellent *New Yorker* piece (April 23, 1983):

> "[This] isn't like the stereotype of a retirement community. The usual thought is that you lose your usefulness. You sit back and rock in your rocking chair and life slows to a stop. But the people here aren't looking for that. Sun City Center has a hundred and thirty clubs and activities. We have a stamp club, a poetry club, a softball club, a garden club—I could go on and on—as well as active branches of the Rotary, the Kiwanis, the Woman's Club, and that sort of thing. The residents form their own clubs and run the Civic Association, so if you've got a particular talent or social concern you can always find an opportunity to develop it. Many people take up painting, and we have some really fine artists here."

If retirement communities do not hold *the* answer to comradelessness for you—they don't for me—they do offer some answers you and I can use right where we are:

Rethink your values.

Try something new.

Get involved.

Be productive.

Think about it. We will come back to those and other object lessons.

III
YOUR
WORSE HALF
Things about Your Wife
That You Had to Learn
from Another Man

HALFWAY THROUGH
THIS BOOK,
I STARTED LISTENING
WHEN YOUR WIFE SPOKE

When I set out to write this book, my viewpoint was, I suppose, strictly that of the male chauvinist pig. I had no plans, none, to dwell on your wife's problems with your retirement.

I didn't know there were any problems.

Oh, I had often heard the gag, "I married him for better or for worse but not for lunch." Big deal, I remember thinking. So your wife might have to fix two lunches once in a while. Poor baby!

But you? Now, you're someone who's got *problems* with retirement.

I would feel bad about being so deaf and blind if it weren't for one thing: we older men are all chauvinists in this respect.

Pighood for us began when our mothers dressed us in blue. That message—that boys are different from girls—got delivered and redelivered. Boys wore pants, girls wore skirts. Boys had short hair, girls had long hair. Boys could not be sissies, girls could.

As we grew up, finished our educations and went to work, the message of our difference was delivered once more, delivered to us like a stone from Mount Sinai: men are the serious workers of the world. Your wife may have a good job when you marry but yours is the vital one. If your employers want to transfer you to another part of the world, it's your wife's duty to quit her position. It is your job, your hours, your duties, your pressures, your needs around which the whole household is destined to revolve.

After forty years of that, you and your wife may be forgiven if you confuse the importance of the job with the importance of the job *holder*.

The problem with such a misapprehension at retirement comes when you go right on acting the part of the first-class citizen, the only one in the house.

Think about it.

I was far along with this book when understanding began to come.

One evening at dinner, I finally started listening to your wife—really listening.

For more than a year, my dinner party partners had listened very attentively to me when I talked about retirement and about my writing. They agreed that retirement *is* a problem for men. They were concerned for their own husbands and their concern showed. They taught me a lot about your feelings, your ideas.

But I listened only to what I wanted to hear.

To be sure, I did see what happened to their faces when the subject of retirement came up. The muscles would contract, particularly the muscles which squint the eyes, twitch the nose, and purse the mouth. I did notice it but I misread it. I put it down to their anxiety over *your* well-being.

Also, the words registered when an occasional wife would say things like these:

"What about the wives?"

"What are you going to say about *us*?"

"I hope you're going to write about us, too!"

"It's my retirement, too, you know."

I heard the words but I literally did not know what they were talking about. Not then.

Finally, I heard your wife saying those things to me and I started wondering. Was I missing something important? Something very important? Maybe I'd better start asking questions. From then on, I resolved I would do some probing when a wife said, "What about us?"

"What about you?" I would ask.

"Well, you know. My life changed a lot when Jack retired. It was awful for a long time. I could tell you a lot about wives and retirement."

"Please do! Tell!"

(Long pause. Mental gears clearly meshing.)

"Well, it was the telephone."

"The telephone?"

"The telephone. He was on the phone about his investments all the time. I couldn't call my friends and they couldn't call me. It was awful."

"What did you do—put in another phone line?"

"No. We just worked it out. We worked out everything. After a while."

(The curtain comes down—*zap!*)

Here the conversation would cool down and she'd lead me to a safe subject. Loyalty had set in. She could not criticize her husband to another man and that was that.

In time, I got better at drawing out the wives I talked to. I saw that I had to stop asking my questions on a you-and-Jack basis. I had to let my conversation partners speak in general terms, impersonally, as experts on women.

From there, patterns began to emerge. But the loyalty barrier still got in the way, still prevented my getting candid reactions. At one point I thought a very bright friend of ours, herself the wife of a retired man, was ready, even eager, to interview other wives for me. But, no soap. She began to worry that she might, without intending to, betray her friends' confidences.

In the end, my old friends at Leo Burnett Company provided the solution: they offered to conduct two group interviews for me. What they did that I couldn't was to provide an impersonal business setting, a guarantee of anonymity, and a professional group leader who was a woman.

Group One consisted of eight women, all of whose husbands planned to retire within two years. Group Two also numbered eight women. Their husbands had retired in the period between twelve and twenty-four months before.

The results were all I'd hoped and then some. The groups not only confirmed the main hypotheses I had formed but they also gave me several important new ideas. They were open with each other and, by being open, gave me revealing anecdotes and quotes.

At last I was ready to write about wives. As a bonus, the sixteen women also offered some very good advice—for both you and your wife.

God bless you women who participated in the groups. I hope your husbands read this book. And pay close attention.

MY HUSBAND
THE TIME BOMB

As I write, there is a commercial that shows up almost daily on the news show I watch.

We see a middle-aged man get out of a car and walk toward a house. The door opens, a middle-aged woman runs out. The two put their arms around each other.

"Honey," he says, "I'm home! (Pregnant pause.) *Forever!*"

"I know," she says, her whole face smiling and her voice a butterscotch sundae. "I know."

What goes on here? Are we to think that the couple are newlyweds and that the man has quit his job so they can spend all their time together? Or that the man has had an extramarital lark, that the affair has soured, that his wife has qualified for sainthood by forgiving him all, and that the reconciliation will be rapturous? No. What we learn from the body of the commercial is that today is the man's retirement day!

As fairy tales go, this one ranks right up there with Cinderella and Snow White.

The day you retire, you become a massive threat to your wife's serenity. No matter how much she loves you, she worries that your lack of plans and programs is going to make a hash out of *her* plans and programs.

One group discussion member, trying to express what she felt, came up with "he's a ticking time bomb." The other members wished they'd said that.

Before that concept raises your blood pressure too high, think along with me about the typical wife's situation before her husband retires:

The kids are grown up, out of the house, on their own. For years now, the wife has had the house, the car, the telephone, and her days to herself. She has been able to conduct the business of her life with a minimum of interference and a maximum of privacy. She has adjusted and she likes it.

She has been her own boss. If she wants to spend the day shopping and lunching with a friend, who's to complain? If she is a club person, or a volunteer, or a part-time or full-time job holder, or all of those things, she can go at it full tilt. If she wants to go out first thing in the morning and leave the house-straightening for the hour before you come home from work, what's the difference? If she's continuing her education, she can exercise her mind to her heart's content. She is becoming the rest of the person she always wanted to be.

Then comes retirement day.

(The "Dragnet" theme is heard offstage. Dum-duh-*dum*-dum).

On my own retirement day, my wife did *not* run out to meet me with open arms. Her face did not smile and her voice did not sound like an ice cream sundae, butterscotch or otherwise. I offered to take her out to dinner that night but she declined. (With thanks, though.) She'd had a busy day and would have a busier one tomorrow. We took our dinners on trays in front of the TV and she went—sensibly—to bed early.

What my wife knew—and I didn't—was that my new lack of routine was going to conflict daily with her old, established one. If I wanted to sleep a little late, she wanted to get up and get going. If I went into the library to read after breakfast, she had to sit at her desk there and make her telephone calls in a goldfish bowl. Or she had to ask me to sit elsewhere. (A man's home is his castle?) Or she was obliged to use another phone without her papers and calendar at hand. If she had a lunch date and knew I didn't, she'd keep it, but (she told me a year later) she felt guilty about not including me.

I have tried to imagine having had our roles reversed.

There I am in my office and there my wife is, depending on me for direction and amusement. She sits across the room, reading a book, when a client calls. I try to smooth his feathers or to answer questions without looking at her face, across which runs a stream of nonverbal editorial comments. Unthinkable.

Or I make a lunch date with a fellow worker whom she knows to be my pal as well. "Really," I try to tell her, "he and I have to talk business." Unthinkable.

My wife is not the only one. Listen to the group discussion members:

Q. Any changes in your life since your husband retired?

First woman: "Well, little things—like the phone rings and I talk and he says, 'Who was that on the phone?'—little things like that that I didn't have before. Sometimes that gets a little (ha-ha) irritating."

Q. You say husbands resent the telephone. Why do they?

First woman: "Well, I think it takes your attention away from them. That's one of the biggest taboos when they're home."

Second woman: "My husband says the same thing: 'You spend half your life on the phone.'"

Third woman: "Well, they don't have the people to talk to that we do."

Q. What else?

Fourth woman: "Well, I have a part-time job, I see a lot of people, I serve the schools. And he became a little jealous. I have these places to go to—these are commitments I had over the years. And he couldn't understand it. Finally, it got so I'd have him drive with me and he liked that. I see a lot of people and some of them say, 'My husband's retired and, Oh God, I'm going crazy' and some of them went out and got jobs just to get out of the house. These men are so busy and suddenly they're retired and they don't have any continuity in their lives and they don't know what to do with themselves."

Fifth woman: "One of the big adjustments I have—I never ate lunch and now I've gained twenty pounds. (Rueful laughter from the others.) When we eat breakfast, he says, 'We won't eat lunch today.' Then comes twelve o'clock and he says, 'Don't you think we'd better have a little snack?' (Laughter.) That's the only thing I find perturbing. Come twelve o'clock and I've got to drop whatever I'm doing and get lunch. And he doesn't gain an ounce.''

Sixth woman: "When my husband retired, he was looking forward to it but I wasn't. I love to clean the house and he's always criticizing me for that. 'You've always got a rag in your hand,' he says."

Second woman: "Whatever he wants, that's what we have to do."

Fourth woman: "Retired men lead such boring lives, they have nothing to do . . . nothing productive, nothing constructive. All they do is bug their wives. They are *bored*."

Fifth woman: "I wouldn't be able to keep up with my activities—my husband doesn't have any of his own. It'd always be, 'Where are you going? What are you gonna do?' "

Sixth woman: "My husband would love it—I'm fighting it. He's already up early on weekends and vacations."

Seventh woman: "Mine wouldn't love it. He's ready to go home after one week of vacation."

None of the quotations above is as trivial as it may seem on the surface. Underneath the ladies' complaints about the telephone, there is real fear. They see their husbands and themselves as carrying on a power struggle, a struggle they think they, the women, may lose. For example, they fear for their relationships with their friends.

WHY CAN'T A MAN BE A FRIEND LIKE A WOMAN?

By the time you retire, your wife will have behind her thirty-five to forty years of close friendships with other women—all her married life and more. These relationships have not been just the icing on her cake. They have been a big slice of the cake itself.

A woman's friends do a lot more for her than a man's friends do for him. They are to pass the time with, sure. And yes, they are for laughs, for lunch, for card-playing, for bowling, for tennis, for golf, for gossip—just as your friends are for you.

But there is a big, big difference.

The discussion-group women talked about that. They were so much of one mind about the difference that I have put their thoughts together in the composite "speech" below:

"You asked why men resent the telephone so. Maybe they resent the fact that the calls aren't for them. But, my gosh, most of them wouldn't make a telephone call if their lives depended on it. How do they expect to get calls?

"I don't know how women got along before the telephone was invented. For women our age, it has been our salvation, the way out of isolation, the lifeline to our support groups.

"When we had our babies, we raised them communally. We shared information, experience, ideas. And we shared baby clothes, cribs, high chairs, everything.

"We're not like men with our friends. Men don't make lasting relationships. Close acquaintances—that's what men make.

"If a woman needs a friend, she'll find a woman. If a man needs a friend, he'll find . . . a woman. (Much laughter.)

"Women are close to each other and they talk closely. Men don't trust their friends with anything private, just surface things like sports and politics. Men have friends all their lives but they're not close. They put on armor and they don't let other men penetrate it.

"Women get into today, what's going on today. With men, if it isn't sports or the stock market, it's the past, always the past. Women share the real, personal things in their lives. For instance, if a woman had a retarded child, she'd reach out to her friends for support and advice. The man would avoid it. I think it shakes up a man's masculinity if his child is not perfect and he certainly wouldn't share that with another man.

"Caring and concern—that's what's important to a woman."

These differences are not just theory or idle abstractions to the wives of retired men.

They cause two big, practical problems.

The first of these is jealousy.

Your wife can see that you resent the time she spends on the telephone. She can see that you compare how long she spends talking to female friends with how long she spends talking to you. She can see the jealousy and she worries that it will smother her female relationships in a blanket of inhibition.

The second problem is what they see as too much dependence— of you on them. "Retired men are just tails to their wives' kites," one woman said. "It's like having another baby in the house—a 200-pound baby," another said.

Still another woman asked the rest of her group, "Why do we have to do their programming for them, why do we have to define their day?" Answers tumbled over each other:

"They feel inadequate to do the planning—so they look to you to do it."

"Maybe their mothers did all that for them."

"You're a mother figure—they're the child."

"When he gets too bored, I even have to make him go out and take a walk."

In spite of their complaints, the two groups of women do not see their husbands as heavies so much as they see them as victims. It's just "the way they were brought up," one said.

"That's right," said another. "Material things are the measure of a man's life. For him, the end of earning is the end of life."

"His self-worth," another woman added, "is measured by his paycheck. So, no job—no status. But maybe our children will be different. Don't forget that it's the Depression children who are retiring now."

"That's right. I hate to think that human beings can't change."

The message to men is clear: change for God's sake. Change your attitudes when you change to retired life. Change for your sake. Change for our sake.

Change, yes. But don't take charge. . . .

WHO'S IN CHARGE HERE?

Vignette from one of the group discussions:

Wife: "You didn't retire—you became a professional thermostat setter."

Husband: "You're right that I didn't retire—but what I am is a professional errand boy."

Earlier, I used the phrase "power struggle." In the nature of things, there is bound to be a power struggle when you retire. You're used to having your say-so at work, your wife has her say-so at home. Now there's only one arena for the two of you. Who's going to be in charge?

If you think you're too smart to fall into that trap, you're half right anyway. You would certainly not be so dumb as to rearrange the living room furniture while your wife's out for the day. Or to call the painter on your own and change the color of the front door.

However, it isn't the big, obvious stuff that will get the two of you into trouble.

One retired husband put his foot into it by offering to go to the supermarket for his wife. She had another urgent errand so she thanked him, gave him a detailed list of brands, sizes, and quantities and kissed him goodbye.

When she came home, he said proudly, "Well, I got everything you wanted and I saved a lot of money besides."

"That's good, dear. (Double take.) Wait—you saved a lot of money? *How* did you save a lot of money?"

"Well, you know—I looked for the bargains on the front of the packages. Ten cents off, fifty cents off—bargains like that."

Poor innocent. He had found bargains to be sure—on laundry detergent, paper towels, instant coffee, several other items—and had bought the bargains instead of the brands she had specified.

But he had found something else as well: a surefire, double-edged way to criticize her. In one stroke, he had impeached her judgment of relative brand performance and had denigrated her eye for value.

By the time a man retires, his wife has developed a highly personal and sophisticated set of techniques for managing their home. Purchasing, inventory control, budget control, general maintenance, crisis management, interior design, laundry and cleaning schedules, suppliers, labor, tradespeople relations—she's gotten these and all other departments down to art, science, and business all bundled up into one. Her skill gives her a consequential part of her sense of identity and her sense of worth.

We challenge all this at our peril.

Your wife will be tolerant as you stumble through a week or two of your adjustment period. She will understand that you are at loose ends—no deadlines, no quotas, no routine, nothing and no one to manage. She went through that herself as the kids moved out and a big chunk of her own job moved out with them.

But she doesn't sympathize enough to hand over her hard-won powers to you.

She will see that you are unconsciously looking for someone new to supervise and oversee.

But she is not, repeat *not*, a candidate for the job.

By the time our children come to retirement age, there may be a new kind of social contract in American households.

Among young husbands and wives, both of whom are holding jobs and contributing to the family income, there is a lot of experimenting today with work assignments at home. But I suspect it's too late for you and me and the rest of our generation.

Even after four years of learning from mistakes, I still step on my wife's toes.

After the summer drought of 1983 which traumatized our lawn along with that of everyone else, I took a playing lesson with my golf pro one day. The greenskeepers were power raking, overseeding, fertilizing; their work set off in me an uncontrollable urge to give our own grass a rebirth. I went home and with fine, fresh idiocy, told my wife about the plan I've just conceived—to hire a garden service to do for us what the greenskeepers were doing for the golf course.

Instantly it was fire-and-ice time at our house.

I seemed, she observed, to have forgotten that the lawn was her turf—in both senses. Had I failed to listen, as usual, when she told me her own plans for rejuvenation? Hadn't she already found the answer to the watering problem? Hadn't she already put down two batches of seed on the small bald spots? Did I have my own work in such a state of perfection that I could relieve her of the burden of doing her thinking for her?

Of course, if I really wanted to help with outside things, I could get the wheelbarrow, take it to the trunk of her car, hoist the peat moss from the one into the other and bring the sack to her on the back lawn where the shade-grass package was sitting in plain sight. Then I could get the edger and. . . .

WHEN YOU DANCE
WITH A GORILLA . . .

Listen to the sounds of Late Twentieth-Century Woman:

"I had sworn to myself that I wasn't going to be like my mother. I wasn't going to tamely follow Leland's decisions and hide my feelings. I wasn't going to say yes when I meant no. We did have a long discussion as to where to go when he retired. I remember saying that North Carolina was as far south as I would go, but it turned out that North Carolina was exactly where he wanted to go. What I did hide from him was my realization that I wasn't ready to leave Washington. I guess I went along with the move out of Washington because of my acceptance of the wife's role. . . ." (Martha Bradford)

"John is absolutely determined that we are going to move back East when he retires. He is crazy about salt water and sailing. I'm miserable. I've pointed out that all my friends and activities are here and our children's roots are here and this is *home*. But he doesn't want to hear that. He says I'll adjust in no time and love it as much as he does." (A Chicago friend)

"I'm a big-city girl. I'd lived in New York and Chicago all my life and loved our life here. But Bill was determined to get away from the snow and the ice. When he found a place he liked down south and we voted on it, I voted no but he voted yes. So we moved." (An ex-Chicago friend)

"He'll always find something he likes to do. Whatever that will be. I just take each day as it comes. No sense in worrying." (Group discussion)

"We went to Florida to look at a place and my husband said he wouldn't live there. Oh, he'd rent a place and stay there for a little while. But live there? He'd never do that." (Group discussion)

"I want to keep going and doing, but he won't want to do much. He's tired. Who's going to say anything that'll change him . . . ?" (Group discussion)

"My husband had a big job in a highly respected company. One day he came home and announced that he was going to retire early—at age fifty-seven! I was stunned. Sure, I had been president of a charity and president of a woman's club and I guess I had some standing of my own. But I loved being the president's wife. I liked the trips we took and the parties we went to and I loved how his associates looked up to him. Then, out of the blue, I was just the wife of a retired man." (My wife)

"Sure I'd hate it if Roy retired early. Some day? Sure—everyone has to retire someday—but I *like* being a college president's wife." (A friend)

"I think just about every woman of our generation gets a lot of her own identity from what her husband does. When I was a girl, the thing I was most proud of was the big job my dad had. He was *somebody* and everyone knew it, including my friends." (A Chicago friend)

How much of the above did I hear before I retired? None.

How much did I hear before I started working on this book? Nothing.

It was one of the surprises of my life to hear all this. It forced me to construct a new image of Late Twentieth-Century Man.

Instead of a gentle knight in shining armor, I saw a fellow in a gorilla suit.

MR. BONES: If you start dancing with a gorilla, Mr. Interlocutor, when do you stop?

INTERLOCUTOR: I don't know, Mr. Bones . . . when *do* you stop dancing with a gorilla?

MR. BONES: Why, Mr. Interlocutor, you stop dancing with a gorilla when the gorilla wants to stop. Yuk, yuk, yuk.

Whatever happened to Betty Friedan and Gloria Steinem? Did Carrie Chapman Catt live for nothing?

WE ALL MAKE MISTAKES, EVEN WOMEN

By now you may think of me as a bearded fellow with a lighted bomb in one hand and, in the other, a banner reading "Women Power!"

Forget it. Forget half of it, anyway.

I may have a bomb in one hand, but my banner reads, "Partner Power!"

God knows I have had my consciousness raised and that I am sympathetic as a man can be to what women have told me of their feelings about retirement.

But, I say, let them speak up. And let them ask their husbands to speak up.

In general, women are the most practical, realistic people I know. They have tough minds and tough spirits. They know how to understand another woman's point of view. They are willing to express their true feelings and they have had a lot of practice at it.

They are more durable than men, more patient than men, more able to postpone self-gratification than men. That is what they say about themselves and I agree with every word they say.

So why don't they use their native talents to deal with retirement?

After several hundred hours of conversing with dinner partners, listening to tapes of group discussions, reading anything and everything I can find that is relevant, I have concluded that women have a collective mental block on the subject. I don't know what it is.

Do women still think of retirement as being a code word for death? Possibly.

Does a woman feel old and unattractive when her husband retires? Could be.

Does she really regard retirement as a man's concern pure and simple, something that only he is entitled to make the decisions about? It is not beyond the realm of imagination.

Assuming they do think and feel these things, does that overload the circuits?

After all my research, I have yet to hear any woman say, "Five years before my husband retired, I asked him to start a dialogue with me. I said, 'Please tell me your feelings about retirement and please listen while I tell you mine.' "

In fact, I have yet to hear a woman say, "Long before my husband retired, I sat myself down to write out what I thought the problems and opportunities would be. Then I tried to figure out what I should do about them."

Most surprising, I have yet to hear a woman say, "As my husband approached retirement age, I thought I had better get the subject on the table with my women friends, particularly the women whose husbands were already into it." Far from hearing anything like that, I have heard the following:

"You can't ask anyone else for advice or information—everyone is different."

"Is it useful to share experiences? Not to me. We're all individuals. We can't learn [about retirement] from others. Marriages are closed corporations."

"I don't want any information—it'll all fall into place."

"Whatever will be will be."

Do our wives think that we men are so self-absorbed that they can't pierce the wall? Do they think it's hopeless to approach?

That may be true of all men some of the time and of a few men all of the time but it definitely isn't true of all men all of the time. A brief demonstration:

I have conducted two group discussions with retired men. My objective in each instance was to gather up wisdom for inclusion in this book. In the second of these discussions, I added the question, "What has retirement meant to your wives?"

First man: "My wife was very apprehensive about it. She thought I wouldn't have enough to do. She had been observing a couple of neighbors who retired and, in each case, saw how retirement changed the wife's way of life. The wives no longer were available for lunch and they no longer came to visit my wife. One of these men even wants to be included if his wife has a lunch date with women friends! And that woman has gone right downhill physically.

"Well, I made up my mind that I wouldn't have that effect on my wife's life. I bought an old house and set out to rehab it and I've done a lot of the work myself, so I've been out of the house a lot. And I have a stack of other things saved up to do when that project's finished.

"My wife has quite a bit of time to herself and she's been going on as before. Her worries haven't applied yet.

"Besides, I'm trying to encourage my wife to pursue interests of her own. She's even talked of going to college and getting a degree of some kind and I hope she does.

"The fact that I don't have to work for our living anymore and that the children are grown means she has the possibility of a wider life than in the past. We can even be away from each other for a month or two if it's useful for one of us—no hangups about that."

Second man: "Retirement has improved our relationship, if anything. It used to be that I was so wrapped up in my work that I was at home in body only. I was always thinking about the laboratory. Now that I don't have to worry about it anymore, she thinks I'm really at home and she thinks I'm reasonably good company. I myself don't get out much, but she does. She's a registered nurse and she's very dedicated to the cause of family planning. She works at a hospital two or three days a week. I believe in having something to do away from the house. It's not that I don't enjoy the company of my wife, but the company of just one other person constantly and forever would wear very thin."

Third man: "I realized about the second day that I stayed home that my wife's reaction was something I hadn't thought much about. I was surprised that she was apprehensive. That had to do with little, mechanical things—my role in the house. Of course, she still works in a bookstore three days a week—that's a factor.

"We got past that. Then she started asking me what I would do with myself. 'Well, I'm going to work on this book,' I said. 'Maybe you'd like to learn to cook,' she said. 'Maybe I would,' I said. 'Might be intriguing.' 'Maybe you'd like to help with the housework—put the laundry through the machines for instance.' Looking back, I realize she didn't want me to do any of that. I'd better not cook except as a minor hobby. And I'd better not do very much housework. She needs that as her reason for being. I am responsible for cleaning the study, though, because that's where I write.

"Now she's asking whether she should retire from the bookstore. It seems to me that my retiring has forced her to ask that question. Interesting thing, though—I'm not sure I want her home while I'm working!"

There you are. You wife isn't exactly the heroine of the piece. And you aren't exactly the villain. If that's any comfort to you.

On the theory, however, that there can be more to retirement than the cold comfort of equal guilt, I'll have a lot more to say about marriage in retirement later. I will offer the best advice I have been able to find, whatever the sources.

What do you and your wife need to bring to that party? Only these: Willingness. An open mind. Good will. That's all.

Piece of cake.

IV
THE SURMOUNTABLE OPPORTUNITY
All You Need Is Willingness, Wisdom, and Guts

YOUR OWN
BOSS
AT LAST

It does not matter how big a wig you have been.

It does not matter if you have filled in the *Employer* blanks on this or that form by writing "self-employed."

You have always had a boss.

Even if you have not had a plain, ordinary boss-boss, you have had patients, clients, customers, voters, directors, trustees, committees, stockholders, bishops, memberships—something or someone looking over your shoulder, giving you the fishy eye and deciding your fate.

Therefore, retirement day, dear citizen, is your personal Fourth of July. Your Bastille Day. Your Cinco de Mayo.

As Gerald Ford put it to me, this is the day on which you get "the option to say no."

The option to say no has this supreme advantage: it permits you to get busy because you want to rather than because you have to.

On the day you retire, you may turn around and take on some other kind of responsibility. Arthur Wood did that when he retired as chairman of Sears and Arthur Schultz did it when he stepped out as head of Foote, Cone & Belding. One after the other, the two Arthurs accepted the unpaid chairmanship of the Art Institute of Chicago, a tough job. But both had the option of saying no.

It is a terrific feeling when you can say no to other people's goals, rules, and standards.

No.

NO.

NO.

Even on paper it looks terrific.

"No, I will not set the alarm clock. No, I will not wear a tie today. No, I will not see him. No, I will not take that phone call. No, I will not write the checks today. . . ."

Ironically, the greater fun is in having the option to say yes—to yourself.

Phil Schaff set himself the goal of making as much money in retirement as he had in his best year on the job—so he could go on making significant "investments" in outstanding education for outstanding students. "Making money is a marvelous game for me these days," he told me. "But what I love is giving lots of it away."

George S. was retired early from the steel plant in which he'd worked for thirty years. He became a professional caddy "because I like golf and I like to keep physically active," and he set himself the goal of becoming a first-rate typist "because I can use typing all my life."

After Royal Little had stepped down and away from two big-wig jobs, he rented an office and set himself up as a part-time venture capitalist and deal maker. His rule now was simple: he would help only with deals he believed in. At other times he would play golf.

For me, the ultimate gift of liberation is the option to say both yes and no—to the same question. It is not that I am given to wishy-washiness. It is that I am partial to my new flexibility. Most of the work I do now can as well be done on a rainy day as a sunny one, on the weekend instead of a weekday, at night rather than during the hours from nine to five. One way or another I get it done.

If you call me on a nice day and you ask what I'm doing and I say "working," don't say you're sorry, say "golf." I'll meet you on the practice green in half an hour.

To me, there is a new sort of dignity in being my own boss, a new feeling of responsibility, too. It does something for my sense of self-worth to lay my own neck—no one else's—on the line, to be the only player who has to take the heat. (When France fell in 1940 and England was alone, Winston Churchill admitted that even that catastrophe had its up side. Ghastly as the war was, at least he didn't have to prosecute it by consent of committee.)

There is, naturally, a catch in all this.
In order fully to enjoy being your own boss, you have to be doing something you think is worth doing, something you can feel passionate about.
That is a catch. But it isn't a catch-22.
It can be done.
All it takes is willingness to look for the "something," the wisdom to recognize it, and the guts to get on with it.

WORK FOR ITS OWN SAKE

There are a lot of witless ideas about retirement. Most of them are left over from the days when "retired" was a euphemism for "useless."

Chief among such ideas is this one: your last day on the job is your last chance to do serious work.

What a crock.

If good, hard, serious work is your idea of fun, retirement is the opportunity of your lifetime.

For the first time in your life, you can put all your time, talent, and energy into work itself. You can put behind you all the pet peeves that went with your job—politics, committees, paper-pushing, administration, travel—whatever the aggravations may have been.

You may not even have to give up making money, if that's how you like to keep score on yourself. An account manager at the William Esty advertising agency retired to his sculpture studio in

Connecticut and promptly started generating more income from his art than he ever had from his job.

Whether or not you work for pay, the critical factor in your opportunity is that *you no longer have to put money considerations first*.

I am aware that this sounds a lot like Alice in Wonderland. ("Why is he talking about working in a book about retirement? Does he think words mean what he wants them to mean?")

The point we stick on here is the product of history, of conventional wisdom, and of one-track-mindedness: The work we do on our jobs is the only kind of work there is. For us. Advertising men do advertising. Doctors do medicine or surgery. Lawyers practice law. Store owners run the store.

Therefore, anything else is make work. Pastime work. Mickey Mouse work. Lots of people simply can't get past that idea. It might as well be engraved in bronze in the lobby of every plant and office in the country.

There is, of course, a trick to seeing retirement as an opportunity to work for the love of it: you have to redefine your idea of what work is.

In my own case, I had to see that what I liked about my own job was not advertising as advertising. I had to see that what I really loved was to generate ideas. To write. To visualize. To solve problems.

Dr. Charles Huggins, a Nobel laureate in medicine, was, for a great chunk of his life, a star surgeon and professor as well as head of a team of cancer researchers. As he grew older, he retired from all those jobs—but, at eighty-one, he was still working fifty to sixty hours a week. He was still working, alone in his own laboratory, on cancer research. "Research has always been my pleasure as well as my job," he says. "Nothing matches the thrill of discovery."

Daniel Ruge, a former neighbor of mine, might have missed some of the most interesting work of his life if he had clung to the idea that neurosurgery was the only work for him. When he judged himself too old to go on performing surgery personally, he retired from the operating room and accepted an offer from the Veterans Administration. As its chief authority on spinal surgery, he traveled all over the country as a consultant to other doctors. Then, Ronald Reagan became president. And there, in Washington, was Dan Ruge, whose long-time mentor was Nancy Reagan's father, Dr. Loyal Davis. The news that Dan had become the President's personal physician came to me when I saw his face on TV after the assassination attempt.

In the last part of this book, you can read about an astronaut who "retired" and became a star in the telephone business. An advertising account manager who "retired" and became the un-paid, *de facto* mayor of Captiva Island. The head of a small manufacturing company who "retired" and became a power in senior golf. You can find here a dozen other stories of people who have transferred their skills to new arenas.

I have not said that your opportunity will fall into your lap.

I have said that you may have to work at it. Paradoxically, it may turn out that retiring successfully is the hardest job you've ever had.

What's so bad about that?

If work is your schtick, retiring is, *ipso facto*, the work for you.

THE FIRST OF THE SECOND-CHANCE GENERATIONS

Your head and mine carry around ancient tape recorders, loaded with old wisdom about retirement and the course of life.

"*Carpe diem*," our forebears chant at us. "Life forgives you not. Blow today's opportunity and that's it, son. You never get a second shot."

For all of yesterday's generations, that was wisdom. Back then, only the rich could retire in solvency and good health and with twenty-five percent of their lives ahead of them. Most people stepped off the treadmill into disability, or worse.

Of course, the old wisdom is still half wise. When will it not be rewarding to live in and for today?

The rub comes when we retire ("it's all over, son") and we live by the old idea that our futures, our chances are all behind us.

Expect vegetablehood and you will become a vegetable.

Let us reminisce together about how our lives have gone.

As toddlers, we had all of the questions, none of the answers. And we burned to learn it all. Overnight. (How does a cigarette butt taste? How do Daddy's glasses feel? What kind of sound would the glass make if it fell?) The line of our curiosity stretched from infinity to infinity.

Things changed when we went to school. Now *they* had all of the questions and we did have some answers. In theory, the line of our curiosity still stretched from infinity to infinity, but in practice *they* limited it to a single short segment.

At work, we were introduced to specialization with a vengeance, and our curiosity line grew shorter and shorter. In the end, we knew a lot about pediatric hematology or tax exempts or management by objective and very damned little about anything else.

Our part of the curiosity line looked more like a dot.

Inside every sixty-year-old head is a three-year-old mind yelling to get out. "Learn to fly," it shouts. "Become fluent in French, live beside the sea and look and listen, get your hands into clay and paint, and and and . . . ."

Inside every sixty-year-old head a ninety-year-old censor croaks, "you'retoooldit'stoolatethat'stoohardwhatwouldpeople-thinkbetterjusttakeiteasynosuchthingassecondchances."

Three-year-old or ninety-year-old: who's right?

Dr. Robert Butler, the gerontologist, says, "Creativity can often be found in older persons, not only in the famous, but also in the daily lives of ordinary people. A person may in fact *first become creative in late life* when burdens and responsibilities lessen."

Leo Tolstoy never stopped growing, learning, and creating. His biographer, John Bayley, says that all his long life Tolstoy invented and reinvented himself. "Tolstoy is not a fixed point; he is constantly on the move, carrying us with him."

Bernard Berenson was another who never lived on old laurels. His ideal was "getting out of myself all that goes to turn an animal into a human being, a work of art." He lived his ideal into his nineties.

T. S. Eliot said: "Old men ought to be explorers/Here and there does not matter/We must be still and still moving/Into another intensity/For a further union, a deeper communion/ . . . In the end is my beginning."

For most of us, survival came first, the spirit second, while we still held jobs. Most of our ancestors never got a chance to change that.

Those of us in the second-chance generation have a luxury they never had. When we retire, we have the time and resources to reverse the order of our priorities, reshuffle our hierarchy of values.

That's true as true can be, but it's tough to get our minds around. (We are pioneers after all.)

With the best will in the world, many of us never get past the sunshine-and-magnolias approach to reversing and reshuffling. We move down south or out west and we expect the new places and things to make us happy or at least content. Unfortunately, that is not the way life works. The only geography that counts is the skin we live in. The only clement climate is the one we create inside our heads and guts.

The happiest retired people I know are those who have used their second chance to help, to teach, to create, to start living for others as well as themselves. Whether or not they have moved their bodies away seems to make no difference. If they have allowed their minds and hearts to move and grow—that's where it's at.

When I was just beginning to work on this book, I wrote a letter to Reginald Jones, the retired chairman of General Electric, a man I've never met. I asked him to write back, telling me something of his thoughts on second chance. Here is what he said, in its entirety:

Dear Mr. Shank:

I have your letter of November 19 and regret the delay in my reply. My retirement life has become so active and hectic that since the date of your letter I have been in my new office on only two occasions.

I'm not at all sure that I can be particularly helpful to you in the development of your proposed book. I can only say that it is my personal experience that individuals retiring from positions such as you and I have held can be as busy as their constitution and their family will permit. Since retirement I have joined the boards of directors of nine different companies and have carried on a host of *pro bono publico* activities with which I have been associated for some years. I have also found that it is most rewarding to spend as much time as possible in academia. Making oneself available to faculty and students is both stimulating and worthwhile. Questions come from left field and really keep one on the *qui vive*. It is also a way to keep *au courant* with the thinking and concerns of a younger generation. I find that we draw great interest on campus and are afforded a genuine opportunity to advance our points of view. Alan Greenspan once made the remark to me upon leaving Washington: "All legislation originates in academia." This comment highlights the significance of explaining democratic capitalism to the youth of our nation. Socialism sounds so attractive, even though it has been an abject failure as an economic system. On the other hand, capitalism has no "theology" and to young minds appears to be based on self-interest and greed. We do have a most convincing case for our economic system and the need to present that case by experienced practitioners. I know that many retired businessmen are doing this and I hope that you can encourage others in the development of your book.

You have a worthwhile project and Godspeed with your efforts.

Sincerely,

I do not know—and may never know—whether my own second-chance years will turn out to be the best years of my life.

What I do know is this: living with the opportunity day by day is joyful for me.

To paraphrase the title of a best-selling autobiography, I am an "unfinished man." Trying to finish the job in style is an *experience*.

VICTORY OVER EGO

With a Capital "E"

The habit of going for the gold dies hard.

When we retire and "has been" replaces "is," the old slogans still ring in our ears:

Big is beautiful!

Winning isn't everything, it's the only thing!

Make no little plans!

We're No. 1!

After sixty years of that, we find it hard to define new goals and construct new ways to keep score. Even the living saints among us find it hard. Which is OK for a while. A little pain is a powerful teacher.

The pain ends on the day we learn the name of the enemy. The enemy is Ego—with a capital "E."

My former associate, Sir Niall Lynch-Robinson, also retired, had a recent battle with the enemy. Niall wrote this to me:

"I got involved quite recently in an almighty power struggle in a school of which I was chairman of the governors.

"It was insidious because it wasn't a power struggle between me and anyone else, but rather a see-sawing between two or three quite tenable points of view which eventually got disastrously out of control. Right away, at the back of my mind, there was, I think, a little man who never had been there before, saying, 'Go on, you can beat them if you keep at it!' I saw no way of resolving it, my blood pressure started to go up, and in the end I left them to it."

If Ego is the enemy, ego (with a small "e") is the friend.

Ego says, "If it's not important in the eyes of the world, it's not worth doing." ego (with a small "e") says, "Whatever I can do and do well is important, at least to me."

Another former associate of mine, Dewitt Jones, stressed this to me as follows: "What was the magic ingredient that, in my case at least, made retirement a happy and fruitful experience?

"I talked long and hard to you about getting involved—that there are hundreds of opportunities and needs in any community that are crying for people with talent and ability—or just plain will—to pitch in and help out. But the key is not just involvement. You must believe that what you are doing is very important. You can't feel the job is beneath you—otherwise you'll do a lousy job and be frustrated and discouraged. I know a number of high-powered guys who feel the only thing they can do, having been chairmen and presidents of big companies, is get on some fancy board that 'fits' their image. That's baloney!

"When you come from a high-powered field like advertising where you dealt with chairmen, presidents, and exec VPs for huge stakes, how do you adjust the muscles to deal with a fire board that consists of two real estate salesmen or a conservation board with twelve people from different walks of life? Quite a challenge in itself. Well, in my view, you do it by saying to yourself that this is the most important thing I can do right now and I'm going to bust my butt to make it work by setting some attainable goals and then exceeding them.

"The satisfaction comes from doing just that and it's as satisfying as selling a $25 million campaign to a big client and just as tough. Maybe it's not important in the *big* picture but the fact is that it is to me and that's what counts."

There are two great things about making this kind of capital contribution rather than the money kind.

The first is that, as you give it away, your capital grows.

The second is that putting your intellectual capital to use again is simply wonderful for your ego.

The wife of a retired friend of mine said this of her husband: "When he goes to those meetings, he's always done his homework. He knows the problems, knows the facts, knows what he thinks is right for our little corporation. He presents all that and if everyone agrees, he's happy. But he's just as happy if they don't agree. He never makes it an Ego trip for himself."

Once you start sending out clear signals that you are willing to contribute your intellectual capital, the word will not take long to get around.

Your telephone will ring. And ring.

And when it does, you'll never again have to wake up in the morning and wonder what there is to do all day.

Later, I will discuss some of the ideas I've collected on how to send clear signals.

Your part's harder than mine.

You have to bring the willingness.

FOR WORKAHOLICS: THE JOYS OF GETTING THE MONKEY OFF YOUR BACK

"You are so busy making a living that you don't have time for living itself."

Who said that? Wife? Kids? Friend(s)? You, yourself? Probably none of the above. Not in years. All of you have accepted the primacy of The Job in your life. When someone offers you the old advice, "Take time to stop and smell the roses," you say, "Sure. Tomorrow for sure."

Sure you will.

Then you retire. Kicking, screaming, fighting the panic. For you, the smell of roses cloys both nose and mind. So what are you going to do? Load up your calendar with rigid commitments—paid ones, unpaid ones, or some of both? There is a man in our town who has done that. His wife and my wife are friendly and here is what his wife tells mine: "When he was still chairman, he worked every night from 8:00 to 11:00. Now he's taken on so many civic and charitable jobs that he works every night from 8:00 to 1:00."

There is another way to go. And it is fun.

Royal Little has gone that way, and this is how he describes his life today: "I'm not on the job all the time the way I used to be. I'll work like hell on a deal for three or four days and take a week off for golf."

Gerald Ford has gone that way, too. To be sure, he is still so busy that he needs—and has—a full-time director of scheduling and arrangements, Rowena Evans. On the day I interviewed him about his retirement, Ms. Evans showed me the schedule with my name on it. Mr. Ford had already been in front of a video camera that morning and would have a lunch meeting followed by a telephone interview. But from 2:30 on the day was blocked out for "personal time." It's a good guess that he had exercised his "option to say no" and had gotten up a golf game. That's one reason he lives on a golf course.

By now, I have interviewed, heard about, or read about a great many certified workaholics who could describe themselves as Mr. Ford does: "Retired but not unemployed."

I can't speak for all of them. I know only about myself.

But I suspect that most of them would agree with the principles involved in the following nine statements about me:

1. Work is more fun when I break it up with play. I even work better.

2. My main work is more fun when I break it up with other assignments.

3. I can take a five- or six-week vacation and love it—provided I work at writing for half the day most days.

4. I can't work as many straight hours as I once did. But a half-hour nap restores me to full working speed for several more hours.

5. When I find workaholism and single-track-mindedness creeping in again and staling my mind, I invoke Shank's Law: "Thou shalt knock it off for one day a week and paint canvases instead."

What fun the work of painting is for me! And how restorative.

6. I have more fun at parties now. No one ever wanted to hear me talk about my old passion, advertising. But people seem to be fascinated with hearing what I've learned about retirement.

7. Practicing golf is a great outlet for a workaholic. I can get as grim and determined at that as at any other job. And it does wonders for my pleasure on the golf course.

8. By giving myself one main job and several lesser ones, I have increased my circle of friends. This has a very yeasty effect on my general outlook on life.

9. Spontaneity is a powerful ally. When my mind rebels and won't work the way I want it to, I have learned to get up, get out of my office, and do the first thing that comes to my mind: run errands, take a walk, call a friend, go hit a bucket of balls. What it is doesn't matter. What does matter is that I not only return to work refreshed but I discover again this incredible—for a workaholic—truth: having fun can be *fun*.

The fact is that retirement is a terrific boon to a workaholic. You can work whenever the spirit moves you—nights, weekends, early mornings—and work 100 percent of the time at work *you* choose. And still find time to smell the roses.

Welcome to the club.

THE ODDS
FOR HAPPINESS

I am about to reveal the best-kept secret in the world: Older people are the happiest people.

Specifically, people in their sixties, seventies, and eighties are happier than people in their teens, twenties, thirties, forties, and fifties.

The differences are not small. Or ambiguous. Or full of ifs, buts, and maybes. They are clear and they are significant.

Does that shake you up? Does it do violence to your most cherished prejudices? Or does it merely make you want to close this book and file it on the shelf with your kids' old collection of fairy tales? I wouldn't blame you.

When I was twenty-one, no one asked me how I thought I'd feel about my life at various ages. If someone had asked, I'd have had a ready answer. I could even have put down my answer on a piece of graph paper and it would have looked like Figure 1: a steady increase in happiness right up to age sixty-five, then *ZAP.*

Moreover, I never changed this concept while I was still working at my job. I assumed that the older people I knew were just hanging in there, trying to make the best of a bad thing.

In the course of doing research for this book, I paid a visit to The Menninger Foundation, a renowned mental health clinic and research center located in Topeka, Kansas. I went there hoping to load myself up with information and wisdom that I could then pass on to you. For a long while, I didn't realize that my trip was a success; I had arrived there with questions that have not yet been answered and may never be.

Now, however, I see my trip differently. For one thing, Dr. Paul Pruyser and Mr. Tom Dolgoff put into my hands two documents that completely turned around my ideas of the emotional climate in the older years.

The first of these documents is a graph, taken from Gail Sheehy's *Pathfinders.* Based on interviews with 50,000 men and women of all ages, it speaks, eloquently, for itself. (See charts.)

Happiness Among Men
(Shank View at Age 21)

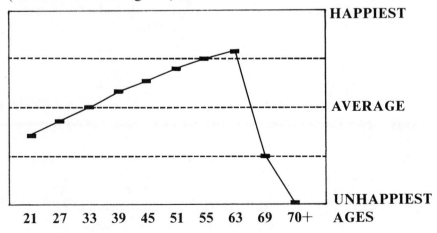

| HAPPIEST |
| AVERAGE |
| UNHAPPIEST |

| 21 | 27 | 33 | 39 | 45 | 51 | 55 | 63 | 69 | 70+ | AGES |

Happiness Among Men

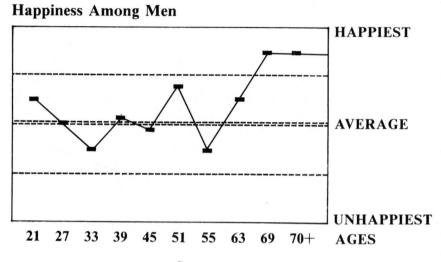

Some caveats
These are not guarantees.
These are the averages of all male
replies to the Sheehy questionnaire.
All it says is that the odds are good for you and me in retirement.

Happiness Among Women

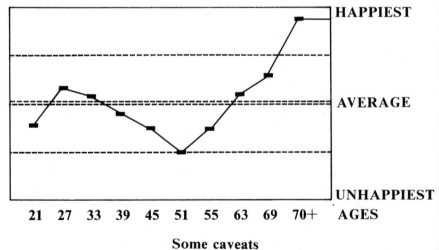

Some caveats
These are not guarantees.
These are the averages of all female
replies to the Sheehy questionnaire.
All it says is that the odds are good for you and me in retirement.

The second document is a reprint of an article by Pruyser, originally published in the scholarly journal *Pastoral Psychology*. In this piece, Pruyser says that we human beings have an "overruling conviction that life has a peak somewhere" in the thirties, forties, or fifties with "an upward slope on one side and a downward slope on the other." He had such a conviction himself. Halfway through his article, he writes, "Much as I struggled to extricate myself from it, I have demonstrated how much I am still its captive."

Trying to extricate himself, Pruyser turns to Jung, Erikson, Gandhi, Coles, Freud, Karl Menninger, Einstein, and Goethe for insights. He also cites the work of Ernest Hirsch, a colleague at Menninger's. Hirsch, says Pruyser, finds that an "*amazingly* [my emphasis] large proportion of quite ordinary people over the age of sixty-five emphatically declare in a psychological interview that their later years are the happiest ones in their lives." Pruyser had supposed that such satisfaction in later years would be "the special situation of the 'happy few' who are highly endowed and whose knowledge and skill remain in demand and, therefore, *do not actually retire.*"

In trying to explain all this to myself, I have had to do a lot of tough thinking. Myths and misconceptions die reluctantly. The thinking has been worth the effort, at least for me.

I now can see and accept the happiness-value of the following "freedoms to" and "freedoms from." These are unique perquisites of older people:

Freedom from the pressures and constraints of job-holding.

Freedom from the anxieties of child-raising.

Freedom from striving and struggling.

Freedom to go and to do.

Freedom to develop oneself.

Freedom to devote major chunks of time to others.

Freedom to speak one's mind.

Freedom to set one's own goals.

Freedom to believe that "it's OK to be me."

Freedom to reidentify with the idealism of youth.

(Not to mention the freedom to add to this list as one's insights come along).

However, the most convincing explanation for the older-is-happier phenomenon is something else, I feel.

We learn the truth of what Blaise Pascal said in 1670, "We never really live, but only hope to live. Always looking forward to being happy, it is inevitable that we should never be so."

We learn that Anonymous, too, was right: "Success is getting what you want; happiness is wanting what you get."

We learn to live in the here and now.

In spite of all this, you may find ways, lots of ways, to be unhappy in retirement. I did. Lots of people have.

All I say is that age is on *your* side. As I've tried to demonstrate—and will demonstrate further in the retirement stories to come—the odds of your being happy/happier/happiest are a lot better than you might have thought.

Better that than the alternative, I say.

Agreed?

V
WISDOM
Mostly in the Form of Dutch-Uncle Talk

HOW TO READ
THE NEXT THREE PARTS
OF THIS BOOK

For quite a while now, this book is going to read as though they'd passed a law against the words "if" and "but." There will be no verbs in the subjunctive mood, no either/or sentences, no hedging words—legal or otherwise. The only colors will be black and white.

The purpose of this is not to make me sound like a know-it-all or make you feel like a know-nothing—God forbid.

My purpose is to save us both a lot of tedium and, in the doing, to save us both a bundle on paper and printing costs.

Demonstration

I could say, "If you suspect that your priorities may have gotten a little out of balance and that you may have let your job muscle other good things out of your daily life, you could conceivably profit from a review of many of the parts of your value system. May I suggest you give it some thought?"

73

I will say something more like, "You've let your job dominate your life. Overhaul your priorities! Overhaul your values! Now. Not later."

You get the idea.

Therefore: When you read what follows, please have on hand a full supply of caveats, subordinate clauses, and such useful words as "tommyrot."

And remember what Cicero said in 50 B.C.: "No one can give you better advice than yourself."

VI
WORKING IN RETIREMENT

"GIVE UP THE TITLES. BUT GO ON WITH THE WORK."
—Monsignor Vincent Cooke

Back in the heyday of auction bridge, silent movies, and crystal radio sets, you and I learned how to think about retirement and we learned our lessons well.

Retirement, they told us and showed us, was a word that meant old and sick and poor.

Retired farmers moved to the nearest small town, sat in a rocking chair on the front porch, and watched life go by. Rich retired people went to Florida and played shuffleboard or sat on the benches in the sunshine. Other retired people lived in old folks' homes or moved in with their children, and a lousy time of it was had by all.

In all cases, retirement and work were mutually exclusive, by common definition.

This stupefying and stultifying concept haunts millions of us still. Monsignor Vincent Cooke said to me in my interview with

77

him: "We think the proper role of the retired person is to go away somewhere and take it easy. That's a big problem we have. We figure we've always worked for other people and now other people are supposed to work for us."

One crucial reason why this 1920s idea has lived into the 1980s is as follows. Our ancestors made the words "job" and "work" synonymous. The job that called for an eight-, nine-, or twelve-hour day and a five-, six-, or seven-day week was what they meant when they spoke of "our work." Therefore, despite the fact that the great majority of us still are vigorous in mind and body at retirement, we behave as we were programmed to behave. When age brings us to the end of the job, some cobwebby quirk of thought says that we have come to the end of real, honest, hard, worthwhile, important, pleasurable work as well.

And so we permit ourselves to enter second childhood. As retreaded children, we try to act the part. We try oh, so dutifully. And in the trying, we cut ourselves off from one of the great opportunities in life: to be our own bosses, to work for the love of work.

Forsooth.

So, my first—and best—piece of advice for you is to retire from your job but not from work.

Work for the good of your self-esteem. Work to get some structure in your life. Work for the fun of working. Work to get out of your spouse's hair. Work to satisfy your survival instinct and your work ethic. Work for any or all of the above reasons but *work!*

THE IMPORTANCE OF IMPORTANCE

A flat prediction: When you retire from your job and start looking for work to take its place, you will have a problem with your attitudes, your value system, and your priorities.

The problem has a name. The name is Importance.

Your successes, your standing in the community, your friendships, your earning power, your busy schedule, your feelings of being *somebody*—all will, in retrospect, look more important, more valuable, indeed more indispensable by the day.

You can try to shake all that off with a figurative flick of the wrist but it's not going to work. You might as well stick your hand in flypaper and try to wave it away.

Remember the bus driver who acted out his dream, retired to Florida, and took it easy? Leland Bradford wrote of him, "He began to realize how important his work had been in the lives of many. He realized he had had pride in his work. Nothing took its place for him. He didn't find situations in which he felt he had significance in other people's lives. He didn't try very hard. He lost his self respect and was unhappy for the few remaining years he lived."

The key words in the above paragraph are these: *Nothing took its place for him.*

There is no better statement of the number one danger that presents itself to you and me and all of us at retirement time.

And there is no better testimony to what we most need: to find at least one thing, one important thing, that will allow us to live in and for the present.

This means that we have to change.

The problem is not to *find* important work. The problem is to *see what we find* as important.

That's where our ability to change attitudes, values, and priorities comes in. If we look with a haughty eye at every possibility that crops up and measure it by our old standards, we are going to wind up like that bus driver. Or like those friends of Royal Little's who ran big corporations, went off to Florida or somewhere, and died in two quick stages—minds first, bodies second.

Now, I realize that this is not altogether news to you. You have often heard that it's important *before* you retire to take up a hobby or two and to have something vaguely called "other interests." You may in fact, have taken the advice and you may take a lot of comfort in that.

Sorry. I'm going to make you uncomfortable.

There may be someone, somewhere on the face of this earth, who has retired and who has replaced his job in his scheme of things with a menu of hobbies and "other interests." May he have a long and happy life!

But there is a difficulty with hobbies: they are, by definition, pastimes. Now, pastimes can be absorbing, I know that. My own hobby, painting, is the greatest passer of time I have ever found and I take a certain pride in the results of my efforts. But my mind couldn't live on a diet of painting any more than my body could live on a diet of cream puffs.

What's missing for us in hobbies and hobby-type interests is, of course, importance.

If you think you have problems in defining the word, "importance," as it applies to your life, go get your fattest dictionary and see what the professionals say. Poor guys. It's easier to define "will o' the wisp." Which is part of our problem.

To illustrate: I know a man who serves on a number of boards in his retirement. Two of the companies surround their directors with all the standard, big-deal props: Paneled walls. Leather executive chairs. Directors' names engraved in brass plates on the chairs. All the hush and plush are designed to tell the meeting-attenders what important people they are. But there's one problem as far as my friend is concerned. The management looks for directors with big names rather than big ideas, people who bring to the party big reputations rather than big contributions. My friend, not surprisingly, finds those companies *boring* because they don't give his head anything important to deal with. Happily for him, his other boards provide all the challenge he wants and needs.

Importance, clearly, exists only in the eye of the beholder.

If the beholder gets a thrill out of solving problems—if good, meaty problems are important to his intellectual well-being—he doesn't need a big title or a big leather chair to tell him that they *are* important.

If the beholder has dedicated his life to helping other people, he doesn't need a big parish or a big practice to feel good about the act of helping, however trivial the act may look to others.

So, the responsibility for finding and doing "important" work in retirement rests squarely on us. Others can propose, but only we can dispose. If you are holding your breath, waiting for me to announce the One-Size-Fits-All Magic Formula by which you or anyone else may discharge that responsibility, please stop. There ain't no such thing.

However, I do have a suggestion for you, starting on the next page.

HOW TO WRITE
YOUR OWN DEFINITION
OF "IMPORTANT"

First, get some paper.

Second, get something to write with.

Third, go someplace where it's quiet and will remain quiet. No telephone. No television. No one who will talk to you and thus rescue you from the hard, lonely work of thinking. You are about to design the new-model You, and that calls for all the focus and concentration you can bring to bear.

Fourth, write at the top of a page the following words:

Important. Now.

Fifth, do not let my playful tone fool you. I am dead serious about this but I don't want to be a deadly bore.

What you're trying to accomplish is to get your mind to focus on your own new wants and needs. You will be surprised to find that your faithful unconscious has been working on the subject even if your conscious thoughts have been a million miles away. As you write and rewrite your list, you will, I guarantee, find that the exercise gets and keeps your attention. As one man said to me after an interview, "This has been fascinating—what could be a more fascinating subject than me?"

To help you get started, I offer herewith a sort of checklist. It is by no means global in scope—do add and subtract according to your own lights. The numbers after each item are simply the familiar one-to-six scale. If an item is very important to you now, rate it a six. If it is very unimportant, give it a one. If it falls in between pick a number from two through five. The objective is simply to force yourself to record your ideas in writing. How better than by writing them out to put your ideas to the acid test?

VALUE	1	2	3	4	5	6
Making extra money.	—	—	—	—	—	—
Holding a full-time job (paid or unpaid).	—	—	—	—	—	—
Working for the pleasure of it.	—	—	—	—	—	—
Status. And/or fame.	—	—	—	—	—	—
Power.	—	—	—	—	—	—
Comradeship.	—	—	—	—	—	—
Goals and purposes of your own.	—	—	—	—	—	—
Helping others.	—	—	—	—	—	—
Learning, growing.	—	—	—	—	—	—
Variety of activities.	—	—	—	—	—	—
Flexibility.	—	—	—	—	—	—
Other?............................	—	—	—	—	—	—

Pretty easy so far? Fasten your seat belt.

Now we add in another two factors: candor and realism.

Candidly now, what ratings did you give to status and power? Ones in both cases? Both very unimportant? Really? If it had been me, I would have done the same thing. No way would I admit to being interested in status and power, particularly now. Those are socially taboo, remember? But how do you *actually* feel?

And what about realism? Did you give a six to both helping others and making extra money? Can you give first importance to both those goals in the real world?

How about a fresh checklist so you can consider a few changes?

VALUE	1	2	3	4	5	6
Making extra money.	—	—	—	—	—	—
Holding a full-time job (paid or unpaid).	—	—	—	—	—	—
Working for the pleasure of it.	—	—	—	—	—	—
Status. And/or fame.	—	—	—	—	—	—
Power.	—	—	—	—	—	—
Comradeship.	—	—	—	—	—	—
Goals and purposes of your own.	—	—	—	—	—	—
Helping others.	—	—	—	—	—	—
Learning, growing.	—	—	—	—	—	—
Variety of activities.	—	—	—	—	—	—
Flexibility.	—	—	—	—	—	—
Other?...........................	—	—	—	—	—	—

If your numbers did change from your first chart to your second one, good for you. You now see what this exercise is all about. And you are on your way to thinking yourself into a new set of priorities and standards.

Now that you have started down this road, keep going. You are not going to get where you want to get overnight but you will get there. I recommend that you take out your list at least once a day for two weeks and put yourself to the task of rethinking it each time. I guarantee another thing: If you will put your back into doing this, you will be surprised by the growing clarity of your new definition of "importance."

But don't put away your paper and pencil.

I have another assignment for you.

Next page, please.

COUNTING UP YOUR INTELLECTUAL CAPITAL

Now that you have written a good, sharp definition of what's important to you, it is time to look at how important you can be to other people.

You are now going to take inventory of the intellectual capital you have been storing up for your retirement. Prepare yourself for some surprises—pleasant ones.

You, I, all of us workers of whatever calling, have earned our livings on the strength of three main things:

1. Our professional skills and knowledge.

2. Our ability to play the organizational game.

3. Our mastery of the ins and outs, the crotchets, the "this is the way we do it heres" of the specific milieu in which we have toiled.

It is critical that we see these distinctions clearly and keep them at the tops of our minds. Otherwise, we are going to flimflam ourselves with the classic complaint, "My job is the only thing I know how to do." Or with this variation: "The only valuable work I can do is the work I did on my job."

There is no getting around the fact that, when you and I retire, we do lose a sizable fraction of our value to others. What I knew about Leo Burnett Company and what you knew about your specific situation went right down the tube. *C'est la vie.*

But the rest of our intellectual capital stayed right there in the vaults we call our heads.

Leave it in there and of course it's worth nothing.

Haul it out and reinvest it and that's another story altogether.

I am about to lay another list-making job on you, but this time it will be simpler. Get out your paper and pencil, go to your sanctuary, and write this heading:

Intellectual Capital

Then copy down the following (I'm going to get you off to a fast start):

Judgment. I know how to learn everything that's relevant

to a problem, to analyze what I learn, and to synthesize it into a clear definition of what the problem actually is. I know how to go from there to a solid assessment of the possible solutions and to recommend the most likely one.

Creativity. Having defined a problem, I can create solutions that others have not yet thought of.

Experience. All those years of working in my field of expertise have taught me that all problems tend to repeat themselves, at least in principle. My knowledge of how similar problems were solved in the past makes me valuable in the solution of present problems. This can save large amounts of time and money for those less experienced.

That, of course, is just for starters. You will want to make a much longer list and you will want to be a lot more specific. For example, if you are a first-rate numbers guy, spell that out for yourself in detail. When you look at a balance sheet, do the soft spots jump right out at you? Write that down.

The key thing is that you do a thorough and accurate job of looking at yourself and what you still have to offer. Don't, for heaven's sake, do the old false-modesty bit! You're in much greater danger of underrating yourself than of overrating yourself. No matter what they have said about you at the testimonial dinner, you are still shook up by the discovery that you are not indispensable. You have temporarily forgotten that "valuable" and "indispensable" are not synonyms.

As with your previous assignment, don't try to rush this one to a finish. Treat it with all the respect you'd give to yeast-based dough: give it time to rise.

SERENDIPITY AND OTHER BRILLIANT STRATEGIES

You have a firm handle on what and who are important to you now. You have a new idea of how important *you* can be and to what and whom. Good for you.

"But," you say, "that still begs the burning question. What am I specifically supposed to *do* with this nifty opportunity you keep talking about? I want to get going."

Relax, I pray you.

No one is asking you to make a quick decision and to live with it for life. The next thing you need to do is to get these strategic assets lined up on your side:

Patience

Willingness

Adventuresomeness

The guts to correct mistakes

And an eye for the happy chance

Don't tell me how hard that is. I know how hard it is. I didn't say it would be easy to find your retirement work, I said it would be smart.

The sober fact is that neither you, nor I, nor anyone else can march straight away from his career and into his best new opportunity(ies) without experimenting. None of us is so brainy and foresighted that he can take the big step without stubbing some toes, all ten of them perhaps.

Indeed, toe-stubbing may be a prerequisite to finding one's new *métier*, as you will see in the stories to follow:

Dewitt Jones might never have become "mayor" of Captiva if he had not been willing to take a crack at being a fireman.

Bob Noel might never have started his lucrative little business if he had not seen—by chance—a picture of a rug-covered bench and if he had not then been adventuresome enough to risk a failure.

Monsignor Cooke might never have gotten into marriage-encounter work if he had not first been willing to serve as an assistant pastor.

I offer a little of my own story by way of further example: Whether or not you like this book, I have liked writing it—a lot. But I would never have gotten here on a straight line. One way and another, I had to do a six-week lecturing stint at the University of Southern California, had to try consulting with a small publishing company, had to do unpaid marketing projects for Lake Forest College and Highland Park (Ill.) Hospital. Only then could I see what I wanted for myself: to make writing the new centerpiece in my own life. It was not that I didn't like the other things I'd tried. I'm still doing some of them. But their great value was in helping me get to where I am with my life today.

The more things you are willing to try—in context, of course, with your new knowledge of yourself—the more likely you are to end up with a happy result.

I commend to you, therefore, the following policies:

1. When your phone rings and someone asks you to talk to him about taking on a chore, talk. Even if you turn him down, you will be practicing your new strategy of willingness. The next time your phone rings, it may be the first link in a serendipitous chain.

2. Send out willingness signals. Whenever anyone asks what you're doing, say you're following your new policy of trying a variety of things, seeing where you really want to go. *That* will make your phone ring.

3. Before you try something—whether you think you'll like it or not—leave yourself an honorable escape route. No one is going to get mad when you say, "I'm willing to give it a shot if you are—provided that either of us can cut it off with no hard feelings if it doesn't work."

I know what you're saying: "Leaving things to serendipity," you argue, "does not strike me as the world's most brilliant strategy."

I hear you.

But, I remind you, it *is* at least a strategy. When you embrace it, you are not just pursuing the non-strategy of sitting around the house, practicing grumpiness and waiting for the president of the United States to call and offer you a cabinet job.

You are doing things, two important things: first, you are playing the old spider game, spinning your web and waiting for the right piece of happenstance. You know that it will come along. The only question is when. Second, you are giving your well-honed judgment an opportunity to do its job. Brilliance consists of many things, including the ability to look at the sour apples along with the sweet and then to tell the difference.

Think of Columbus. When it finally dawned on him that he hadn't found India, he saw that he'd at least found a fascinating substitute.

And think of Sir Alexander Fleming. He'd never heard of penicillin before he stumbled over it in the middle of being scientific about something else.

Brilliant pieces of strategy?

Q.E.D.

WORK FOR MONEY BUT DEFEND YOUR FREEDOM

The day you go off the payroll, watch out for irrational messages, coming from within:

"Told you so! You're not worth a plugged nickel any more."

"People respect ants, not grasshoppers. You're a grasshopper."

"Over the hill and out to pasture. That's you."

That, of course, is not how you're supposed to feel about your retirement. You're supposed to take it easy, aren't you? You know the litany: "Take it easy, man. It's time to reap your reward for all that long, hard work. These are your Golden Years."

Isn't that what everybody has always said?

Yes. Well, everybody but retired people.

When you start getting those irrational messages, there is no use asking for a summit conference between the rational and irrational parts of your mind. The Rational You can talk all it likes about how financially sound you are. And it won't work.

The Irrational You doesn't give a damn about pensions and tax exempts and Social Security and all that jazz. It *does* give a damn about the two kinds of respect: respect you get from others, and respect you get from yourself. What the Irrational You wants to see and fondle is paychecks. When it does see paychecks, it says:

"See! You've still got the old moxie, babe." (True)

"Hey, look! You can still pull your own weight." (True)

"Now who's too old to work? Not you, kid." (True)

Naturally, there is a moral to all this. Three morals, in fact.

First moral: The human spirit is allergic to sudden change. It *hates* to have the rules change overnight.

Second moral: Therefore, gradualism is the prudent man's philosophy of retirement. (More about gradualism later.)

Third moral: So work at what you like in retirement—but get paid for some of it.

But wait. There's another part to this, damn it. Who ever said this was going to be easy?

Among the successfully and happily retired people you will read about in this book, all but one works for money some of the time. But there's a second part to their retirement strategy and you've got to look at that part, too. Ignore it at your peril.

Gerald Ford speaks fondly of "the option to say no."

Leo Schoenhofen sees "retirement as an opportunity to do things I could never do before."

Bob Noel cherishes his freedom. "The absolutely great thing about retirement for which I thank God every day . . . is freedom. I love it."

Arthur Wood says, "It's great to be able to work over the weekend if you want to and then go fishing for the next three days."

Furthermore, every person you will read about in these pages also does work without pay. Most of them work longer and harder for the pleasure of helping others than they do for money.

And every one of them finds time to smell the roses.

Therefore, dear reader, defend your freedom. Defend your flexibility. Sign no contracts. And don't forget your honorable escape route.

Sooner or later, even the Irrational You is going to get wise to the following: the retirement opportunity does not yield itself to us stubborn practitioners of tunnel vision and monomania.

The opportunity demands that we cultivate and practice the most underrated and least-pondered virtue of them all: balance.

OF PROBLEMS AND PROJECTS: MISGUIDED POLICIES, MISPLACED PRIDE

So here you are, retired from your job.

You've overhauled your priorities and your values. You've worked out your own new definition of "important." You want to fry other fish now and you want to defend your freedom. But you don't want to retire entirely from gainful employment—for the reasons we've just discussed.

However, the single most logical road to where you want to go is closed. C-L-O-S-E-D. There is not a safer bet in town.

Right now, today, your old organization is loaded with problems that need solving, projects that need doing. They aren't going away and you know why: the press of daily business is—what else is new?—getting in the way.

Furthermore, at least one of these pieces of undone work has your name on it. You are the single most qualified person in the world to get it off the organization's back. So why isn't your telephone ringing?

Pride. (Misplaced.)

Or policy. (Misguided.)

Or both.

Let's take a look at how that works, but fasten your seat belt first. Some of this is going to shake you up.

Here's a hypothetical situation: one of the people you used to work with has a long-standing problem. He himself could solve it by waving his magic wand and making all his other problems disappear for a while. Or a small team could solve it—if he could free them up.

He thinks of you and wishes—in a way—that he could call on you. In another way, you are the last person in the world he wants to see and to confess his problems to. Pride!

Even if he is a big enough fellow to live with a little loss of face, he has to think of his fellow employees. Suppose he did bring you in? How many out-of-joint egos would he have to deal with? How many people would feel threatened by your presence? Tough. . . .

Suppose, however, that all those problems of anxiety, ego, and pride somehow are made to vanish. Suppose you do get a telephone call.

They want you to come in and get their problem/project off their lists. Of course, there won't be a fortune in it for you. They'll have to find you a little place to work somewhere and maybe they can get the typing pool to help. Oh—and they want you to keep a low profile. No sense in upsetting the troops. How about it? ("Low profile" translated: don't stick your nose in any business other than what we're assigning you).

Confess, now. That does shake you up a little, doesn't it? Don't those people remember who you were and what you were?

Sure, it's a tough problem they've got and you can solve it but you used to have *assistants* who did that kind of work!

It is for just such reasons that our national inventory of mothballed talent is going to waste. And that's why so many of the mothballed are sitting around feeling sorry for themselves.

However, there is a glimmer of hope.

Late in 1983, I heard a story from a friend, a story that falls into the category of "if they can do it, we can do it."

A big company has had the same problem, over and over again, for at least fifteen years. It is costly and embarrassing. It affects every division, every department. The government is involved. Consumer advocates have been involved. There have been lawsuits.

It's a bad problem, which I'll call "X" for a moment.

The company itself is tightly structured, many-layered. Its mandatory retirement policy for executives applies to everyone. Period.

My friend had run into a retired executive of this company a few days before. He thought the man looked exceptionally beamish and said so. The man said, "You're right. Haven't you heard? The company has just given me a wonderful project—the "X" problem!"

My friend and I agreed that it was wonderful. Wonderful that the company had been flexible enough to ask. Wonderful that the man had accepted. Wonderful that he had been so pleased.

The name of the company is General Motors.

The name of the man is Richard Gerstenberg, former chairman of the board and chief executive officer.

And "X" is the recall problem, that recurring obligation to call in and modify cars that went out of the factory with some unforeseen problem.

If they can do it, so can a lot of other people.

Think about it. Think hard. And ask yourself how willing you are to take on a tough project with limited authority, limited responsibility and a specific deadline for completion.

You are willing? Really? Good.

Then get a photocopy of this chapter and put it in an envelope with the kind of agreeable covering letter that you write so well.

Say, in effect, "keep me in mind." Mail it—you know who the right person is—to your old organization.

If *that* doesn't make your phone ring, try someone else.

The competition.

GET A
SERIOUS PLACE
TO WORK

Show me where you plan to work in your retirement and I'll tell you in ten seconds flat how serious you are about working.

Take me to a child-size desk in a spare room with a bed, a dresser, and an old football and you flunk.

Take me to your conjugal desk in your conjugal bedroom and I'll have trouble keeping my face straight.

Take me to a showplace den that features a big TV, a trophy case, you wife's needlework, and the family snapshots and—well, you see what I mean.

Exactly the same principles apply to *any* sort of workplace. If you need a workshop, do not treat it as a playshop. If you need a laboratory, a darkroom, a barn, or whatever else, let it be serious.

Serious work cannot and does not take place in frivolous surroundings. Never mind saying, "Yes, but look at Winston Churchill, John Maynard Keynes, and Robert Louis Stevenson. They did a lot of work in bed." I'll come back with, "So what. They were practicing geniuses. And they didn't do their best work in bed, anyway."

Believe me, I tried all the makeshifts, all the halfway measures. They didn't work and neither did I. In fact, there is a clear-cut correlation in my own history of work-in-retirement: on the day I set up my own serious *place* to work, I started *doing* serious work.

What's at issue here is not just bricks and mortar, not paper and paraphernalia. And it's certainly not money. I'd rather see you in a cubbyhole that looks open for business than in some plush place with executive-type fixings and the unmistakable air of being a museum.

What is at issue is attitudes. And the most important attitudes we need to look at are our own.

As every one of us hard workers knows, the hardest thing we have to do is to get ourselves up and running. It is one thing to have other people set the deadlines for us and to lay out the standards of satisfactory performance. It is quite another thing to make our own rules and to live by them.

I am in no way different from you in this department. I have a lot of grasshopper genes in me. I put off working until my conscience starts to nag at the bloody-murder level and I have to protect myself vigorously from beguiling and bedeviling distractions. I have to *seduce* myself into working.

That's why, when I walk into the space I call my office, its message to me is as plain and single-minded as I know how to make it: "The only purpose of this place is to get you to work."

My office is not an ugly place or a bare place or a spartan place. The chairs are comfortable, the light is good, music is always playing, and I keep plants around. There is a private bathroom— although I do share it with my photocopying machine.

It does, however, have three desks: a computer desk with two kinds of printers flanking my Apple Lisa, a counter-style desk, and a "lap desk." The latter is a big chair with writing pads and a dozen pens right at hand. There are three phone lines—enough to keep my wife and myself out of each other's hair. The air conditioner and the electric baseboard heaters are independent of the systems in the house.

If I need a nap, I have to go into the house to take it.

It's not just you who will be asking how serious you are. Your spouse and family, your friends, and even relevant strangers will be asking themselves, "Does he really want to work in retirement? Or does he just *want to want* to work?"

Now that you have answered yes to the former question, I offer the following guidelines for home offices. The very same principles apply no matter where you choose to or have to hang your hat.

1. Make it private. It must be yours and yours alone. No sewing machines. No day beds. No out-of-season clothes or vacuum cleaners in the closet. Above all, no "hers" desk alongside yours. You need to defend your territory with your life and your wife needs to defend hers. In one way, this *is* your new life we're talking about.

2. Have your own telephone, if you need one. This is not a

selfish rule. It is just as important to your spouse as it is to you. It's OK to answer calls for each other as genuine needs arise. But you can't make a career of it. Neither of you can.

3. Get your own tools and get good ones. Even if you have a family typewriter, get another one, a better one. The fewer excuses you have to put off working, the more work you will do and the better you'll feel. Good tools, private tools, tools that are a pleasure to use—it's hard *not* to work when you have them.

4. Have a private entrance if possible. The less you and your visitors get mixed up in the business of the household—or the business of anyone else, for that matter—the better off you'll be. That goes for private bathrooms, too.

I've been as hard-nosed about those four points as I know how to be. I've done so in full awareness that your wife will raise some objections. When that happens, ask her to read Part Three of this book entitled "Your Worse Half." Then ask her to read this section. She will get the point. And she'll respect you for having made it.

More than anything else, your wife wants you to feel good about yourself in retirement. Not just for your sake—for hers as well.

YOU, THE NEW RENAISSANCE MAN

Reader! Now hear this:

From this day forward, you are forbidden to call yourself by any noun which ends in any of the following suffixes:

-er	-ant
-ist	-ian
-yst	-ent
-ive	-or

If you take that as a challenge to look for loopholes, I give you herewith the sole and only exception to the rule. You may call yourself a generalist.

If this be tyranny, make the most of it.

Specialization was all well and good for us when we had kids to feed, to house, to educate. Back then, it made sense to narrow our fields of expertise; to narrow was to broaden our economic prospects. If we wanted to wind up with a two-car garage and two cars to fill it, we knew what to do: hang in there until we became something that ended in "logist" or "ician."

Fine.

But now is the time to knock that off. The price of not knocking it off is awesome (meaning dreadful) and self-limiting (meaning boring). The ground we lose by thinking of ourselves as superannuated specialists is bounded on one side by fun, on a second by self-respect, on a third by growth, on a fourth by adventure, on a fifth by . . . you see where that leads.

Now is the time for us to be modern Medicis, to become twentieth century "universal men."

And we are just the people who can do it.

When you and I came into the world, we were generalists. Every baby is a Renaissance kid.

We didn't think it was hard to grow, to learn, to explore, to experiment. In our view, the world was our oyster and all we had to do was reach for it.

We didn't think it was hard to learn English (or Spanish or Creole or Vietnamese). We could hardly wait to say "mama" and "dada." And it was fun.

"Thou shalt specialize" is not a mandate from that overrated czar, the gene pool. It is merely an economic artifact, a symptom of the Post-Industrial Age. Even Einstein, the ultimate specialist of his time, was a violinist, too.

You and I are now going to demonstrate something to each other.

The list below covers the prerequisites for a certain specialized occupation. Read it, please; put on your thinking cap; and write down all the occupations to which you think it applies.

The Practitioner Must Be Able To:

Learn new techniques.

Learn new facts.

Apply logic.

Analyze data.

Collaborate with others.

Follow and give orders.

Follow approved procedures.

Innovate.

Create as necessary.

Communicate orally.

Communicate in writing.

Persuade.

Make decisions.

Display willingness.

Display open-mindedness.

Concentrate.

See things through.

What's on your list? Surgeon? Attorney? Engineer? Editor? Physicist? Historian? Minister? Salesman? Critic? Production Chief? Actor? Your own specialty?

Wrong.

That is, whatever you put down is wrong unless you happen to have listed "advertising creative director." As I made my list, I was trying to describe the good people I've known who made their livings at my old specialty.

The point of this demonstration is: that the better we get at our specialties, the better we get at all the basic skills. Show me a surgeon, for example, who does not rate highly on all items on my list and I'll show you a bum surgeon.

Therefore, reader, do not let your friends cop out when they retire. If you hear them saying, "The only kind of work I can do is the work I did on my job," do them a favor.

Give them this direct order: "Buy a copy of this book. Read especially the chapter on the Renaissance Man. And get to work."

DO YOUR FRIENDS A FAVOR: LET THEM HELP

As a full-fledged, lifelong, red-blooded, All-American boy (now senior-grade), you have the standard headful of old slogans and old mottos, e.g.:

Stand on your own two feet!

Paddle your own canoe!

Fight your own battles!

In that philosophy, to tough it out is proof of machismo. To ask for help, on the other hand, is proof of wimpismo. To be a wimp is a fate worse than whatever used to be the worst fate.

Taken in moderation, that is virtuous stuff, no doubt about it. The strong of mind have a way of winding up in the winner's circle.

But, when our time to retire comes and we want and need to work, many of us carry virtue to the point of vice. Instead of asking for and taking the help that's there, we insist on going it alone. *If* we get going at all.

That is not strong-minded. It is pig-headed.

This is not to say that you should take hat in hand, knock on doors, and complain, "Hey, I've got this problem. Solve it for me, please." That would wear out your welcome fast, and solve nothing.

On the other hand, you have dozens of friends and acquaintances who would love to help make *your* solutions work.

Think of your friends as a think tank. When your new life is at its newest, you are going to find yourself in urgent need of other ideas to augment your own.

You may, for instance, have decided you want to help today's college graduates with the problem that concerns them most: their need for a job and their difficulty in getting one. Wonderful!

That will make you feel needed and wanted and it will meet every one of your tests for worthwhileness. It will even help you repay all the people who helped you way back when.

But as soon as the first glow of the thought wears off, your Rude But Practical Side is going to get into the act.

"Terrific," your RBPS will say. "But how? Where? When? What? Give me a clue."

You know what happens then—or what will happen if you, like me, suffer from an insufficiency of knowledge. You won't have a clue, not a practical one, and your good idea will starve for lack of nourishment.

That is where your friends and your friends' friends come in—and come in with whoops of joy. There is nothing, nothing in the world, that we human beings love more than to use our brains to feed someone else's good idea.

Think, therefore, of your friends and their friends as your own ad hoc think tank.

Take them one at a time. Or take them in groups of two or three. Do it on a businesslike basis. Make formal appointments. Ask for specific amounts of time. Provide pencils, paper, tape recorder, coffee, and whatever else it takes to signal that you are dead serious and want serious contributions in the form of alternative ways to go from here.

Believe me, this technique works. (As a bonus, it is fun). In my own retirement, I have been idea-seeker or idea-generator many times and I have never seen this method fail to advance the ball. For example, I could never have produced this book without the help of my friends, their ideas, and their lasting effect on my own concepts.

The technique works for several excellent reasons.

First, the simple act of focusing on a subject works magic. Focused thinking produces focused thoughts as nothing else does.

Second, ideas are not monolithic phenomena. They are chains. You may produce the first link but be unqualified to come up with the second. So your idea is going to abort right there. But if someone else has the knowledge and perspective to supply the missing link—wonderful.

Third, the technique has all the allure of a game, a team game. When you tell a friend that you have a big idea game to play and that you want him and his brain on your team—hey! he'll be there with bells on and thank you for asking.

So.

Now you and your think tank have produced several ways to go with your kids-and-jobs plan. You have a list of possibilities something like this:

1. Find a group of college kids who would like to do the kind of work you did. Help them any way you can on a part-time, informal basis.

2. Find a group of retired people with a wide variety of experience and an interest in helping kids get jobs. Organize these friends as a board of volunteer job counselors. Dozens of worthy causes would love to have you.

3. Volunteer yourself as a resource person to the placement office of the college nearest you.

4. Sell yourself as a college recruiter for several organizations that can't spare staff members to do the work.

5. Do it up right. Start your own personnel agency, specializing in the placement of new holders of bachelors degrees.

All things considered, you like number four best. Now what?

Now, (nimbly switching metaphors) think of your friends as a chain of brains. You have two obvious next steps.

First, you need to pick the brains of a number of people on the employers' side. You don't yet have anything to offer them because you don't yet know what their problems are. You need to know facts, priorities, attitudes.

Second, you need to talk to people on the college side. What you need from them is exactly what you need from employers: Information. Real-world stuff.

In both cases, you need first to get some doors open.

Now, there is more than one way to open a door. You know that from experience. You can put your requests for time and advice in letter form. Or you can telephone, cold-canvass style, and try to make appointments.

But the shortest way home is a phone call from one of your friends to a friend of his. As follows:

"Hey, Jack. I have a retired friend who has a nifty idea, really nifty. But he needs some advice. Of all the people I know, you are the one he most needs to talk to. Plus, he might just be able to help you guys, too. Can I have him call you? Great. Here's his name. . . ."

You have now really started something and it will now take on a life of its own. People will see your objective as worthy and your intentions as serious. They will volunteer ideas, warn of pitfalls, *introduce you to other people who can help.*

Moreover, they will be grateful to you for the chance to do something good. Far from thinking that you can't paddle your own canoe, they will admire you as a man who really knows how to captain a ship.

And you didn't want to ask for help!

VII
HOW TO SUCCEED AT MARRIAGE EVEN IN RETIREMENT

CHANGE 1:
THE MALEVOLENT
MAGNIFYING GLASS

It does not matter how long we have been married or how much rough road we have traveled together.

It does not count that we husbands and wives can claim, with some justification, that we "know all about" each other.

Marriage-before-retirement does damnall to prepare us for marriage-after-retirement.

There is no mystery about it.

Suddenly, we two people are spending a lot more time together, day in and day out, than we have since the honeymoon. And how long did that last?

Suddenly, old habits, roles, routines, schedules, responsibilities, and all the other taken-for-granteds go up for grabs.

Suddenly, a regiment of surprises comes marching into our living spaces. Suddenly we find ourselves spending a ton more time than we'd like, waiting for the other shoe to drop.

Now, I know what you're saying to yourself. You're saying,

"There goes Shank, getting carried away again. It can't be that bad. . . ."

Oh, really?

Listen again to the Bradfords, Leland and Martha:

"One person said to us, 'No one knows the bruising many husbands and wives give each other when they retire.'

"Another told us, 'We are like strangers in our marriage going through a ritual without meaning.' "

Speaking of a third couple, the Bradfords wrote:

> Then he retired. He found it difficult. He couldn't always remember where he placed his now sparser correspondence or whether he had already answered it. He missed the finely-tuned organization he had known and the secretaries who did so much. With no intention to be critical of the way the home was kept, he did repeat to his wife fairly often how much he missed the perfect order of his office. She, who had always felt that she had done a more than competent job in keeping the home neat, perceived his remarks as critical and took affront. She felt she saw a new side of his personality she had not observed before—obsessive neatness. She failed to realize that, having become accustomed to all the careful organization in his work, he was almost unconsciously following her around and closing doors and picking up papers. She had intended to do the picking up and had always done so on her own schedule. She felt deflated, irritated, hostile, and then openly angry. She didn't like what her new view of this side of her husband was doing to her. Her anger produced bewilderment in him, then excuses, and finally anger in response . . . Neither listened to or understood the other. Each felt put upon.

Having read or listened to or lived through dozens of such vignettes, I have formed the following image in my mind:

I see a magnifying glass, a monstrous lens that stands between us husbands and wives when we retire.

When the glass is turned upon small faults and foolishness, it blows them up in size, turns them into federal cases. "Do you have to spend so much time on the telephone?" sounds like, "I hate you and furthermore I hate all your friends." "Could you put away the newspaper when you finish?" sounds like, "You are a slob. You've always been a slob. I should have listened to Mother and Dad."

Just what you'd expect of a magnifying glass.

But this one turns in a nannosecond into a minimizing glass. It looks at strength, tenderness, caring, and all other positive things and turns them into trivia.

Will you as a couple look me straight in the eye and say that you guarantee—*guarantee*— that you will never, ever let that magnifying glass into your house? God bless you. And good luck.

Or will you say this: "I know what you're talking about and it's the pits. We hate it when we lose our perspective that way."

When we let the magnifying glass take over our married lives, we have the following options:

Divorce

Formal separation

Ad hoc separation—doing whatever it takes to stay away from each other

Truce—we don't separate physically, we just don't speak to each other

Misery—terminal misery

Change

You say you opt for change? Not so fast, reader.

Change is not that easy to accomplish. It takes work. It takes time.

Before you choose your option, read on.

CHANGE 2:
MEET THE ENEMY

Take a look, a good look, at Marriage Enemy Number One. (Retired or not.)

You will find it, described in living black and white, on page 1156 of *Webster's Third New International Dictionary* (Unabridged).

You and your wife already know the enemy by the effect it has on you. As your Webster's puts it:

1. You "continue in the same straight line or direction unless acted upon by some external force."

2. You have "an indisposition to motion, exertion, or action."

3. You have "the tendency of animals to continue repeating the same action in the same place."

You guessed it. The enemy is inertia.

No matter that your marriage relationship now calls loudly for changes by both of you, you are going to resist. You will resist, passively to be sure. But passive resistance is powerful. Remember Gandhi.

Example number one: In our generation of "traditional marriages," we husbands and wives have accumulated dozens of roles, privileges and prerogatives that are sex-specific. Husbands do only this and that. Wives do only thus and so. Couples, as couples, do whatever is left over.

Our adult children may tell us that they are trying new configurations, lots of them, and that many of their new ideas work well.

"Fine," we say, "that's fine for you but not for us. We do as we do because that's how we were brought up. It's too late for us now."

This is called inertia.

Example number two: Like other married couples, the two of you and the two of us know all about forbidden territory. Forbidden territory is home to the subjects we no longer talk about. You know why:

"I can't speak to him about *that*—he'll just get mad."

"If I try to get her to do it differently, she'll start to cry and say, 'I knew it. You don't love me any more.' "

The thought of stepping into forbidden territory sends involuntary shudders through us all. "I guess," we say, "I'd rather go on gritting my teeth—at least until tomorrow. Maybe next week?"

How about year after next? Or never?

This too is inertia. Be warned.

CHANGE 3:
THE FIRST STEP

You are still reading this section? Wonderful. That proves two things: First, you really do not want to settle for divorce, separation, terminal boredom, or terminal misery. (Some people do, you know.) You prefer serenity, growth, fun. Second, you are still a mightier force than inertia. You have not condemned yourself to mindless repetition of the "same actions in the same place." Three cheers!

But don't rest too long on your laurels. The sooner you get to work the better. Work? Work!

Constructive work. Interesting work. Even exciting work. The kind of work that keeps business in business, politicians in office, doctors in practice, churches vital, colleges relevant.

The work is called renewal and you've probably done a lot of it in your life.

I propose nothing less for you, your wife, and your marriage. The need is clear, the stakes are high and the rewards are quite literally priceless.

I propose that you start now to rethink, renegotiate, reshape, and refresh the conditions of your married life.

Now, I fully appreciate that this sounds like a tall order. And so it would be—if you had to make a giant stride and get it all done and over with by bedtime tonight.

You don't. Ten baby steps will get you as far as a giant one.

The baby step you can take today is simply to make another list. (Believe me, I am not a list freak. I am simply a true believer in the value of writing things down. To write is to think. And this, reader, is a certainty in an uncertain world: retirement is a time for you and me and all of us to *think*.)

The purpose of your list is to get you beyond the general ("I hate the way things are going between us") to the specific ("Things would be terrific if we could just make the following sore subjects go away").

Now, I obviously don't know what *your* sore subjects are. But I do know some sore subjects that appear to be endemic in the retired and about-to-retire population. To help you crank up your own thinking machine, I offer the following (realizing that your wife will have a different list of sore subjects).

Sore-subject Checklist

1. "She says I'm always underfoot when she's trying to use the phone. Why does she have to spend all that time talking to the same people every day?"

2. "She's always complaining that I won't help her around the house. But if I try to clean up the kitchen or something, she says I'm criticizing the way she runs the house."

3. "Every time I go to my desk to do a little work, she's put everything away and I can't find a thing."

4. "When I bring up the idea of taking a little trip, she asks, 'Where?' and it doesn't matter what I suggest. She wants to go somewhere else. Next thing you know, we wind up in a shouting match."

5. "She's always talking about getting together with 'our friends.' What she's really talking about is *her* friends and their husbands. With her, 'our' friends are a one-way street."

6. "One minute she says I'm a big boy now and perfectly able to fix my own lunch or take my own clothes to the cleaner's or something. The next minute she says, 'You're just a great big baby. Here! Let me do that.' "

7. "She's always asking me why we don't do more things together. Ha! Just let me suggest something—a ball game, for instance—and she's too busy. She's got some dumb meeting. Or she's already got a date to go shopping and to lunch with her friend."

Ouch! Enough. You get the idea.

You can, if you like, dismiss all of the above on grounds that they're just a lot of trivia. Teapot-size tempests. You can say that your problems are more global in scope than *that*.

And you're right, in a way.

This is not a checklist of the underlying problems (from your point of view) that the two of you are having. It is a list of symptoms.

But I ask you: When you go to the doctor, does he ask you to tell him what your disease is? Doesn't he, rather, want to know all about your symptoms?

Very well. Now you've written down your own list of symptoms and sore subjects. What next?

Do you put your list in your strongbox and throw away the key? Burn it in the fireplace? Just sit there with your wife, looking at the tube, not speaking, waiting for a bolt of constructive conciliation to strike *her* out of the blue? Please, sir!

Picking your time judiciously, approach her with a kiss and a heart-felt compliment. Tell her that you are eager to do what you can to make your retirement a terrific time of life for her as well as you. Tell her that you are reading this book. Ask her to read it, too, and particularly this part of it because you've found an idea that you think will help you both.

Then encourage her to make her own list.

Above all, make it clear to her that this isn't some sneaky, high-flown new way you've found to criticize and carp. The two of you are to take a constructive, loving, mutually respectful step to a really good life in retirement.

Now you've got your list and she has hers. Super. What next?

Be businesslike. Make an appointment. Set a time to begin and a time to end. Have paper and pencils on hand. Agree in advance on what you are trying to accomplish: to get a joint list down in writing, a list of the things you *both* agree are problems. Agree, too, that it's OK to disagree at this stage of the game. Agree that there is no need to rationalize, criticize, defend, or otherwise behave like a pair of prosecuting attorneys.

All you want right now is to construct a real-life basis for renewal and renegotiation.

To take the next baby step, keep reading.

CHANGE 4:
GET A REFEREE

Now that the two of you have agreed on your list of disagreements, you have three ways you can go with your new knowledge:

1. You can, God forbid, drop the whole subject as too disturbing, too hopeless, or too much trouble.

2. You can, using your own head of steam, try to work through your list of sore subjects.

3. You can find a third party to help you rethink and renew your relationship.

Leland and Martha Bradford took option number two and did well at it. (Any pair of trained psychologists should be able to do well.)

My wife and I, not trained psychologists, have taken option three. We recommend it. We have friends who recommend it. We know that a lot of other couples have found it interesting, constructive, satisfying.

Fair warning, however: you may not be able to take option three without going through a certain amount of sass and back talk from your Inner Self. Here's a sample:

"What does Shank think you are? A pair of nuts?

"You have your disagreements, sure you do. But you aren't, for heaven's sake, sick people. Or bad people."

"You could never do that! Those guys are witch doctors! They brainwash you! What if people found out?"

Even in the mid-1980s, millions of us cling to such ideas.

When someone says "psychiatrist" to us, what flashes first onto the movie screen in our minds? A granite face wearing a long beard and a better-than-thou expression?

"Psychologist?" A fellow ringing a bell and making a bunch of dogs salivate?

"Counselor?" A holier-than-thou type who treats adults like backward children?

What a pity that we perpetuate the stereotypes—what a pity for us. *We* are the losers. Not they.

The fact is that any psychiatrist, psychologist, or qualified family counselor, whatever his or her formal education, is first and foremost a teacher.

What does he teach? The most fascinating subject in the world—us.

To illustrate, let us take a sore subject from one couple's list. The woman has several friends to whom she speaks on the telephone every day. Some call her, she calls others. Moreover, she is co-chairwoman of a benefit affair. It is complicated, involves a number of other women, involves several telephone conferences a day.

The man is spending a lot of his time at home now, is often in the room when the calls come in, and makes what he thinks are humorous faces as he overhears his wife's end of things.

The wife grits her teeth for a while but it gets to be too much. "Damn it, George! Can't you give me a little privacy once in a while? I don't stand over you when you're on the phone. You'd *kill* me."

"Come on, Alice. Of course you don't stand over me! I only use the phone to take care of our business! I don't talk long and I don't talk often!"

"You have a lot of nerve! You never talked to your secretary that way or to any other woman!"

"And you never treat your friends the way you treat me. You've always got plenty of time and sweet talk for *them!*"

This way of dealing with a sore subject is a dead-end street, or worse. Left on that level of mutual aggravation, the soreness on both sides will implacably increase.

When the couple's counselor-teacher-referee hears the story, he quickly sees two things.

First, the counselor sees that the man is judging his wife's priorities and values by his own. Because he doesn't think that the business of her life is important, he implies that she herself is not important.

Second, he sees that the man is feeling left out of his wife's life. Indeed, the man had expected to have first call on her attention, had expected to get it instantly, without notice. His wife doesn't understand that. All she hears is the criticism.

Being an experienced professional, the counselor does *not* say the obvious: "You, ma'am, are treating your husband like an outsider and you, sir, are treating your wife like a second-class human being. Knock it off, both of you."

What he *does* say is, "Let's explore your words and actions and feelings together." He provides a constructive atmosphere, an atmosphere of objectivity. His goal is to help husband and wife to see themselves as he sees them. Only then will they truly understand their problems. Only then can they learn to negotiate a better way to accommodate the needs of each. In short, the counselor helps them learn to help themselves.

Once we have gotten the hang of getting to the bottom of our sore subjects, we can begin to make a new set of agreements between ourselves. We can get to the day when we write up and agree to something like the following:

Retirement Bill of Rights
for Bill and Alice

1. Each of us is entitled to work at the business of his life with a maximum of privacy, freedom, and authority.

2. If one of us wishes to discuss family matters in the daytime, he will (unless in emergency) do it by appointment, just like anyone else. Neither of us is entitled to the other's instant attention just because we're married.

3. When we have disagreements or complaints, we will do our best to discuss them rationally and in a businesslike way. We recognize that cheap shots are destructive and accomplish nothing. When it is appropriate, we will again seek the help of our family counselor.

4. We accept the proposition that what each of us chooses to do with his time is important to him or to her. We will not seek to impose our personal standards of importance on each other.

5. We will re-divide the household roles and responsibilities by negotiation. Once we accept this division, we will not "supervise" each other. If one of us is in charge of sweeping, the other will not tell him how to hold the broom. This does not preclude helping each other as the spirit moves or as needs arise. In the end, we are a team. Thank goodness.

I didn't promise you profundity.

This list is based on nothing more than common courtesy, common sense, and the commonly accepted concept that the marriage license is not a deed, not a certificate of ownership. Your own list will differ in particulars but the principles will be the same.

When you and your wife have done all the above, done it with a will and with love in your hearts, there is one guarantee—just one—that I am prepared to make: you will have changed.

You may still disagree, perhaps often. You may still not say all you mean and mean all you say. But you will have changed. You will know there's a better way.

You may even be ready to go on to advanced subjects in the curriculum.

SECRET INGREDIENT OF HAPPY TOGETHERNESS: INDEPENDENCE

Up to now, we have been focusing on damage control: how to swing the pH level in our marriages over to the neutral point on the dial. How to forswear the acid remarks. How to stop corroding the tie that binds.

And that's vital. It is not, however, the end of the journey. Now we get to the best part: opportunity.

If I had a magic wand and could wave it over the two of you, here is the marvelous thing that would happen:

1. You would find new pleasures, achieve new things, reach new heights as human beings . . . operating as an honest-to-God *team*.

2. You would, moreover, find new pleasures, achieve new things, reach new heights *as free-standing individuals*.

I know, I know. It sounds as though I'm trying to fob off on you a contradiction in terms, a pair of conditions that are mutually exclusive.

I plead not guilty. Think about it.

Isn't condition number two simply the prerequisite for condition number one? Don't we all need to be strong and free as individuals before we can hold up our end of a partnership?

Enough theoretical stuff. How does the theory work in practice? What kinds of day-to-day things happen in the marriage of two independent individuals? What kinds of things don't happen?

I am going to use my wife Hobby and myself as examples. *Examples*, not exemplars, mind you. There's a big difference. We have made a lot of progress since I retired, but we have to work at our problems and opportunities as everyone else does.

Here is a sampling of the things that go on at our house.

1. Each of us is responsible for working out a personal daytime schedule. And each of us has the necessary authority to do it. We don't ask permission and we don't "give" permission. If I want Hobby to do something with me during the day, I ask her for a date. And vice versa. Agreement is not automatic. We don't own each other.

2. When we are both at home in the daytime, we do not interfere with each other's work or privacy or concentration. Her office and mine are entirely separate from each other. For convenience, our telephones ring in both offices. But we respect each other's need to use them in private.

3. We understand that house-management is strictly Hobby's turf. She decides what needs doing, when it gets done, and who does it. If she asks me for advice, I give *advice*. Not direction.

4. I recently thought we needed a new, larger refrigerator and said so. But it was she who made the decision actually to buy one. And it was she who did the shopping, she who picked out the new machine. She loves it. So do I.

5. I recently concluded that I needed to trade in my old car for a new one. I told her so—for information only. In the end, I bought the same kind I'd had before but in a different body color. She suggested the color and I liked her suggestion. I liked my old car. I love my new one.

6. A couple of years ago, Hobby announced to me that she was going to take up the study of Marcel Proust, a novelist about whom I have always had a blind spot to put it euphemistically. As I write, she is still at it, reading him regularly, attending not one but two courses on him, preparing to write a paper on Proust for a women's essay group of which she is a member. During a recent disagreement between us, she said to me: "If you would just read Proust, you wouldn't have such asinine ideas!" I forebore to pick up that brick and throw it back. Progress!

7. We have both gotten interested in George Washington. I do not know whether this will be a hot topic in our lives for long. Doesn't matter. For the time being, we enjoy comparing notes. "Isn't that amazing" has become an everyday phrase around our house.

8. We both like to drive and each of us has definite ideas about the use of car radios and air conditioners. Furthermore, I smoke and Hobby doesn't. Our friends now understand all this. When we occasionally drive up to a distant party, each in his own car, people no longer ask us (jocosely, I suppose), "Aren't you two speaking to each other?"

9. We are now able, once in a while, openly to express our deep respect and liking for each other. For a long time after I retired, we both suffered from lowered self-esteem—a condition in which it is tough just to *see* the value of other people, let alone to verbalize it.

10. In those departments of our life together where the proper possessive pronoun is "ours," rather than "yours" or "mine," we are now able more often than not to negotiate and compromise. In some cases, we are even able to delegate our share of the decision to the other. We trust each other not to make such decisions selfishly.

Believe me, we are not paragons. Nor are we unique. We know a dozen other retired couples who seem to be growing as individuals and who seem, simultaneously, to be growing closer to each other. They are surely, all of them, working on their relationships, just as Hobby and I are.

I don't mean "working at marriage" to imply anything negative. Quite the contrary. By now, you know my attitude toward work: it's the most fun there is.

VIII
HOW TO PREPARE YOUR EMOTIONS FOR RETIREMENT

"START 20 YEARS AGO"

Early in this book, you read a section entitled "The Killer Myth: It's time to retire it."

In that section, you read a lot of good news about the effect of retirement on health. But you also read a warning. Quote: "There is a medical phenomenon called 'the giving up–given up' complex. Severe emotional stesss, such as some people suffer when they retire, can cause feelings of helplessness and hopelessness. This, in turn, can lay the distressed person open to 'activation of neurally-regulated biological processes potentially conducive to disease.' [Dr.] Portnoi notes, however, that even this reaction can be prevented by solid preparation for retirement."

"Solid preparation for retirement!"

That glutinous phrase has found a prominent and permanent home in my memory. Solid preparation! It sounds to me like Napoleon planning his next campaign. Or General Motors designing and engineering a new car.

I asked a friend of mine, a clinical psychologist, how a person should go about the "solid preparation" of his emotions for retirement.

119

"Start twenty years ago," he said. Funny fellow.

"What kind of solid emotional preparation would you recommend?" I asked a happily retired friend. He looked at me with genuine puzzlement. "Be damned if I know," he said. "The only people I know who are mad at retirement were mad at life long before they retired."

Then, one day, I thought my lucky break had come. My brother Max, a professor of biology at a large university, called. He and three dozen colleagues, all about to be retired, were invited to a two-hour seminar on the emotional issues in retirement and I could come and listen if I liked! The speakers, he told me, were to be a gerontologist and a clinical psychologist! *Wunderbar!* Or so I thought.

On the big day, the gerontologist, aged forty, maybe, regaled us with stories of his aged mother and how she dealt with forgetfulness. She put out her pills for the day in a little dish so she'd know whether she'd taken them or not. Put her purse beside the front door so she wouldn't forget it when she went out. That kind of thing.

The psychologist told us about a sabbatical year he'd taken in California. It dawned on me, finally, that he was trying to tell us something: that moving to a warm climate does not solve all living problems.

And that was it.

Dr. Paul Pruyser of The Menninger Foundation gave me one early clue as to why I was having so much trouble finding experts on solid preparation. He said to me (remember?): "Don't expect too much from psychiatry. Retirement is too new. We are learning as everybody else."

Richard A. Kalish of Berkeley, California, provided another clue. In his book, *Late Adulthood: Perspective on Human Development*, Kalish says: "When middle-aged people—adult children, personnel directors, social workers, or gerontologists—try to project themselves into their own retirement years, their projections do not always help them understand people who are presently retired. People with young children, with rising status and power, with increasing income and increasing consumption patterns, and without aches and pains on arising in the morning are likely to lack a real awareness of what retirement offers, both positively and negatively, for the retired person."

So here I am, as close to being an expert on solid preparation as you are going to meet. You already know that I am not a psychologist or gerontologist or any other kind of "-ist." Except generalist. But I am retired.

I did go through eighteen months of depression and boredom and anxiety before I turned around—all for lack of solid preparation. (Do as I say—don't do as I did!)

I have, now, talked to several hundred people about their retirement problems or concerns.

I have read a million or so words, finding a nugget here and a nugget there.

I have, in short, played the part of an intellectual vacuum cleaner.

What I have to offer from here on is a few thousand words based on solid experience.

Plus a double helping of solid common sense.

Plus the solid comfort of this fact: people sixty-five and over are the happiest people in the world.

That's a lot solider preparation than *I* had.

GET A SURROGATE FATHER AND GRANDFATHER

By the time your kids and mine retire, this book will sound as quaint as *The Canterbury Tales*.

By then, our kids will have watched tens of millions of people retire and do just fine. They will have had plenty of yous and mes around to serve as role models.

Our kids aren't going to need me or anyone like me to write a book on how to deal with the emotional, philosophical, and spiritual issues in retirement. They'll *know* how.

Meanwhile, there's us. *We* haven't had happily retired fathers and uncles and grandfathers to watch and to emulate. You and I are the Neil Armstrongs of the age of mass-production retirement. And it's still scary out there. It always is for people who take a giant step for mankind.

Not to worry, though.

There is one thing we can do about our disadvantaged state. There is one stunningly obvious right thing we can do. And the sooner the better. We can find a substitute "father" and "grandfather."

I wish I had been smart enough to do that early on. I wish I had looked around for help in the form of someone brainy and smiling and committed and busy and *retired*. I didn't. My brain took forever to get out of low gear.

Had I had the wit to look for such a person, I would have bought him not one but a dozen lunches if he had let me. I'd have asked him to tell me in detail about his retirement experiences. I'd have asked him to level with me, to tell me the bad stuff as well as the good. I'd have wanted to know what his problems were and how he solved them.

I'd have asked him also to recommend another role model or two. People with different problems and solutions. I'd have asked *them* to share their wisdom with me. And I would have listened hard.

Now, I know what you're thinking and I agree you've got a point. To ask for that kind of counsel is unnatural for men with red-blooded-all-American backgrounds and it isn't easy. We have to get past two main fears: of becoming a nuisance, of sounding like a wimp. Plus which, our know-it-all inner voices will yell at us, "Don't play the dumbbell! You're *smart*. Figure it out for yourself."

Tell your inner voice to bug off.

The fact is that the successfully retired men you ask for advice will be flattered. And they will think you're smart as hell to ask them.

So *ask*.

BEFORE YOU PUT
THE SHOW ON THE ROAD:
REHEARSE, REHEARSE,
REHEARSE

The reality of retirement is going to surprise you—painfully or pleasantly, one way or the other.

I haven't met a single soul who knew *exactly* how it was going to be.

The over-optimistic have seen a lot of castles in Spain come thwacking down to earth. The over-pessimistic have wasted a lot of time on advance anxiety. Both categories have suffered needlessly.

When I suggest that you rehearse and re-rehearse your retirement, I can just see you, nodding in agreement and saying to yourself, "That's common sense." Wonderful! But what does it actually mean—"to rehearse."

Let me tell you a story. When Robert Gage was still in his fifties, he and Rachel Gage decided to retire to Florida, rather than to stay on in Minneapolis. They loved their long-time home. *But . . . .*

And that's the end of the familiar part of their story. The rest of the Gage saga is a textbook case of how to do it right.

For the next few years, they spent each of their vacations in Florida, staying in city after city, town after town; scouting out each of them. They had a long checklist. But they also had a lot of fun, doing their joint research. They visited churches, hospitals, Kiwanis Clubs, and Chambers of Commerce, talking to people, looking for kindred spirits, looking for agreeable ways to be useful.

They found all they were looking for in a small town on the west coast of Florida. Then they researched the neighborhoods and bought the building lot of their dreams.

During the remaining years before their retirement, the Gages went straight to their adopted hometown to spend each vacation. They found their pleasure in making friends, getting involved, getting to know the ropes, getting to feel at home.

They saved the building of their new home until they'd actually retired and moved south for good. "We visited the building site every single day," Rachel Gage told me. "It was a daily thrill to see the progress. We wouldn't have missed that experience for anything."

By the time the Gages' house was built, the rest of their retirement life was well underway, including the project that would be the centerpiece of Bob Gage's life for the next four years: a proper public library.

In the course of making friends, Gage had found three other men who thought that creating a library would be an exciting way to use some of their new free time. And they formed an informal partnership.

For the next four years, they raised money from the other townsfolk. They persuaded the town rich man to give them the necessary land. They found an architect and collaborated on the plans; hired the contractor and worked with him; found people to donate books; found and hired the librarian. All without a cent of public funds.

I asked Rachel Gage whether her husband had suffered any withdrawal symptoms. He had been a sales manager for a dairy equipment firm and had obviously loved the work. Didn't he miss it? Didn't he feel lost without the dealer-friends to whom he'd been so close?

She looked blank for a moment, then looked at her son who had been listening in on the conversation. The two agreed. They had never known Bob Gage to have a down day in his retirement. Neither, for that matter, had she.

RETIREMENT ON THE INSTALLMENT PLAN

Of all possible ways to retire, here's the one that upsets the most, destroys the most, wastes the most; is, therefore, the dumbest:

Do it all at once.

Bang! *Crash!* T-H-U-M-P!

One day a going concern, the next day just gone.

If that doesn't suit our psyches, you and I can do one of two things. We can shrug our shoulders and say, "Well, that's the kind of life it is," and spend the next year or three getting adjusted. Or we can try to find an alternative.

There *are* alternatives.

Many law firms do things a better way. They say to their older partners, "Retire in *stages*. At sixty-five, turn over the management part of your job to a younger person, but go on as a partner. Work case by case. At seventy, step out as partner but become of-counsel. Hang in there."

When the lawyer does become of-counsel, he gets an office, secretarial service, and other prized amenities. The firm keeps its access to an experience-heavy brain. Everybody wins.

You will say to me, "Come on! You know lawyers and law firms fall into a one-of-a-kind category. Legal work is different from my kind of job. It's easy for lawyers to retire on the installment plan.

That I grant you. But I ask you this: Have you and your associates really *tried* to find a way?

Joe Greeley and his employer, Leo Burnett Company, did try. They found a way that worked—in spite of the fact that it flew in the face of all the conventional wisdom.

Leo Burnett Company is an advertising agency. And the conventional wisdom about advertising says the following:

1. Advertising is a young man's business.

2. In advertising, you burn out early. Older people can't hold up their end.

3. An advertising agency must continually make room at the top for the hot young people in the company.

4. Fail to make room and you lose your best young talent.

5. In advertising as in many other businesses, you can be only one of two places: all the way in or all the way out.

Nobody knew all that better than Joe Greeley.

Nonetheless, Greeley wanted to cut down rather than cut out. So he made a proposal. He would, at sixty-five, cheerfully give up his big office, big salary, big title. He would give up his stock and his seat on the Board. He would do marketing projects for whomever the company wanted. That's what he loved most about the business anyway. He asked a few modest things in return: a small office, access to a secretary, more vacation time, a salary in keeping with his new status. Let's try it for a year, he said, and review the arrangement then. If it hasn't worked for one or both of us, no hard feelings.

It did work, for several years. And both parties to the deal were the richer for it.

I freely admit that Greeley's meat can be another man's poison. Not every ego is strong enough to accept such a package of "demotions." Not every organization can and will be sufficiently flexible.

What about someone who wants to take his retirement in installments but can't arrange the Greeley solution?

There is another way to go. Overlap the old and new. Don't wait for the end of your career to get involved in other kinds of work. The closer you get to retiring from the old, the more involved you get in the new.

To overlap does not make for a laid-back kind of life in the last few years before retirement. But it *will* pay big dividends later.

You can think of it as a gilt-edged investment.

BEWARE THE GEOGRAPHICAL "CURE"

I have nothing whatsoever against insurance companies and real estate firms. I carry no brief against those seductive ads with the sun all a-shine and the people all short-sleeved.

Nor do I have objections (beyond esthetic ones) to "living the good life," "golden years," "reaping the rewards," and other such language.

Hey, there's *truth* in those concepts! A lot of retired people *can* be described in exactly those words. Some climates *are* more salubrious than others.

My problem is with *us*, not the insurance or the real estate people. It's *we* who kid ourselves that a dramatic change of scene is the answer.

Elsewhere in this book, I said, "We move down south or out west and we expect the new places and things to make us happy or at least content. And that is not the way life works. The only geography that counts is the skin we live in. The only clement climate is the one we create inside our heads and our guts."

I stand behind every word of that.

Please do not think you have caught me in the act of talking out of both sides of my mouth. You haven't.

It is true that many people you will meet in this book have chosen to live in sunny places. And it is true that all are happy with their new lives. That's why I want you to meet them.

But which came first? The sunny places or the happiness?

You know what my answer is.

In sad fact, geographical change has compounded, not cured, the adjustment problem for a lot of people. Not only have they been cut off from their jobs, they have cut themselves off from friends, family, familiar roots, familiar routines. For them, it's a case of too much too soon. Once past the fanfare and flurry of moving, they get up one morning and the inner self starts whining: "In God's name, what is there to do today? Already I'm bored. I wish we were home."

"Home" is the key word. Home is not a building, not a town, not a state.

The only state that feels like home is a positive state of mind and that can exist anywhere in the world. But you know that.

TRIUMPH
OVER THE PAST

On guard, reader.

Your past is always trying to reach up and bite you.

One morning soon, you are going to wake up and begin a deadly dialogue with yourself. It will go something like this:

Voice of the present: Well, sir. Another great day of retirement ahead. Up and at 'em.

Voice of the past: Up and at 'em? Why?

Present: (as to a child) Because. Quote: "Let us then be up and doing/With a heart for any fate . . . ." That's Wordsworth.

Past: Sure. But do *what?*

Present: I don't know. Haven't decided. There are lots of important things to do. Errands. Chores. Get organized.

Past: (helpfully) Good. Let's make a list. What's the first most important thing?

Present: Well . . . .

Past: And the second? The third?

Present: Don't bug me. I'm only half awake.

Past: Does it matter?

Present: Don't use that smirky tone of voice. What do you mean, "Does it matter?"

Past: Does it really matter what you do today?

Present: Quiet!

Past: It *doesn't* matter.

Present: QUIET!

Past: It doesn't matter. And you don't matter, either . . . .

Present: Bastard!
Past: . . . not any more!
Present: Shut *up*! I'm going back to sleep.

When the deadly dialogue starts up in our heads, we should welcome the experience; it will warn us.

It is not enough that we continue to work in retirement. It is not enough that we get our marriages into a new state of health.

We have got to train and retrain ourselves to live in and for the here and now.

TRIUMPH OVER THE FUTURE

Of all the dumb habits of thought that we acquire early in life, the dumbest is this: to regard the future as the be-all and end-all.

Think back. How many of the following fat-headednesses have come out of your mouth—as they've come out of mine?

1. Just wait till school's out. *Then* I'll have a really good time.

2. Just wait till I meet the right girl. *Then* I'll really be happy.

3. Just wait till I get my raise and my promotion. *Then* life will really be good.

4. Just wait till I get this problem off my back. *Then* I'll be a really happy man.

The habit of postponing satisfaction and fulfillment can and will follow us into retirement ("Just wait till fishing season comes—*then* I'll be happy.")—unless.

Unless and until we learn to live in the here and now.

Preoccupation with the future takes another and a sinister turn when we do what our mothers called "borrowing trouble." You know how that goes.

You say to yourself, "Well, the alarm clock's set and the clock radio's set and I guess I'll wake up early enough—unless the traffic is a lot worse than usual and unless I have trouble starting the car. Lord! I don't want to miss that plane."

Never mind that you've already allowed an extra half hour for traffic problems. Never mind that your car has just been tuned and it never started more willingly. Never mind that there are twenty planes a day that go where you're going and that you could catch another and still have plenty of leeway on the other end. . . .

When we let ourselves fall into that trap, when we let tomorrow's problems cut us out of today's pleasure, when we do it over and over again, well *hey!*

Now is the time to learn to live in the here and now.

TRIUMPH IN THE PRESENT

"What is the secret of those people—those evergreen people—who become more and more alive as they grow older, in contrast with those who experience psychological death at an early age?"

Roy Larsen, religion editor of the Chicago *Sun-Times*, asked that heavy question in his column of January 25, 1976. In considering it, he analyzed a list of ten older people whom he knew and who "never abandoned the search for everything green." As he saw it, they had in common eight traits which I list, in part, below:

1. "The meaning of their lives is derived from several sources—family and friends, work and leisure, private interests and public concerns."

2. "They have a capacity for intimacy," for forming "a truly satisfying bond with another."

3. "They are rooted in at least one community where they know how it feels to be 'surrounded by a whole circle of approving eyes.' "

4. "They define prestige and success in terms of vitality, not in terms of social status, financial position, or professional achievement."

5. "They do not allow their lives to be 'trivialized.' They do only what their time and talents allow them to do well."

6. "They do not try to fashion the rest of the world in their own image."

7. "Once their competence is proved, they are freed from the curse of earnest striving and can develop a talent for taking themselves lightly."

8. "They remain in constant communication with their insides. Without becoming narcissistic, they have learned with Theodore Roethke to 'stay alive, both in and out of time, by listening to the spirit's smallest cry.' "

In the last paragraph of his column, Larson recognized that his "list of common traits" begged the really tough question: "OK, that's fine, but how do you get that way?" To that, he offered this reply:

"Each day there is set before us the choice between life and death, vitality and sterility. Somehow we have got to get ourselves into the habit of saying 'yes' to life."

"Saying 'yes' to life" and living in the here and now are one and the same thing in my view. When we look only to the past for pleasure and self-esteem, we are saying "no." And when we worry the stuffing out of all our tomorrows, we are also saying "no."

In a word, life *is* today.

Let me confess. What you are reading here are the words of a reformed sinner.

For more years than I like to think about, I had another kind of habit, a lethal one. I *compared* my todays. I contrasted them with great days from my past or with red-letter days coming up. And, somehow, today was always boring by comparison.

That monkey on my back was bad enough when I was pursuing my career. But at least I never had to wake up in the morning and ask myself what there was to do that day. There was always work.

In retirement, the monkey on my back became a gorilla. The great days became further and further between. The boring days piled up. I was depressed. I turned more and more inward. Even the occasional red-letter day did not help.

If someone had then said to me, "Howard, what you need to learn is how to live in the here and now," I would have thrown up my hands. What I did not need, I'd have said, was a bunch of platitudes and other super-simplified pap.

Looking back now, trying to identify the symptoms of my coming out of it, I think first of natural things that I saw or felt as though for the first time: a single shaft of sunshine, drilling through the cloud cover. A hummingbird at work an arm's length from my face. The hue of the moon at a certain angle of inclination (not silver, not cheese-like, *moon-colored*).

In time, more complex things started to happen. When a friend asked if I would be willing to do some consulting with his firm, my habit-pattern told me to say "no" but I actually said "yes." I finished a painting I had started a year before and had not had the heart to complete. I began to laugh again—even laugh at myself from time to time. I began making a plan for the next day before I went to bed at night. *Mirabile dictu.*

Once I came to realize what was happening to me—and that I *liked* it—I decided to put words to it. For my own benefit. If I did that, I thought, I would do more of what was making me happy and do it on purpose. Over a long period of time, I wrote a sort of "owner's manual" for the days of my own life. I'll share some of my manual with you—but don't expect profundity. You already know it all, anyway:

Howard Shank's "Owner's Manual" for Howard Shank

1. When you go outside to get the newspapers in the morning, walk the long way round. Check out the bird population. If it's snowing, kick your feet through it. If it's raining, describe for yourself how it feels on your face. If it's sunny and warm, *bask*.

2. Do not gulp the first cup of coffee. Taste it.

3. Allow at least ten minutes for rumination between breakfast and getting going. Don't rush, damn it! Ask yourself why you are glad to be alive. Listen to your answer.

4. Kiss your wife and pet your dog before you leave the house.

5. Stroll, do not dash, to your office. The black squirrels may be back.

6. Sneak up on your work. First, finish the job you deliberately did not finish the day before. That'll get you into the rhythm faster.

7. Do each day's filing before you quit for that day. Then it

won't pile up on you and you won't hate it so much (I'm still working on that one).

8. If someone calls you in the middle of a sentence, do not grit your teeth. Be *flexible*.

9. If a friend calls—or if a friend of a friend calls—and asks for help, don't debate it. If you can help, do it. You know it'll make you feel good and you can catch up on your work later. Be *flexible*.

10. If it's a super nice day, don't be grim about working—do something nice outside. You can always catch up on your work. Be *flexible*.

11. If you have somewhere to go and something to do and you *really* don't want to go and do it (see the dentist?), plan a special treat for later, something you'll really look forward to.

12. When you are really down and grumpy, write a list of the things in your life for which you are grateful. Anything and everything you can think of. Great for the perspective.

13. When you have a problem ahead, a really tough and complicated one, do as much to solve it as you can possibly do today. Trust yourself to take the next right step tomorrow. It erases anxiety like magic.

14. Kiss your wife and pet your dog when you come in from work.

15. Before you go to sleep, make a mental list of the things you liked about your day. (The cardinals are back. The sun came out. You did a good job on thus and so. Anything, large or small). And kiss your wife.

Actually, there's more to my manual than that. But that ought to be enough to get you thinking about your own. Here. Be my guest. Write down the first thing that comes to your mind:

My Manual

1. _____

_____

_____

Good luck with the rest of it.

I hope it brings you joy and happiness in your retirement. One day at a time.

ADVICE ON TAKING ADVICE: WORK ON YOUR WILLINGNESS

You can complain—you probably are complaining—that it's a snap for me to hand out all this advice. *Giving* advice is like falling off the famous log. *Taking* advice is the hard part.

Agreed? Agreed.

"Why is that?" I have asked myself. "Why is it still so hard for me even to listen to good advice, let alone take it?"

"Why does a part of me think I'm so smart and all-together that I can handle any problem and all problems by myself?"

"Why does the macho part of me still think it's wimpy to seek and follow counsel?

"Why do I keep on courting big pain or big trouble before I get willing to get help?"

Is it that I am:

Bullheaded?

Prideful?

Incurably optimistic?

Or am I guilty, only, of being only human?

What do you think?

Still and all, when I think about what goes on inside my head, my heart, and my gut today compared with what went on in the first eighteen months of my retirement, I am filled with gratitude. I am happier than I have ever been. I understand the meaning of the word, "serenity." I approach my day-to-day problems with a wider and widening perspective. I progress in *spite* of being bullheaded, prideful, overoptimistic and human.

Wonderful Howard, right?

Boy, how that thought seduces me!

When the thought of how wonderful I am gets too seductive, I have an unfailing defense: I start listing in that fat head of mine the people who have helped me, guided me, counseled me, instructed me, advised me in my retirement.

I think of GW, KH, AA, JN, VS, GD, BL, JB, KL, JL, PS, HS,

MHS, BN, CF, JC, DM, LS, GB, PP, RG, PB, MS, BP, MCS, JK, PD. . . .

And if that is not enough, I go on to others—people who probably do not realize how much I have learned from them. GH, EB, DM, JB—an even longer list.

Somewhere in my chain of days, I developed, without knowing it, a trace of willingness to learn, to grow, to ask for advice, and to take it. When I saw this and saw how that trace was helping me to help myself, I became a little more willing. With a little more willingness came a little more progress. With a little more progress, a little more willingness . . . .

Free advice, reader. terrific advice:

Don't do what I did to get acquainted with the magic of willingness. Don't suffer through the endless nose-bumping, the ever-churning stomach, the boredom, the daily down-in-the-mouthness that I put myself through.

Work on your willingness. Give it all you've got, intellectually, emotionally, spiritually.

Let willingness work for you in your retirement—from day one. Don't be like me.

IX
BROTHERS AND SISTERS UNDER THE SKIN

In Which You Will Meet 29 Retired People with Only One Other Common Denominator: Gumption

"A BALLGAME OF THE HEAD, THE HEART, AND THE GUT."

That is what I said about retirement, very early in this book.

Now I am going to demonstrate the truth of what I said.

In the pages which follow, you will meet two professional babysitters (retired) and a president of the United States (also retired).

You will meet a retired astronaut and a former railroad worker. A recovered cancer patient and a seventy-nine-year-old monsignor who still plays golf every day—in spite of a repaired arthritic hip. You will also meet the former chief executive officer of one of America's largest companies—a man whose number one plan in retirement is to start up a non-profit clinic for the treatment of alcohol and drug abuse.

You will, in short, find twenty-nine definitions-by-example of the word "gumption."

Gumption is that quintessentially American blend of shrewdness, common sense, courage, ambition, enterprise, initiative, resolution, effort. To quote Mr. Webster, "Gumption [is the ability] to defend the position against the odds."

Metaphorically, all 29 of these people came to retirement as naked as the day they were born.

They came stripped of the old powers, the old supports, the old securities, the old adventures.

The titles were gone.

The perks were gone.

The signs and symbols of status were gone.

It was prove-yourself time all over again. Who-Am-I time again. Grow-and-learn time again. And here these people are. *Smiling.*

Jim Lovell, the retired astronaut, made a statement that seems to me the very essence of gumption. Speaking of the time when he was leaving his old life for his new one, Lovell said:

"I did *not* want to trade on the past, although I could have. I could have been a glad-hander. Or I could have been a door-opener—someone who could get you in to see important people.

"But I didn't want that.

"I wanted people to want me for what I was now, not what I had been." [My emphasis.]

Now, I acknowledge that to retire with a pile of money is not all bad.

And, yes, it would be terrific to have a forty-year-old body in a sixty-five-year-old skin.

An ever-shining sun is nice. So is a view that just won't quit. So is a houseful of creature comforts.

But those, I hold, are only the frosting, not the cake.

In retirement, the truth about happiness is no different from what it is at every other time of life.

It's what's inside us that counts, not what's outside.

If it gets down to a choice between the buyable goodies of this world and the priceless quality of gumption, well . . . .

Please read on and see what you think.

DEWITT L. JONES

The "Mayor"
of
Captiva Island

Of all the present-day wars between those who see change as progress and those who see it as plunder, the quietest and most gentlemanly war may be taking place at Captiva Island, Florida.

In February 1983, the chief umpire in the struggle was my friend and fellow alumnus of Leo Burnett Co., Dewitt Jones. By then an honorary native of ten years' standing, Jones was incumbent president of the Captiva Civic Association.

I went there to spend two February days with him, not as an amateur social historian but in my role as chronicler of happily retired people. As matters turned out, I could not really understand what he was doing in retirement without learning something about how his island home deals with Florida-style change. This is a state where progress comes in tidal waves, whereas he is committed to the concept of "reasonable change."

That concept is the centerpiece of his life today.

The approaches to Captiva and its larger island neighbor, Sanibel, speak of progress or plunder (your choice) in a voice too loud to ignore.

Houses, streets, shopping centers, high-rise apartments spread out along the route to the causeway, most of them clearly new to those flat, recycled farmlands. The big bucket, the golden arches, and other predictable landmarks have grown out of ground where, only yesterday, cows, gladioli, and other crops defined the scene.

In spite of that, vacant land was everywhere and the highway could surely handle several times the number of cars I saw. Its planners have put their bets on the come line: the boom is at the beginning, not the end, they are signaling to all comers.

The contrast between mainland and islands is vivid, especially at the point where I crossed the few yards of bridge between Sanibel and Captiva. Abruptly, old trees start to border the roadway, growing so close to one another that they have created a living parasol. I knew that houses also bordered the road but a stranger would have had to infer their presence. Postcard-size name signs stood at the feet of cunningly casual, dirt-and-shell driveways. They were the only clues.

Change was not new to southwestern Florida. It had started coming centuries before Dewitt and Barbara Jones began spending vacations on Captiva.

The earliest-known inhabitants were Caloosa Indians who ate the local conchs by the millions and, according to Jones, tossed the shells over their shoulders when they finished. Whatever their method of disposal, proof of their appetites lives on: shells are still the all-purpose building material here.

The next wave of change arrived in the form of Spanish conquistadors who, armored, plumed, and speared, won all the battles of the day except for the one against the mosquitoes. And they, too, left their mark. The name, Captiva, refers (or so local legend says) to the captive women whom the Spaniards insisted on keeping at their sides.

The change was deadly for the Caloosas. The twentieth-century brand of change might have been equally deadly to Sanibel and Captiva themselves. Like sand-and-shell-based islands everywhere, these have only their complex ecosystems to guarantee the vegetation that defends them against the caprices of the sea.

In June 1982, a nameless sub-hurricane marooned the inhabitants of Captiva and Sanibel. There were four-foot tides, gale-force winds, and breakers that gouged boxcar-size chunks out of the coastal roads. Ancient trees fell like saplings. The issue of beach renourishment reached a new level of urgency and the wisdom of the "reasonable change" doctrine took on fresh luster. Dewitt would tell me later how the big storm had helped him to resolve the "density issue" in favor of the resident's point of view.

On the surface, there seemed to be little connection between Jones's previous life experience and his unpaid job as *de facto* mayor of Captiva. Childhood on the North Shore of Chicago. Dartmouth. A major's rank in the Air Force. Piloting bombers in Italy in World War II. A salesman's job in the promotion department of Walt Disney Productions. Managing such accounts as United Air Lines, Allstate Insurance, and Oldsmobile at Leo Burnett Co. Nothing in this past would have predicted Jones's present to me.

Nor, in fact, had the Joneses come to Captiva planning new careers in civic work. They had simply liked shelling on the beach, liked fishing together, had found the people of the community congenial. The house they would build would, they knew from experience, demand huge outlays of time and energy. For Dewitt, there were three well-established hobbies: ham radio, photography, stamps. They were all set, they thought, for things to fill their time.

What Dewitt Jones had not taken into account was his urge to be in the thick of things, a part of his nature that had not retired when his body did. In time, restlessness overtook him.

At first, it was photography that provided an outlet. This was not entirely accidental, I think. The Jones' son Dewitt, known as Wif, is a star contributor of photo layouts to *National Geographic* magazine.

"There's a beautiful bird sanctuary over on Sanibel," Dewitt *père* told me. "And I spent hours and hours photographing birds. After a while, I used some things I'd learned in advertising and put together a one-hour slide show which I presented at the local civic association on Sanibel and then at the Audubon Society. I've shown it probably fifteen times since then—all around Florida— and it's pretty good and I'm proud of it. The reception was good, too, and it helped my ego a lot."

It didn't help for good, however. He could not think immediately of an encore.

His first direct step to where he is today came when he received, and accepted, an invitation to be a volunteer fireman. "On an island where the average man's age is sixty-five, volunteers were hard to come by," he said. (So, I gather, were people who were willing to take responsibility. In what was to become a familiar pattern, Jones was soon elected president of the fire department.)

"I did that for a couple of years," he told me. "We managed to keep it going and it was an important adjunct to the community. But I retired after I found myself at three o'clock one morning, holding a fire hose on an LP gas tank which was surrounded by a burning building. I said, 'I guess I didn't retire to do that kind of foolishness' and I came home and told Barbara that it looked like my days as fire commissioner were numbered and I gave it up. A younger man took over but we have paid firemen now and it's a blessing."

By now, Jones's pattern was set, although he had to go through a time of trial and error before he found the next right vehicle for his talents.

This happened when he joined the Sanibel/Captiva Conservation Foundation. If marriages ever were made in heaven, this was one of them.

The S/CCF was, he found, a "vibrant" organization with 1,200 members who were attracted to it by the progress-or-plunder issue. They knew the value of their wetlands, knew they were vital to the local ecosystems, knew that the then-policy of the county government was to encourage aggressive development by builders. The members had read ruin in all this and they had organized to head off what they perceived to be a clear and present danger.

When Jones joined the foundation, the present needs were two. The first was to raise $150,000 to repay a debt. The money had gone to purchase 500 acres of still-natural wetlands. The second need was a building to serve as a focus for research, education, and tourism. He addressed the problems with commitment and enthusiasm, qualities that—the pattern again—led to his election as president for a three-year term.

"I approached that job as I approached client problems at Burnett," he said. "And that proved invaluable."

As we talked, I could see the parallel. His concept of the president's job had nothing to do with "running" things as a boss runs a company. He viewed his fellow members literally as clients. It was his task to understand their wants and needs, to generate strategies for reaching their goals, to arrive at consensus, to work alongside the other committed volunteers.

He applied the same idea to money raising. In making proposals to prospective donors, they were his clients, he their agent. He was helping them to do good things that they really believed in—now that they thought of it. This worked. In his first-ever attempts at money raising, Jones brought in one check for $20,000, another for $50,000.

When he and I visited the center on our sightseeing trip, I could see that he had been the in-house Jack-of-all-trades. He had helped to get the building and landscape designs drawn and approved, had written and laid out a brochure, had taken photographs for that piece and postcards. He even had written the inscription for the commemorative plaque in the entry way.

"It was a hard, involved, full-time job," he acknowledged. "But it really paid off for me in self-respect."

As grand finale to our tour, we drove through the Ding Darling National Wildlife Refuge, a 4,000-acre spread run by the Department of the Interior. This was where Jones had taken the slides for his show and the birds obliged us by putting on a show of their own.

We saw an anhinga, a bird that must swim underwater to feed but, unlike ducks, has no oil glands to make its feathers buoyant. To avoid drowning, it must hang itself out to dry from time to time, looking like so much wet wash on a clothes line.

We saw a flock of roseate spoonbills, those shy rare birds that feed by moving their spatulate bills back and forth through the water like metronomes, filtering their food from the mud.

And we saw a hunting osprey hanging above the water, holding its station like a helicopter. Suddenly, the helicopter became a Stuka, glided steeply, then plummeted—pow!—into the water where it had seen a fish. I hope it hasn't starved. In three bombing runs, it came up with nothing. Jones did not seem worried; rather, he reminded me of myself-as-grandfather, showing off the talents of the progeny.

The Jones's house seems small from the outside, a perception caused by the scale of the surroundings. The house sits in a clearing just large enough for it and a handful of cars. Among the old, large trees all around is a species nicknamed "tourist" for its two stages of bark-growth: smooth in one stage, peeling like sunburned skin in the other.

The main rooms of the house are seductively informal, cozy but with faces turned toward trees and salt water. Jones's own room looks out and beyond in a different way; his amateur radio station can stretch his voice or fingers halfway around the world, sunspots willing.

I had asked him for a demonstration of his fifty-year hobby.

As I watched and listened, we heard a man from Caracas, speaking liquid English, congratulating someone for his "beautiful, clear signal." We raised Genoa and Tanzania (which posed no challenges) and India, the latter garbled by sunspots. We went on to Russia where the operator was speaking English. English? Russian hams speak to each other in English because it is a nation that has far more languages than the rest of Europe put together.

At 5:00 P.M. sharp, we made the regular daily contact with the "Dartmouth Network," made up of fellow alumni, fellow hams. Finally, Jones made his electronic sending key imitate a machine gun. I marveled. I gave up Morse Code after becoming a Boy Scout, Second Class.

After dinner, Jones ran through his presentation on the latest great concern of Captiva residents, the "density issue."

The storm of the previous June, he told me, was the most powerful of the last fifty years, name or no name. It cut off access to the mainland and thus to food, medical supplies, other essentials. Even if travel time had been normal during the storm, it would have been impossible to evacuate the population if things had come to that. Everyone agreed that someone had to do something about holding down residency until better emergency measures could be taken. The "someone," it turned out, was Dewitt Jones.

At the time of the storm, Lee County (the official governing body of Captiva) had statutes on the books that restricted building on Captiva to six units, residential or commercial, per acre. Beginning with this number, with the number of existing units, and with traffic-count data, Jones had drawn up a series of charts that made a compelling case for change. They demonstrated that any emergency that called for evacuating the two islands could only result in calamity. The one route out was never intended for mass exodus.

After Jones had presented his story to several Lee County administrative bodies, the door to the commissioners was open to him at last. All through the process, everyone knew that there was a hidden agenda. The concerns of the evironmentally minded and those dedicated to elbow room were well known. However, the evacuation subject was the only one that was clear-cut and, for now, impossible to debate. The Captiva Civic Association came away with what it wanted: a reduction in permissible-units-per-acre from six to three. Jones' "client approach" had worked here as well.

Events of this size do not make up the monthly menu of the Civic Association board members. By chance, I was able to see that for myself. It happened that my visit to the Joneses coincided with a regular meeting of the board. While I knew that this was a "government" that had no force in law, I also knew that its influence in county affairs was substantial. Captiva votes and tax payments are important and the county people address careful ears to the views of its association. I was curious to see how it worked.

At the table, all but one of the twelve members were present. Each was originally from somewhere else. Many were semi-retired or completely so. Owing to a cocktail party we'd attended the night before, I knew that one member was an architect, another a jeweler, another an emeritus professor of history. A fourth had been a partner in a large firm of management consultants.

The big event of the meeting was a surprise. A young lawyer came in, seeking the board's endorsement of a client's request for a zoning variation. He made his case well but the case itself was not persuasive. The relevant law was too loose for his purposes. Questions brought out the fact that a variation would allow a retail bakery, a convenience store, a day-care center, or any of a number of other traffic-creating enterprises. I could see the member-homeowners wincing.

"You could file with the county without our approval, you know," a member said.

"I know," the attorney said. "But my client and I are sensitive to your feelings and those of the community."

As it turned out, the board did vote to withhold endorsement for the time being. Luckily, from their point of view, they did not have to base their vote on distrust of the owner's—and fellow resident's—intentions. Instead, the new density-per-acre regulation gave them an unarguable reason for saying no.

Working his way down the agenda, Jones presided in the manner of an executive secretary rather than that of a company chief. "Volunteer officers," he said later, "have to depend on the power of ideas and persuasion to get things done. No one gives them a big stick."

Other questions before the board that day were as follows: Any objections to the sign on the new post office and real estate company building? ("I almost threw up.") May such-and-such group use the town hall? ("Only if they clean it up when they leave this time and pay for the damage.") Any progress on that pier that needs measuring? (No.) How do you like the new librarian? ("So far, so good.") Are we ready to vote on new car-parking regulations? ("Not yet.")

I wondered how many thousands of such small matters had had to be dealt with in order to preserve the low-key, natural look and feel of Captiva in the face of sustained population growth. Evidently, the price of reasonable change is eternal vigilance.

I had asked Jones more than once whether he'd had any problems in adjusting to retirement. He had said sure, he had a brief low spot when the excitement of the move wore off. He'd felt at loose ends for a few weeks, but that was all. No regrets. No boredom. No loss of self-esteem.

As things turned out, I hadn't been asking the right question.

The right question was: "How about you and Barbara—as a couple?

Well, yes. They had had some problems and they had seen a psychiatrist, together and separately, seeking counsel.

They discovered that twenty-four-hour-a-day companionship is great for vacations but not for retirement. The need of each for independent time made itself urgently known.

Which turf was whose became a heated subject.

They found that the division of labor and responsibilities that had worked for thirty years no longer applied.

It was Barbara who suggested they get professional help. "There were things we just couldn't cope with without the aid of a third party," she told me.

"You were right, Barb," Dewitt said. "I admit I raised a lot of dust, talking about witch doctors and all that. But I was wrong and I'm glad I was wrong. What that guy gave us was not a lot of theory but a lot of practical, common sense advice."

"We both felt we were pretty smart to go to someone to help us live our last years together and do it well," Barbara said. "We still annoy each other with little things, but we are usually able to concentrate on the big picture. We have a lot to be grateful for. Dewitt's alive and well and doing things he enjoys and so am I."

On the way to the airport with me, Jones did express one worry. In a matter of months, he would have done his tours of duty as a member of the Civic Association and as president. The by-laws were specific. He would have to step down and out.

It seemed to me a needless worry.

I thought that there had never been enough people with his willingness to work. There never would be.

I doubted that he would ever have to depend on golf and his other hobbies to keep him from being at loose ends.

I doubted it very much.

BILL MARQUIS

"If my photography helps the medical profession in any way, it's only a small part of the debt I owe."

For Bill Marquis, retirement came in 1970. He was not given a choice. Cancer cost him his left lung.

After the surgery, he gave up his job as general manager of commercial marketing for the Amoco Oil Company of Chicago, moved with his wife to San Diego, put himself in the hands of a doctor recommended by his surgeons, took with him "a roomful of darkroom equipment," presented by his associates as a retirement gift.

All of which is relevant to what he's been doing ever since.

By 1983, Marquis had become a landmark in the operating rooms of Scripps Memorial Hospital in San Diego—as a volunteer surgical photographer, not as a patient. He ranked as an important part of surgical teams, photographed everything from open heart work to childbirth ("you should see the looks on the parents' faces"). He even carries a pager in case of emergency.

In one dramatic case when Marquis' pager beeped, a helicopter had landed on the roof of the hospital, carrying a young man who had dived off a cliff into shallow water. "I got my equipment ready in record time and shot the surgery," he said. "The boy lived and that was some great feeling."

Marquis' retirement "career" began when the regular photographer suffered a heart attack and his new doctor asked Marquis to fill in. He's worked in operating rooms for two or three days a week ever since. And every operation he's "done" has called for additional hours in his darkroom.

Marquis' photographs are used as teaching aids and in presentations. In one case, slides he made of vocal-chord surgery were part of a presentation at an international medical conference in London.

Beyond his daily routine, Marquis has had the satisfaction of contributing to the techniques of operating room photography. "Some surgeons didn't like the flash—it distracted them and, of course, we couldn't have that," he said. "Because of our and other requests, Westinghouse developed a special fluorescent bulb that allows for photographing the full-color spectrum." Marquis uses a 200-millimeter lens and a magenta filter to warm up the light. No distractions now.

Marquis' motivation in doing the work? About as fundamental as motivations get: "If it weren't for the medical profession—and some help from God—I wouldn't be alive today," he said.

RETIREMENT A LA MENNINGER

"... the here and now of things"

In August 1982, I paid a visit to the new Menninger Foundation campus on the outskirts of Topeka, Kansas.

As I drove up that harmonious hill of old trees and new buildings, I believed that somewhere in the worlds of psychology and psychiatry there had to be a solid, settled body of research on retirement. If not at Menninger's, where?

My plan was straightforward. I would learn everything I could about the problems and the solutions and I would then dish up my new knowledge in clear, readable language for my readers.

Dr. Paul Pruyser got me down from the clouds, quickly.

"You should not have too high an expectation of psychiatry," he said. "Retirement is too new a subject. We are just beginning to learn, as everyone else. But I'm not unprepared for this conversation. At least I am aware of my ignorance."

Thud.

Still, I had been right—very right—to go there, even though my reasons were wrong.

There is a Menninger *philosophy* of retirement and I, for one, am greatly inspired by it.

Simply put, the concepts are these:

1. Give up position, power, and perquisites when it's right that you do so.

2. But don't give up the important things.

3. Go on learning, teaching, doing, helping in whatever ways you're able.

4. Never rest on your laurels.

5. Live for what you can do in the here and now.

The founder, Dr. Charles F. Menninger, lived by these principles until he died at ninety-two and their influence on Menninger professionals has been palpable and profound.

Charles F. Menninger was a farm boy who became a professor at the new Campbell College in Kansas in 1882. He was twenty. He first taught German, geology, botany, mineralogy. Later, when three students wanted to do premedical work, he put together a course that met the new requirements of medical schools. It meant having to learn the subjects himself—and quickly enough to stay a jump ahead of his pupils. He did. And all three young men became successful physicians.

When Menninger decided that he, too, would go to medical school, he was married, and because he had to depend for expenses on his teacher-wife's earnings, he picked the cheapest medical school he could find, Hahneman in Chicago. The homeopathic medicine he learned there qualified him only for the lowest place on the medical totem pole. But he overcame the handicap in the way he would always know best. He continued to learn. And learn.

By 1920, when Charles F. opened the original Menninger Clinic, he was fifty-eight and may well have been the most respected doctor in Topeka. The move had nothing to do with starting a mental health hospital. He had always admired what he had seen on a visit to the Mayo Clinic and thought group practice would offer better medical service to his patients. Furthermore, his hope of many years had been to bring his sons, Karl and Will, into practice with him. The new enterprise took its ultimate direction by chance: both younger Menningers chose to specialize in psychiatry. Typically, Charles F. went to the most logical source for his own training in the new subject: Karl Menninger became his teacher.

In the next fifteen years, The Menninger Clinic became famous. Karl Menninger had written his best seller, *The Human Mind*, and conducted a regular column for *The Ladies Home Journal*. All three Menningers poured out articles for professional journals. *Fortune* published an article about private mental hospitals, ranking Menninger's among the five best in the United States and the only one outside the East. Its reputation was growing by word of mouth as well—just at a time when the new arts of healing the mind were creating a demand that outstripped the supply of psychiatrists, in spite of the Depression.

By now in his early seventies, honored and respected, with both his sons and his clinic going from success to success, Menninger would have raised no eyebrows if he had retired to Florida to pursue his old hobby, gardening, and his new one, conchology.

Nor would it have surprised anyone if he had stayed right where he was, at center stage, running the show. His health was excellent; in fact, he had another twenty years to live.

In the event, he did neither.

Instead, he preferred what he called "gradual retirement" and set about taking it. His first act was to demote himself and promote his sons. His biographer, Walker Winslow, says:

> Having entered psychiatry so late in life, Dr. C.F. had no illusions about the contribution he had to make to psychiatry as a clinician. For over forty years, the doctor had taxed himself to keep up with the developments in general medicine. As he decreased his medical reading and attended fewer conferences and conventions, he felt that he was falling hopelessly behind. . . . His best role, as he saw it, was to function in such a way as to give his sons a maximum amount of freedom.

To satisfy his need for teaching, doing, and helping, and to get out of his sons' way, Menninger took on other, less-exalted jobs at the clinic. He discovered, for example, that he was good with depressed, elderly patients *who had never prepared themselves for retirement*.

Here, his age was an advantage. It is unlikely that such patients would have accepted firmness and leadership from a younger doctor. He, however, could persuade them to try hobbies and studies and to keep working at them until they became genuinely interested.

Menninger's own hobbies gave him a natural basis for patient therapy. For years, he taught classes in them at the foundation. "Even if he had only four or five students," Walker says, "he prepared his lectures meticulously. As he saw elderly patients who were depressed by what they thought was their growing ineffectiveness, he could explain that aging men . . . simply needed to try their effectiveness in new areas, areas that were dominated by eternal values." The great reward for such study was serenity, a quality that Menninger himself had achieved to a high degree.

To mark his ninetieth birthday, Menninger was asked to lay the cornerstone for a new $1.5 million hospital that was to bear his name. There were many eulogies. In response, he simply asked all present to join him in a prayer and, as on all occasions, he planted a tree. "If events had to be commemorated," Winslow says, "he felt that the least man could do was to plant a monument to beauty."

It was probably inevitable that Karl Menninger should become an unusual man. As if the example of his father were not enough, he had Flo Knisely Menninger to look to as well. She, too, was a born teacher who became as well-known in her field of Bible study as her husband did in psychiatry. When the mother was in her late seventies, she was persuaded to write her autobiography even though she complained that she was slowing down. She did so, however, on one condition. First, she insisted, she would have to learn to type. Which she did.

At Harvard Medical School, Karl Menninger was exposed to the idealism and humanism of such professors as Richard Cabot and Ernest Southard, "men who had immense compassion for all sufferers," according to Paul Pryser, "especially those who suffered from social neglect: the mentally ill, the poor, prisoners, members of racial and ethnic minorities." Menninger would identify with those feelings right up into his nineties. Late in 1983, I watched him on a television show whose interviewer called him "famous for being a bleeding heart." When asked how he felt about that, Menninger said that darn right he was a bleeding heart. His heart bled for abused and deprived children, for the poor, for prisoners, for . . . .

The clinic alone could not satisfy Karl Menninger. His activism drove him to wider and wider fields. He wrote two more books *(Man Against Himself* and *Love Against Hate);* raised money for the clinic; spoke widely in medical schools; crusaded for reform in mental hospitals; became chairman of the committee on reorganization of the American Psychiatric Association; was elected president of the American Psychoanalytic Association; gave almost daily counsel to his brother, Will, who became director of psychiatry for the U.S. Army during World War II.

As dean of The Menninger School of Psychiatry, he conducted seminars on the relationship between religion and psychiatry. This was dangerous, in a way. According to Pruyser, "one of the worst professional smears was to be accused of piety."

In his seventies, Menninger had gone his father one better: he had retired from all official duties at the foundation. First his brother, Will, then his nephew, Roy Menninger, had taken on the running of the foundation with its more than 100 psychiatrists and psychologists and nearly 1,000 staff members in all; its graduate school; its psychiatric hospital; its clinical and research programs devoted to alcoholism, genetics, biofeedback, psychosomatic medicine, family therapy, community mental health.

In his own version of gradual retirement, Karl Menninger returned to an old field of interest. Preparing to write *The Crime of Punishment*, Menninger looked freshly at prison inmates as human beings, many of them with mental health problems as agonizing as any of those in the general population. Later, he became heavily involved in the problems of runaway children, collaborating with W. Clement Stone, the Chicago philanthropist.

On the day of my 1982 visit to the foundation, Karl Menninger was, as Pruyser described him to me, "still coming to his office almost every day, bored with the past as always, still writing articles, speeches, and letters if not books, still looking for new projects, determined to outdo his father in longevity, triumphant at having overcome a brain tumor that laid him up for a year."

Dr. Gilbert Bowen, pastor of the Kenilworth (Ill.) Union Church, had suggested that I get in touch with Pruyser. When Bowen was doing doctoral work in pastoral counseling at McCormick Theological Seminary, he had had Pruyser as a mentor and admired the quality of his mind. Furthermore, Pruyser had done some work on the psychology of aging and was himself retired.

"Gil Bowen was mistaken. I'm not retired," Pruyser told me on the phone. Again when I got there, he said, "I'm not retired, even though I could retire now—I'm sixty-six. But I have no inclination to do it. There is no mandatory retirement at Menninger's. Professional staff members have always been able to keep on working here part or full time. Even when they stop doing formal work for the foundation, they can keep a small office here so they have a place to pursue their own projects.

"As for me, I have too many irons in the fire to retire. They load more and more work on me and I have another book with my publisher and I must see it through. For now, my division between work and play is very satisfying."

As I later thought back to that day, I could see that the Menninger and Pruyser definition of "retirement" must be very similar to their definition of the word, "disablement." It was true that Pruyser, like Karl Menninger before him, had retired as head of the Menninger Department of Education. But that didn't mean that he was ready to quit *working!*

Listening to the tapes of what Paul Pruyser called "our brain-storming session," I thought I could see why he had been right at home in Topeka and at Menninger—in spite of having been born, raised, and educated in the Netherlands.

Pruyser, too, is a scholar, teacher, activist. Like the Menningers, he radiates warmth, concern, enthusiasm. He is an elder in the United Presbyterian Church and, like Dr. Karl, is fascinated by the relationship between psychology and religion. His book, *Between Belief and Unbelief*, which he gave me as a memento of my visit, is scholarly and subtle, written with a passion that lies just below the surface.

Even Pruyser's personal enthusiasms seem appropriate to an "adopted" Menninger. He told me that he and his wife had gotten sick and tired of staying in motels with nothing but signs for scenery and that he had just come back from a "real" camping trip to Kit Carson National Park. They had bought an ultra-light, "space-age" tent and a "space-age" cooker and had set up camp among the campers and trailers of less avant-garde vacationers. A young couple had approached them one evening: "You must be Europeans, right? We thought so. In this country, only the very young and Europeans are willing to sleep in tents."

At home, the Pruysers had embarked on another against-the-grain experiment. They had converted their heating system to make important use of passive solar power and of woodburning stoves. The stoves serve a second purpose. Pruyser is a wood-chopper, a pruner, a thinner, a cutter-up of the excess trees on his four acres.

"Isn't it strange," he observed, "how different cultures tend to treat different activities in age-specific ways? In America, older people aren't supposed to sleep in a tent or have a lot of woodburning stoves."

"Or ride around on ten-speed bikes," I said. I told him about my own new Trek and the smiles it gets me when I ride.

"Very different from Copenhagen, for instance," I said.

"Yes." he said. "That's where they're born on a bike and die on a bike."

After a solid morning of yeasty conversation and lunch in one of the crisp, white, open-face buildings, Pruyser had to consult with a patient. He turned me over to his associate, Thomas Dolgoff, a kindly man who was seventy and looked sixty. Dolgoff, who is an expert on aging and speaks regularly at the Menninger Seminars for businessmen, loaded me up with helpful material from his own files as well as with encouragement and good wishes.

He also left me wondering whether the real fountain of youth lies somewhere under that hill outside Topeka.

When Charles F. Menninger was past ninety, he had an experience that reminded him all over again of the need to deal with life in the here and now:

Last night Karl and Jean were here for dinner. I told them some stories of my boyhood and early medical practice. They were a good audience. I can't say I didn't enjoy myself for a while. But when they'd left and I'd gone to bed, I couldn't sleep as I usually can. I was back in the past, lost in a bog of recollections. I couldn't be sure whether I'd see some room of the past or the room of the present if I switched on the light.

In recalling useless memories, some men of my age become senile without organic cause. For that reason, I'm grateful for the experience. I saw how the things I'm doing could become of little consequence, how the work that awaits each awakening and makes it joyous could become unimportant. My sanity, my health, my happiness, my productiveness rest on the here and now of things.

I will never go into the past . . . unless something that happened or something I did has a definite relationship to the here and now.

THEODORE AND HELEN KUNTZ

"All we need now is one day a week that is entirely ours."

In 1982, at sixty-nine, Theodore Kuntz had been retired for four years from his job as a block operator at Chicago's Union Station. He was a volunteer counselor in a hospital, sang in two church choirs, had his hand in a number of volunteer jobs at his church, was a fifth grandparent to kids all over his neighborhood.

Kuntz's wife Helen had gotten so busy with both housework and homework that she had had to retire as a part-time babysitter. Now, as a full-time undergraduate at Truman College in Chicago, she spent evenings reading to herself—Shakespearean plays and Mozart librettos—rather than reading bedtime stories to the children of "clients."

The Kuntzes recognized that their approach to retirement was unusual. In his church work, Theodore had always had problems trying to recruit volunteers, even among retired people. They may be good church members, he said, and they may have the time, but they don't want to "break up their routines."

The Kuntzes believed that their habits in retirement went straight back to habits they formed when they were much younger. "We were involved before and we're involved now," he said. "Some [people] wait until retirement to become active, but by then it's almost too late. Their habits are formed: work, sleep, survive."

If early involvement had been the Number 1 secret of success in the Kuntzes' retirement, their Number 2 secret could not be far behind: they had always made younger people a part of their lives.

Helen Kuntz had read thousands of stories, corrected reams of homework, taught catechism at St. Mary's of the Lake Roman Catholic Church. Even with those experiences, she had had worries about starting college at her age, worries that turned out to be needless. Her fellow students "treat me as a contemporary," she said proudly.

As for Theodore, "a generation of children has gone to the Waveland Golf Course with [him] to search for treasures like lost golf balls in the weeds outside the fence," according to the Chicago *Sun-Times.* "It's commonplace for parents to look out the window and watch one of their children take a flying leap into Kuntz's arms and see his ruddy face beam."

The couple did have three regrets in their retirement:

First, in setting their priorities, they had failed to save one day a week for themselves.

Second, when they went to Ireland, they "didn't stay long enough. It was so beautiful."

Third, they should have learned to scuba dive when they were younger. "I always wanted to see the bottom of the ocean," Helen said.

JOHN W. HANLEY

"I continue to want to be an optimist."

Several people had thought of the metaphor before me.

One security analyst had opined, "Bringing Hanley [to Monsanto] is like trying to turn the Queen Elizabeth around with a rowboat."

Then an old friend had sent Jack Hanley a leatherbound, gold-embossed book entitled *Trying to Turn the Queen* . . . . etc. Inside the book was a bottle of Jack Daniels. Hanley still kept it on a bookshelf.

Nonetheless, the Queen *can* be turned around that way; Hanley had always said so. "It takes a lot of effort but it can be done."

Now, after eleven years as chief oarsman, he was passing the job to another man but he felt serene about Monsanto's future. In not too many more years, he expected "to see Monsanto recognized as the best-managed chemical company in the United States, perhaps the world. I'm stepping aside with full confidence. I'm investing in Monsanto personally."

When Jack Hanley arrived, Monsanto was suffering from a

classic case of commodity-itis. Although the company was huge, its profit margins were now low and going lower. Many if not most of its products lacked uniqueness. Only two of its offerings—Astro Turf and Acrilan—were household words at my house. It was very vulnerable to price-cutting and other profit-depressants.

Hanley's prior business experience—at Procter & Gamble—had been very different. *Its* household words included Tide, Cheer, Crest, Zest, Secret, Crisco, Duncan Hines, Folgers, Comet, Pampers, thirty more. Commodity marketing was entirely foreign to its business strategy.

When he set up shop at the showcase campus on Lindbergh Boulevard, just outside St. Louis, Hanley had three agreed-on missions:

1. "To persuade my new colleagues that we could turn this baby around, that we didn't have to be in commodity businesses forever."

2. "To develop younger people. Managers not only had to *agree* it was part of their job, they also had to *do* it."

3. "To install disciplined management. To get the number of guesses down to a minimum."

In the pursuit of these aims, Hanley had gotten modestly rich. Had rubbed shoulders with the McDonnells and the Busches of the St. Louis world. Had acquired his share of honorary degrees, company directorships, other kudos. Had made some "gaudy mistakes" along with the right calls. Had not found it "a routine assignment." "Dynamic" and "dramatic" were appropriate words for it.

When I arrived for my appointment that October day, I was watching for signals of emotional letdown. I was not surprised when I heard some. (We hear what we expect to hear.)

Hanley's secretary: "I apologize for not being at my desk when the receptionist called to announce you. I used to have an assistant to do the errands. But with our new status around here . . . ."

Hanley himself (at various times in our talk):

"Just to show you how I'm stepping back, our guys are meeting with the New York security analysts this afternoon. The thought of me letting those guys go up there without Father is unthinkable. But I have no reservations about their ability. . . ."

"I suppose my chances [of suffering from] culture shock are very real. . . ."

"A lot of people have said to me, 'Oh, my God, you're heading for one of the traumatic experiences of your life'. . . ."

"I say to myself, 'You're going to face a hell of a lot of changes. Your environment will be *very* different. And you'll have troubles you don't expect.' But I try to remember that I've faced all that before."

In spite of what he said, he sounded cheerful as he spoke the words. Ebullient, in fact.

"I continue to want to be an optimist, to think things can be accomplished," he said. This was an attitude that had served him well in his career. "It has helped greatly to carry people along with me."

He had made his plans for the future. (Boy, had he made plans!)

He would continue on several boards. Would do some consulting. Was going to write a book, mostly for his family's benefit. Had his personal affairs to manage. . . .

And he had some new enthusiasms.

"You know where my office is going to be?" he asked. I didn't.

"That's it—right there," he said. "It" was an IBM personal computer plus peripherals, sitting in a place of honor alongside his desk. Later on, he would move it back and forth between his two homes. He had gotten a carpenter to build a foam-lined container for the purpose.

"Why a computer?" I asked.

He had decided that it would be too slow and complicated to use the mails and a dictating machine to get his paperwork done. Instead, he would be his own secretary-bookkeeper. He hadn't yet mastered the machine. But he was learning. Even now, while winding down at Monsanto, he was improving his typing. He had discovered that a typing program had come with the computer. . . .

He was also determined to learn to play the organ.

The *organ?*

Yes. He'd always wanted to read music and to play a musical instrument. He'd bought not one but two organs, one for their winter place in Florida, one for the summer place in North Carolina.

Hadn't he found it tough going?

Yes. The hard part had been the physical problems in playing: "You know, it's the old business of patting your head and rubbing your stomach at the same time." But he was not intimidated. He was looking forward to working away at it three or four times a week. . . .

So. Keeping busy would not be a problem for Hanley in retirement.

But wait. He had still another plan, I knew. When Monsanto had announced his retirement, it had said he planned to start a center for the treatment of alcohol and drug abuse. That, I thought, had to be a first in the annals of retirement. I was delighted to get out of bed at 5:00 in the morning and fly to St. Louis to hear about it.

The story had begun many years before when Mary Jane Hanley's use of alcohol had descended into the misery—for her, for him, for their children—of active alcoholism.

That had cost the Hanleys seven or eight years of "very difficult times." Their marriage had been "on the verge of rupture."

"Then, shortly after we moved here, Mary Jane recognized that we had gone as far as we could go. And—using her God-given good sense—she got herself into a very well-structured [rehabilitation] program here and she's now been sober for more than nine years.

"It's been my thrill to watch an adult human being start to grow again in a really thrilling way. I've watched her build self-confidence and the ability to manage herself and others. As a result, we've become very good friends—she is my confidante and I am hers.

"You mentioned the importance to women of their friends. Mary Jane has a network of women friends who are also recovered alcoholics and I have a great respect for that. I've seen how that has strengthened her and made it possible for her to resume her independence. I want very much to avoid threatening any part of that—and [my retirement] does have the potential to impact that if I—if we—are not careful."

Was he worried that his retirement would threaten her sobriety?

"Oh, no. She is a magnificent human being—damn it, I really— these are not platitudes—I really *admire* her and what she's been able to accomplish. And she's *continued* to grow. I used to worry about what would happen if I were knocked off—who would take care of her? Well, I'll tell you who will take care of her. *She* will. And she will do a damn good job of it.

"My concern is that I will louse up the relationship and I'll be the loser, not she. She can handle it. I don't want to warp in any way our relationship because of my own enjoyment of it.

"No, I'm not worried about Mary Jane at all. She has an inner peace and an inner strength that will permit her to handle almost anything. My concern is self-interest, purely and simply self-interest. . . ."

"Well," I said, "you've answered my question. I certainly understand why you want to open a treatment center."

Yes. But there had been still another factor.

"We are all complex beings," he said. "I had been suffering more than a little puritanical guilt because of the resources I had been building up. I really had a problem with that.

"Then one day, I was asked to participate in the mayor's prayer breakfast and to read something from the Old Testament. Well, I am not a Biblical scholar, not by any stretch, but I found my way to Ecclesiastes. And right after that chapter about a time to sow and time to reap I found the observation that—in contemporary parlance—if you've made a pile and made it legitimately, it's OK to enjoy it. A man is worthy of his rewards. Well, that had a powerful effect on me. It eased my pangs of guilt. I stopped worrying.

"Of course, Mary Jane said, 'Well, you immediately found something else to worry about—that's just the kind of person you are.' But the guilt problem did disappear.

"Still in the back of my mind—even though we thought ourselves generous givers—I had a conviction that we should do more. I suppose I unconsciously was looking for something. Well, as our rejuvenation went on—and I really mean *ours*—it seemed to me that the benefits we had gotten and were getting from Mary Jane's treatment program were crucial in our lives. It troubled me that that kind of treatment was so hard to come by where we live in Florida. Mary Jane told me what her Alcoholics Anonymous network told her—that they have terrible problems down there. . . .

"Oh, there is a facility that treats the silk stocking trade for profit. Wilbur Mills went there after his Fanne Fox episode— thanks to the courtesy of some constituent of his—at $600 a week or some such outrageous figure. . . .

"The net of it is—there is an opportunity there.

"Mary Jane and I thought we ought to fund a not-for-profit clinic. But in addition to putting up the money, we thought we ought to get some guarantee of quality. And I got an idea of how to do that."

He had been familiar with the Hazelden Institute in Minnesota, "one of the two or three places with the best success records."

"I went to see them. They said yes, they had been out consulting with Gerald and Betty Ford about the clinic the Fords were sponsoring in Palm Springs. And they were willing to consider helping me.

"But I said, 'I don't want you to consult with me, I want you to come in and *manage* the place. I'll take the responsibility for raising the money. I'll either put it up or raise it, or a combination thereof. But I want you to manage it. That's the only way I can be absolutely confident that the quality of service will be available.

" 'Well, we've never done anything like that,' they said.

"I said, 'Think about it, talk about it, see if it isn't time for you to stretch out from Center City, Minnesota.' Well, they took it to their board and while it wasn't unanimous, they said yes.

"But they also said, 'Hanley, don't put up all the money yourself, even if you've got it. It's got to be a community-based activity. You gotta get other people involved.' Well, OK. Fine.

"I got the United Way into the act—I had been involved in the United Way a long time—I got the national United Way into it because they saw it as a demonstration project. If it worked, it would show that an individual can have an impact on a community, and they were willing to help me. They also got the local United Way into it and *they* have been helpful.

"I did make one big mistake—not a fatal one, thank goodness. In typical Hanley fashion, I began to postulate that this was a success and that we ought to start looking for the next one. I said I was willing to put up the funding money for the next one and I said that it ought to be in Winston-Salem because they have a problem, too, and it's right there in our backyard so we can manage one clinic in the winter and one in the summer.

"Well, that aggressive attitude concerned the Hazelden group and I could see they wondered what they'd got a-hold of here in Hanley. Would he lead them down a trail where they would dissipate their energies and wind up with less than quality?

"So I've backed off for the time being."

For now, he would focus on Palm Beach and see whether the combination of Hazelden, Hanley, and community effort works. If it did, though, "it would be a shame not to expand it. . . ."

The Hanleys had gotten a "very reassuring, very nice" bonus from their project. Knowing it could siphon off a lot of money, they had felt they should tell their children. "They were terrific," Hanley said. "They said, in effect, 'Take the whole darned shooting match if you have to. We don't need it. Go!' Not only that, two of the kids made contributions out of their own limited resources."

The word "confident" is never very far from John W. Hanley's tongue. Nor is the word "optimistic." Both seem appropriate. His *curriculum vitae* reads like something out of Horatio Alger. Even the dark years of his wife's active alcoholism were followed by recovery and "rejuvenation." On the surface, he seems to be a man blessed with luck.

In fact, it pays to listen to him with more than half an ear. Luck and a positive mental attitude account for only part of his story.

Near the end of our conversation, he said, "I am a sort of introspective guy in the sense that I step back periodically and look at my reactions at what I'll call 'circumstances of consequence.' I am currently examining my concern—my fear of failure—for this funding operation [for the clinic]. I'm having an emotional-psychological reaction to this concern and it is exactly analogous to a number of other experiences I have had.

"The way things work for me, I have—not a lot of times, but half a dozen times—faced circumstances where I had a concern. Didn't know quite how to solve the problem. Worried with it a little bit, put it aside, came back, worried with it a little more, still had no idea of how to deal with it. Then all of a sudden, I don't know why, but all of a sudden, after the passage of some meaningful period of time, I'd come in here [his office] one day or I'd wake up one day and there it was. The answer isn't always right but it always *seems* right and we begin to move. As I say, the direction of movement is not always right. But we undertake it with confidence that, by gosh, we know how to do this now. I'm sure the pattern will repeat itself with this new project.

"I'm able to step back periodically and look at myself and this whole process and—I suppose it sounds egotistical——I find it *interesting* to be able to analyze Hanley and his problems and the way he deals with them.

"One thing though: I've never been able to identify this mysterious middle part where I pick it up, put it down, pick it up, put it down, not knowing what to do with it, and then, at some later time, I wake up and there it is."

What he had described—and eloquently, I told him—was the unconscious creative self at work. In my own younger days, I said, I had frequently gone through the same "mysterious middle part" myself. Even though my track record had been pretty good, I had sweated a lot over that business of "picking up and putting down." Then I discovered that the process is natural and that every problem-solver goes through it. Knowing that had helped, I said. A lot. I started sleeping better, for one thing.

A few weeks later, I got a letter from Hanley, thanking me for a book I'd sent him. The letter said:

> Until our visit here, I had really never had a melancholy thought about retirement. Then, provoked by your observations, I began to speculate that if almost everybody else had a "problem" of some kind, then why was I not having some troubling vistas.
>
> Yesterday, two things happened. I got that [Bradford] book you sent—and I thank you for it, and I'll read it with interest—but it evoked a touch of uncertainty. Then, last evening was the annual Chairman's Christmas party for the small group in "my building." For the first time in all the years this party has been going on, I did not preside. Dick Mahoney did—and he did a fine job—but it was different. Not exactly sad, maybe melancholy is the right word, but in any event, I am joining the ranks of retirees, at least in terms of recognizing that I will be facing a very important and significant change.
>
> As I progress through this, I will be grateful for your counsel.

Getting this letter has cost me no sleep at all. Nor, I suspect, has Hanley's "melancholy" thought disturbed his own repose. I am sure that he will do very well in retirement—with the help of "the mysterious middle part."

And I wrote back to tell him so.

"MRS. SHERIDAN"

"What you don't use, you lose."

When "Mrs. Sheridan" agreed to let a reporter interview her for the Chicago *Sun-Times*, she did it with one proviso: that the paper could not use her real name. She wanted to avoid telephone calls from crackpots. That, at age eighty-five, was one of her few worries in life.

At sixty-two, Mrs. Sheridan had retired as a medical records clerk for the old St. Luke's Hospital in Chicago—and promptly started her own business. For several years, she baked Christmas fruitcakes, an enterprise that left her with plenty of free time. In other seasons, she traveled around the world with her late husband, who was a retired musician. "We had some wonderful times," she told the reporter. "I never feared retirement. Adjusting to it isn't hard. What you make of it is up to you."

After a significant span of years as a volunteer at a church-sponsored day-care center, Mrs. Sheridan turned pro and commenced a third career, as a baby-sitter. That had started as a "fluke," she said. She began by pinch-hitting for a sick friend. As time went by, her name passed from family to family and in the last five years, she had helped to raise ten children. She had been so greatly in demand that she had had to put strict limits on the number of jobs she'd take. She did have other things to do. . . .

After baby-sitting, what?

"Perhaps volunteer work. I always thought it would be nice to work with shut-ins. I would like to take people out who couldn't get out otherwise. What you don't use, you lose."

GERALD R. FORD

"The option to say no . . ."

It was surely worth another try, I thought.

I would write Mr. Ford yet another letter and attempt, one more time, to convince him that he and his retirement story belonged in this book. This is what I wrote:

Dear Mr. President:

The example you are setting for other "retired" men and women continues to impress me. I am still hoping, therefore, that you will be willing to let me interview you for the book I am writing. Again this year, my wife and I will be spending all of March at Del Safari Country Club, just ten minutes from your house. I'd love to get on your schedule.

The central theme and thesis of my book have to do with opportunity. In this unprecedented era of mass-production retirement, millions of people are still prisoners of the ancient concept that to retire is to plant one foot and both lobes of the brain in the grave. Poppycock, say I. You, for one, are living proof that the years after one's peak of power can be uniquely satisfying and fulfilling for anyone who is willing to learn, change, and grow as a human being.

Not just any ex-president would fill the bill for me. Mr. Truman seems to have rested on his oars, as does General Eisenhower. Mr. Johnson appears to have died a sad, disappointed man. Mr. Nixon's shell gets thicker and thicker. Mr. Carter seems to be making a career of trying to justify the unjustifiable. Of all the old-timers, only Mr. Jefferson demonstrated the glory of the opportunity.

On the other hand, you, sir, are leading a life that I admire and respect for its balance, its new interests, its continued involvement with the other lives around it. You may not have thought of yourself as a role model for others, but I think you're a good one. A very good one.

If you will give me a little time in March, I'll send you, well in advance, a list of the questions I would like to ask you and, if there's time, I'll share with you some of the surprising and interesting things I've learned in the year and a half I've been working on this project.

Meanwhile, good luck at Pebble Beach, if you're playing again this year . . . .

The letter worked.
Or, at least, something worked.
There I am on March 24, 1983, driving west on Country Club Road. The Little San Bernardino Mountains in the distance. Thick slices of raw desert still sandwiched between the man-made oases on either side of the road.

This is exotic country in more ways than one. To get from our rented house to Sand Dune Road in Rancho Mirage, I pass Eisenhower Hospital and the Betty Ford Center for the treatment of chemical dependency. Crossing Bob Hope Drive, one is no more than four wood shots from former ambassador Walter Annenberg's place with its private golf course and its echoes of Queen Elizabeth's recent visit.

On Sand Dune Road itself, the receptionist is a Secret Service man wearing a careful expression and a walkie-talkie.

Inside the converted ranch house that serves the former president as office, the staff are casual but busy this day, and so is a small girl wearing a badge that says: "Kiss me. I'm a Republican." I tell her I'm a Republican, too, and I give her a kiss. She gives me a photocopy of a drawing she has just made for her uncle, one of the Secret Service men.

Mr. Ford, too, is dressed casually. He has removed the coat and tie he'd worn earlier for a videotaping session.

But he is all business.

He knows who I am and why I'm there, has reread my letters, seems to want me to make the most of my opportunity. "I don't have any extra time today," he said. "Let's get right down to it."

Later on, I concluded that Gerald Ford must *never* have had any extra time. At the University of Michigan, he had made the good grades it takes to get into Yale University Law School, but he'd also been a star football player, good enough to play in the 1935 College All-Star game. At Yale, he'd relieved the law-school grind by serving as an assistant varsity football coach and freshman boxing coach. In Washington, he'd played the non-stop game of national politics for thirty years, played it well enough to become both a congressman's congressman and a Republican's Republican. He'd been minority leader of the House of Representatives and twice was permanent chairman of Republican national conventions.

Now, in 1983, I knew that he was still busy enough to need a full-time director of scheduling and that he still took those punishing "red-eye" flights from California to Washington or New York in order to meet his commitments.

My first question for him was intended to be a warmer-upper, nothing more: "Of the new things you're doing in retirement, which do you like the most?"

"I like them all. I like everything I'm doing," he said. "That's the great thing about retirement for me. Now I have the option to say no."

Then he launched into statistics. And left me wondering when he ever exercised his option.

"I've spoken on 101 college campuses since I retired from politics," he said. "I've taught more than 600 classes, answered more than 6,000 questions from students and faculty members.

"I've been to big and small, public and private colleges, including four for black students. It's very interesting to me and I expect to continue though on a slower, smaller scale.

"Also, I'm now on the boards of seven corporations, something I thoroughly enjoy. It gives me the opportunity to see what's happening in the business community, to have a good feel for what's transpiring in the economic system in the United States.

"I do quite a bit of fund-raising for charitable organizations, the Boy Scouts of America, The United Way, Boys Club, various others—arthritis, cancer, etc.

"I make three, maybe four, speeches a month to various organizations, trade associations, and business groups. That's also a good opportunity to see what's happening in the business community.

"In election years, I work for Republican candidates and organizations. But that comes only in election years.

"And I try to play a little golf and do some skiing."

Gerald Ford came away from his thirty years in Washington with his enthusiasm for capitalism and democracy intact. "When I go to campuses, I unabashedly speak up for our governmental system and our economic system. And I enjoy meeting head-on the questions I get from students or faculty members when they're downplaying the United States," he told me. "I often quote what Sir Winston Churchill once said and I'll paraphrase it: 'Democracy is the worst form of government in the history of mankind but it's better than any other that's ever been tried.'" Ford had pursued the same theme with James Reston a year before my visit. In his column, Reston wrote of Ford, "No sensible book publisher would have dared to print such a Horatio Alger story [as Ford's] and even Jerry Ford can't quite believe in his mirage [a pun on the name of Ford's town, Rancho Mirage]. How did it all happen? he seems to ask. How can I pay it back? So he keeps flying around the country, telling young people in the universities that everything is possible, and all would be well."

When Ford left Washington in 1977, his savings could not have been large. Nonetheless, he had a large nest egg of another kind: his rare (if not unique) knowledge of the way things work both in Congress and in the White House. This knowledge, he told me, "is, quite frankly, why I have the opportunity to serve on various boards."

"Every board I serve on," he said, "has a very, very vital interest in what is transpiring in our nation's capital. I can give every board I serve on an analysis of what *has* happened and an appraisal of what I think *will* happen. That contribution to the various boards is very meaningful. Company policies today—I don't care what industry it is—have to reflect what's going to take place or what has taken place in Washington D.C."

If the companies he works with did not get this knowledge from him, he said, "they would have to go out and buy it someplace else."

I had no doubt, as we talked, that Ford was aware that some people criticize him for making money as a corporate director and as a speaker at business meetings. "Commercializing the presidency," is a phrase I have heard. I felt sure that Ford would reject this criticism out of hand. He had worked hard—at government wages—to learn what he'd learned. As a laborer, he was worthy of his hire. He had done nothing and would do nothing to tarnish the presidency.

Up to this point in our conversation, everything Ford had said sounded as though he'd heard the questions before and had had plenty of time to polish his answers. Then I got lucky. A few months before, I had watched as Diane Sawyer interviewed Richard Nixon on television. In their conversation, Nixon had said that he thinks this country, unlike Great Britain and other countries with parliamentary systems, wastes the experience and talents of its former heads of government. Gerald Ford, he said, is a master of domestic affairs. Jimmy Carter knows a lot about the Middle East. He himself had always been very interested in foreign affairs. Too bad, he said, that we don't have some formal way to use those resources.

I described this interview to Ford and asked what he thought.

"I am not in favor of setting up a council or formal structure.

We've got enough commissions, boards, and what have you. That's not the way to utilize this talent or this experience. If the president or the Congress want a former president to make a contribution, they can simply call on the individual to give advice or to serve. I'm *very strongly* opposed to another commission or whatever. I know from my own experiences and I know from talking to other former presidents—whenever they're asked, they are more than willing to help in whatever way is requested."

It was here that I finally surprised him with a question.

What, I asked, had Ford thought about the Hoover Commission?

For the first time, he paused several seconds before answering.

"Well, I was in Congress when the report of the first Hoover Commission was made and that was a fine illustration of President Truman calling on former President Hoover to serve as chairman of a commission to take a look at the reorganization of the federal government. The reports that were submitted to the Congress in 1948 were very helpful—but that was a one-shot operation. Two or three years later, we had another commission under President Hoover but again it was a one-shot.

"Something like that I can understand, but to have a perpetual organization of former presidents with a staff and all that, I'm opposed to it."

Another pause. Then—

"There is pending legislation to have a follow-up to the several Hoover Commissions and there have been some rumors that I might be asked to head it up. There is a need for some outside group to take a look at the structure and so forth of the federal government, but so far the legislation hasn't been enacted."

If the bill were passed, I thought I knew someone who would have a hard time saying no to the job.

Gerald Ford is not the only member of the family who has the option to say no but still says yes a lot. Betty Ford, he told me, "is as busy as I am. She is very active" in raising money for charitable and educational organizations. "The Betty Ford Center for alcohol and drug addiction is completed now and she spends a lot of time over there. Besides her work on alcoholism, she does a lot of lecturing on cancer and ERA and things of that sort." And the Fords are "very family-oriented. We get our family together at Christmas with the four children, the two spouses, and four grandchildren. And we have each family out to spend a week with us in the summer. When we slow down, we hope to spend more time with them. . . ."

Somewhere in the back of both the Fords' minds, there is a "problem" with all this: they don't fit the stereotype of retirement.

"Both of us wonder when we're going to have the retirement everyone expected us to have," Ford said to me at one point.

And at another point: "We keep saying, 'Well, as soon as we get this project done, why we won't take on any more, and therefore we'll have more time as in an ordinary retirement.' "

And at still another point: "I hope to do more of the things that traditionalists say you're supposed to do in retirement." Golf, for instance. "I'm hoping I can concentrate more seriously on getting my handicap down. I'd like to get down to about an eleven handicap, which means you can play well enough to get some good scores as well as some bad ones."

If not fitting the retirement stereotype is a problem for the Fords, it doesn't seem to worry them much.

Ford said, "Since we left the White House and we've had less official burdens and responsibility, we've had the opportunity to catch up on some of the things we missed in married life when I was in politics. It's a less-regulated lifestyle and therefore we're enjoying it more. To be honest with you, we couldn't be happier. We're very happy with our current lifestyle."

"Happy" is a word that seems to come readily to Ford's mind.

After James Reston had visited Ford in 1982, he wrote, "The happiest politician in the United States today, without question, is Gerald Rudolph Ford. Jerry has it all figured out. He is 'retired but not unemployed.' He has all the prestige of the presidency without any of the agony. . . . He thought the best job in America was not president but ex-president."

Thinking back on my own visit with Ford, I thought that Reston had gotten much the same feeling for things on Sand Dune Road as I had.

Except for one thing: the frustration in Ford's life.

"I get *very* frustrated," Ford told me, "that I can't hit a stationary ball more accurately more often."

Mr. President, I can identify with that.

JAKE AND HELEN LUTZ
Varooooom. Varooooom!

He was sixty-three, a retired agent for Standard Oil Company (Indiana). She was sixty-one, the retired owner of a five-and-dime store.

If you had seen them in summer of 1983—astride their Honda Golden Wing motorcycle, towing a cargo trailer, dressed in matching helmets, jackets, and pants—you would have been hard put to it to have guessed the following:

They were great-grandparents.

And they were out to become the first married couple, the first grandparents, and the first great-grandparents ever to ride a motorcycle around the entire perimeter of the lower forty-eight states—20,000 miles. Jake and Helen Lutz had bought their first bike only eleven years before, but they had tried to make up for being latecomers. In those years, they had missed only Alaska, Hawaii, and Nevada in their travels around the United States.

The Lutzes are rare but not unique.

Jimmie Lafal, sixty-nine, of Blue Springs, Missouri, has owned thirty-three motorcycles since 1928. Among other jaunts, he has made the 1,600-mile round trip to Mount Rushmore seven times. His wife Elsie, often joins him in his adventures.

There are 25,000 other members of the Retread Motorcycle Club International which refuses membership to anyone under forty. What are these folks like?

"Older motorcyclists just tend to be a gutsy bunch of people in a nice kind of way," says Ona House, sixty-five, secretary of the "Retreads."

ROBERT J. NOEL
"A typically Noellian solution"

Bob and Peggy Noel had flown in the face of a lot of conventional wisdom when he retired.

I thought often about that as Hobby and I made the all-day,

drive-fly-drive trip from Palm Desert to Pebble Beach. We were looking forward to a long April weekend of reunion with our good friends, but I was eager as well to hear Noel talk at length about his retirement problems and solutions. The last time on the phone, he had sounded like a happy man.

That day, as we drove around the Monterey Bay end of the peninsula and entered the 17 Mile Drive at Carmel, the sun shone as resolutely as though rain and fog had just been legally banned. Indeed, the whole of what we saw looked like the movie set of movie sets. Forest thriving. Houses discreet but plush. Golf course lush. Carmel Bay glinting. Mountains swaggering. Reminders of past romance and present glamour marching past the car windows. I could see what would happen in any argument between head and heart. Should we retire here? Or not? Heart 3—Head 0.

If you and I were second-guessing the Noels on the basis of the conventional wisdom, we would say the following to them:

"You made three big, basic mistakes.

"First, you changed too many things in your life too fast. Bob retired. You sold your old house. You moved to Pebble Beach and left all your old friends and activities behind. All within a few months.

"Second, you knew almost no one in Pebble Beach except for a real estate man, your architect, and your contractor. Furthermore, you didn't belong to anything—not a club, not a church, not a civic organization. Nothing. You came here almost completely unconnected.

"Third, you had no plans, no ideas for how to occupy yourselves. Sure you had to decorate your house. And sure, it would be wonderful to explore a new and beautiful part of the world. And sure, Peggy would have a house to manage and your two girls would be spending part of their time with you. But what will you, Bob, really do with your time and talents and experience day in and day out? What'll you do for fun, let alone for the health of your self-esteem? Why, you don't even play golf! Or tennis. Or have a boat."

Now, a little more than three years after their move, I knew that the Noels had done a lot more than survive the radical surgery. The transplant had taken and was looking better all the time. But I knew that it had not been easy for Bob Noel. The next day, we started our conversation on that note.

"I certainly had some problems with retirement," he said. "But I don't think they were so much the loss of identity or the giving-up of power—things that trouble so many other people in the situation. My problems had more to do with giving up the feelings of security I had when I was working for the company.

"When I was working, I used to have bad dreams occasionally about this. . . . Suddenly I was no longer working for Burnett and I felt cast adrift and I had trouble getting back to the feelings of security that I apparently cherished. When I retired, suddenly all those bad dreams came true. There I was—out of the office, out of the job, out on my own, having moved to a new state and a new house and a new situation. For me, there was plenty of anxiety and depression associated with it.

"I've always found it hard to sort that out. How much of the problem was simply what you associate with having too much time on your hands? And how much of it was just getting to a very introspective time in your life? You start asking yourself all those momentous questions: 'What am I doing here? What do I do from here on? What's my purpose? What's my role?' Whether you want the questions to be there or not, there they are and you have to ask them. The nature of your life simply changes and I felt that greatly. I think it's foolish for anyone to think he's not going to have those transitional problems."

As Noel talked, I knew from earlier conversations that he missed, more acutely than most, the people and the jobs he'd known at Leo Burnett Company. For all the stress of the advertising business, he loved the work he did and he loved the writers and artists and other people who were also attracted to that world.

Bob Noel was an advertising man with a firm commitment to doing whatever would work best for the client. But his special passion was for campaigns like those that involved the Green Giant and the Little Green Sprout; Ernie and the other Keebler Elves; Charlie the Tuna; Morris the Cat; the Maytag Lonely Repairman. As a writer, he had a large, well-nourished bump of feeling for seemingly guileless humor, for character design and development, for dialogue, for music. One of his favorite stories tells how the Green Giant came to say "Ho, ho, ho." Our old boss, Leo Burnett, had heard an early version of a new Green Giant song in a meeting and said he liked it but it didn't sound giant-y enough and what was Bob going to do about that? What Noel did was to analyze the song all over again. He saw the opportunity he was looking for in a three-note, lyricless segment that had been taken by the oboe. What more natural than to have the giant do his three-syllable thing in the oboe's place? The result: "In the valley of the jolly . . . HO, HO, HO . . . Green Giant."

A former player of the tuba in the Northwestern University band and a lover of jazz, Noel was at home in a recording studio full of professional musicians. A pioneer writer of television commercials, he was equally at home with directors, cameramen, editors, and actors. If cartoon characters were involved, some specialized facet of his talent made him comfortable with animators, and voice-over actors like Mel Blanc and Mason Adams.

As much as he enjoyed being a part of all that, Noel foresaw that he would pay a price for his sense of belonging.

"Carl Hixon and I used to talk about that, about how we had a place only in an advertising agency, maybe only one agency. Our abilities and our finely honed judgments and that kind of stuff—they didn't have any application in the rest of the world. You come here to Pebble Beach in a world of retired dentists and chemists and car dealers and bankers—that's what my neighbors are—and it's difficult to talk to them on any kind of professional level. The kind of thing I did doesn't have any meaning to those people at all.

"Even when I was in the advertising business here, briefly, getting out a batch of ads for local hotels and banks and restaurants, I was aware that I was ill-equipped for that. It's an entirely different set of muscles that you use. We were so adjusted to thinking about the best ways to whomp up an advertising campaign to spend $25 million for a client that it's hard to get accustomed to spending $500 for someone who thinks it's all the money in the world.

"If I feel any loss of power, it's that. I can't engage the clutch any more, I can't make the connection between the engine and the wheels. The engine that's in my head doesn't have any relevance to my world today. I can't apply what I know any more and make anything happen. And I can't believe it's just me. It's got to be a problem for all kinds of highly professional people who suddenly don't have to go to the office anymore and now all they have to do is putter around in their garage and play golf or whatever. It's a big sense of loss of power when this body of knowledge that you've built up in your work no longer gives you any feeling of relevance. I think that's a very important shift in people's lives."

And then there is the homesickness for the people he worked with.

"I go back there to the Burnett offices and I stand there in the lobby at lunchtime and I see one person after another whom I haven't seen in two or three years and I'm struck with what a lot of wonderful people there were and are. I thought there was very much of a family feeling in that world. It's a very different kind of family but it surely is a family. And the family feeling was deliberately fostered by Leo and other people who ran the company. How could you not miss that?"

This prompted me to ask Noel to tell again about his Navy experience. He had stayed in the Navy for two years after the end of World War II. He had been a lieutenant commander and a communications expert, but that had never explained to me why he had stayed on at a time when everyone else I knew had tried to get out as soon as possible.

"Well, there I was, not long out of college and I had had my first taste of success. It was the first job I'd had. And at the time I was getting ready to leave the Navy, I was actually in demand. The admiral who was in charge of the Navy in the northwest Pacific wanted me to come and join his staff. I was the most qualified, most experienced communications expert in that part of the world. In the Navy, anyway. To be requested, to be wanted, to have some accomplishments, and a track record to prove it was very important to me.

"Besides, there was all the security of a large organization. You didn't have to make a lot of decisions about your life—the Navy did most of that for you. It was a highly structured kind of life. To leave that and go out and be just another Joe Blow on the street (as I was) wondering what do I do now—I see a lot of parallels between that and retirement. I retired twice in other words. I left a situation I was comfortable with where I had some success and some identity and you have those blue suits with all the gold braid on them and it was pretty nice in a lot of ways."

Noel knew that, for all his attachment to the Navy, it was not the right lifetime career for him. He left, admiral or no. Right away came the what-now and who-am-I questions he would face thirty years later when retirement from advertising came. According to him, these were always tougher questions for him than for some people.

"There are people in this world whom I call the self-starters, who can organize themselves and who can set their own directions. They're sure-footed and confident and they've been that way all their lives. I'm just exactly the opposite. I've always been the victim or the beneficiary of happenstance, fate, circumstance, luck, or whatever you want to call it. I've always felt I should just do my work as well as I can and see where it gets me. I never once thought of running the Burnett creative department. If anyone had ever suggested I'd do that before I retired, I'd have said they were crazy.

"Things have always happened to me. I've never made them happen. Or at least I've never planned for them to happen. I've always waited to see if fate would smile on me.

"When you retire, that set of characteristics doesn't stand you in very good stead. When you're that way, it's much harder to find your way than it is in business.

"The absolutely great thing about retirement, for which I thank God every day and can't get over—my appreciation for it hasn't abated one whit—is freedom. I love it. But the other side of the coin is that too much freedom is not a good thing. Unless you have some kind of ability to chart a course and use that freedom, you've got a problem, and I had that problem. My solution to it has been typically Noellian. Like my furniture business. I just said to myself, 'I'm going to make a few of those and see what happens.' "

The "Noellian" approach to the freedom problem has led Noel down his share of blind alleys. Homesickness for the advertising agency business accounts for several.

When a small advertising agency in Monterey invited him to work with it on a project basis, Noel thought it was worth a good hard try. It would give him an interesting place to go several times a week, and if all went well, his big-league experience would give the agency a chance to grow faster. As things turned out, there was a problem: the barrier of specialization. He was like a microsurgeon trying to remember what he'd learned in medical school about whooping cough or a sprained ankle. Blind alley.

Leo Burnett Company asked him to prepare a presentation on the use of animation and trade characters in advertising. He was to present this work to Burnett people in Europe and then to make a videotape of it for future Burnett generations. He did all that, thinking it might lead to more of the same. It hasn't and he no longer thinks it will. Blind alley.

Noel's old friend and collaborator on jingles, Dick Marx, asked him to write lyrics for some small-city clients of the Marx musical organization. Noel did. And had fun. But those occasions seem to have dried up. Blind alley.

The American Association of Advertising Agencies, knowing that Noel is a master speechmaker, invited him to make presentations at two of its regional meetings. He did and he enjoyed it. And will do it again if he's asked. But the semi-professional speaking circuit offers a tough life and Noel probably thought of that as a blind alley from the start.

Noel's feelings about all this are not bad ones. If they were experiments that didn't work, they haven't soured him on trying new things. One of his experiments, a highly unpredictable one, has worked well. His decorative benches and stools are solid, steady sellers in the world of interior decorators. Visualize a boxy frame of two-by-fours covered with pieces from antique oriental rugs or kalims and you will get the idea.

Noel got the concept from "somewhere," possibly a magazine. It doesn't matter. At first sight, he said to himself, "I think I'll make a few of those and see what happens."

What happened was a hobby-turned-business that satisfies a lot of Noel's needs.

"Staying busy has a value in itself," he said. "Work has a value beyond the tangible things it produces because it also produces self-respect."

I said I understood that, but the human spirit rebels at staying busy just for the sake of staying busy. What you stay busy doing has to click with something inside your psyche.

"You're right," he said. "It's gotta click. You've got to want to do it. And I wanted to make those benches. I have a *need* to make things. Writing doesn't satisfy that need for me in spite of the fact that I did it all my life and liked it a lot.

"I'm really happiest when I'm at my workbench making things, physically making them. I get enormous satisfaction from seeing the benches come back from the upholsterer, all done and ready to ship. And I like sending them out.

"Obviously there's some creative strain in me that wants to be satisfied, but I also like the mindless activity that's involved. Back in the beginning, I used to drive over to Salinas a lot to deliver the frames to the upholsterer. I like—really like—the truckdriver part of the business. Peggy and I go to San Francisco quite frequently with three or four pieces of furniture in the back of the car. We go to the Galleria—the showroom—get the freight elevator down there, put the furniture in the elevator, ride the elevator up, and get the man in the receiving room to give me a receipt. And I like that. I like it a lot. I don't know why but I like it a lot."

There's a good deal more for him to like. He enjoys finding oriental rug dealers who own damaged pieces from which good parts can be salvaged for benches. He has found and bought from such dealers in Chicago, New York, and London, as well as in San Francisco. He gets a sort of childish pleasure, he says, from having his name on the directory in the showroom lobby. He likes to have cards and letterhead that say "Robert J. Noel, Designs" on them. He likes "having people buy the things and write me letters about how much they like them." And, while he doesn't need the income to live on, getting paid for his work feels good. It tells him that what he's doing is of value. "It's been a whole new schtick for me and it's become the cornerstone of my retirement life," he said.

No blind alley this time.

And he may have another winning Bob Noel design underway. While we were there, a twenty-four-inch-high construction of redwood took up a section of his workbench. It looked to me like a cross between a bird cage and a gazebo with a suggestion of pagoda in the "roof." Whatever it was, I thought it handsome.

"It's a driveway lantern," he said.

He had gotten the idea because Peggy Noel had suffered a painful injury one night while getting out of her car in the dark. Looking around for an outdoor light to protect against another accident, Noel rejected everything he could find, most pieces because they clashed with the surroundings.

This one fit.

Redwood is, of course, a major building material in northern California and what he had designed and made from redwood scraps not only served the practical purpose but also seemed to be decorative in the way outdoor sculpture is decorative. He contemplated making each design in limited editions. By hand.

"If I have any criticism of my adjustment to retirement, it is that I don't have enough people in my life," he said. "It's my fault and

I feel guilty about that. But I'm doing something else that interests me and I'm making a new group of friends that way.

"I'm what they call a senior fellow of the Monterey Institute for International Studies." This is a highly specialized college with an enrollment of about 400, most of whom are postgraduate students, mostly foreign, mostly bilingual. They are there to study international business management. Noel, who did considerable work in the international side of Leo Burnett Company, responds to the air of wordliness at the institute. While we were there, I thought I could see Noel working himself up to volunteer to help with the marketing of the institution. I could almost hear the ring of the fire bell.

The morning before we left, Hobby and I took a walk with Noel around several holes of the Pebble Beach course, probably the most photogenic and photographed course in the world.

It is, as every golf fan knows, the scene every year of the Bing Crosby invitational tournament that draws not only the grand dukes of professional golf but a large slice of Hollywood nobility as well.

The eighteenth green is no more than a driver and a three iron from the Noels' house. Another 550 yards or so down the curved rock pile that forms the shoreline of Carmel Bay, the seventeenth green sits, hallowed forevermore by Tom Watson's U.S. Open-winning chip shot for a birdie. We paid it the obligatory homage, taking photographs of each other pantomiming the Watson stroke.

Elsewhere, the Monterey Peninsula brand of glamor was in full working order. Across the bay, the roofs of Carmel-by-the-Sea shone back at the sun. The Lodge at Pebble Beach was awash in attractive guests. Around the bend of the peninsula, the seals lay barking on their rocks and the Pacific waves flexed their muscles. In Monterey itself, Fisherman's Wharf was doing a healthy business and the Victorian houses nearby had fallen into the hands of people who could afford fresh paint. At Cypress Point and Spyglass, golfers struggled as cheerfully as they could with those rocky and watery menaces; the scenery offered magical balm for shots gone astray.

As we walked, I remarked how much at home my non-golfing, non-tennis-playing friend seemed to be in this mecca of golfers and tennis players. Wherever we went, people knew Noel and nodded or spoke; at The Company Store, the clerk's "Hello, Mr. Noel" told the world that this was a steady customer. As we passed the glorious houses alongside the sea, Noel could pull out mental files on most of them and tell us about the owners. At the excellent Club XIX Restaurant in the Lodge, the Noels were old friends to the maitre d' and to several of the diners. It was the same at Easter luncheon at the Beach and Tennis Club.

It was true, I thought, that Bob and Peggy's moving here as quickly as they had was a high-odds roll of the dice. But this time—for the first time—they were not just long-term tourists. This was home and Chicago was for visiting.

The Noellian way had worked again.

THE FOWLERS: LYMAN AND THEO

Trees, trips, and togetherness

If you live near Salinas, California, chances are you get your Christmas trees from Lyman and Theo Fowler.

If you are an older member of the First Presbyterian Church of Salinas, you are likely to have visited Alaska, Hawaii, Oberammergau, the Grand Canyon, Yellowstone, or the Canadian Rockies on one of the Fowlers' tours.

If you have a child or a grandchild who goes to school around Salinas, he or she may well have learned about cones, conifers, and propagation on field trips to the Fowlers' farm.

In spite of what you have just read, both Fowlers are retired. He was a teacher for ten years and a dean of Hartnell College for twenty-five. She taught in the Salinas City School System for twenty-eight years.

However, Lyman Fowler observes, retirement need not be "the end of life."

The Fowlers' retirement plan began to take shape in 1969 when their youngest son was in university. Fowler had always liked working with his hands, growing things, being out of doors. They lived on a small acreage outside of Salinas. It might be wise to experiment with some small crop that could supplement their retirement income. . . .

He settled on Christmas trees, planting fifty seedlings the first year, just "to give it a try." The try worked. Every year since then, the Fowlers have added additional small plots. By 1984, they had 6,000 trees in the pipeline.

Today, Fowler is an unabashed partisan of his kind of farming. For one thing, he regards it as a "wonderful challenge" to produce the best trees possible. For another, he is able to do his planting, watering, spraying, shearing, and shaping in three or four half-days a week. He can space the work "depending on the weather, on how I feel, and on what I want to do. It isn't like feeding animals, which must be cared for twice a day every day."

And then there are the psychic compensations:

"Over eighty percent of our customers each year are repeat customers. They have appreciated our trees, they have become friends. Almost everyone who comes for a tree finds it an enjoyable time. But the greatest joy for us is that for two weeks our whole family is engaged in a 'togetherness project.' Our grandsons have helped from the time they were only big enough to point the way to the parking lot. Now they are high school and college age and know enough about the tree business to write projects on it for college credit. A couple of the boys . . . could almost take over and run the tree farm. Our granddaughter and her mother help in the office, claiming they are 'office managers.' Our sons and son-in-law do much of the physical labor like netting the trees or cutting them during harvest. I think they all enjoy it. At least they come back year after year on the weekends. It has provided a way for the grandchildren to earn a little extra money and it has drawn all of us closer together."

Theo Fowler had wanted to work and be with her husband in their retirement years but it had been tough for her to make the move. She loved teaching and knew she would miss the children. . . .

Christmas trees have solved a large part of that problem as well.

By 1984, the Fowlers were welcoming more than 1,000 school children to the farm every Christmas season. After meeting each bus and giving the children a ride on a tractor-pulled wagon, they divide each group of sixty-five to seventy into two classes. He demonstrates for one class how to plant a tree, how to shape it, how to raise it to "Christmas tree size." She gives the other class the lesson on propagation. Finally, each group starts back to school with a tree for its classroom.

At about the time Lyman Fowler retired from his job at the college, he and another retired teacher began to provide a day's outing for church seniors who could not drive. Using a church van, they had monthly pot-luck luncheons, drove along the ocean, or sometimes went out to lunch. In the first year, about thirty-five people participated. Eight years later, the number had grown to more than 200 and the trips had gotten more ambitious. In addition to day trips in 1984, the Fowlers had plans for a cruise to Alaska and a flight to the East Coast for the fall foliage season.

Writing up his and his wife's story for the weekend magazine of the *Monterey Herald*, Fowler quoted Charles Kingsley:

"We act as though comfort and luxury were the chief requirements of life, when all we really need to make us happy is something to be enthusiastic about."

Kingsley gets my vote.

So do the Fowlers.

HORACE G. (HOD) BARDEN

"The more you do to plan for yourself the better."

If a talent for tying up loose ends is what it takes to promote laughter—especially laughter at oneself—then Hod Barden is a walking testimonial to the value of tying up loose ends. His penchant for planning, precision, and perfection is housed behind a face that surely has laughed a hundred thousand times.

Barden on his name: "My mother and father couldn't agree for quite a while on what to call me. When I wrote for my birth certificate, it came with a handwritten note at the bottom, signed by a clerk who was a high school classmate of mine. She wrote, 'As far as we're concerned, your name is still Baby Barden—ha, ha, ha!' "

Barden on his wife: "While I was barnstorming with the band after high school, my mother kept pushing me to meet good, wholesome girls. Well, I wasn't always interested in 'good, wholesome girls' but I did let her introduce me to one and we hit it off so I decided to take a flyer on her. She's still my wife."

Barden on his job: "When I graduated from Wisconsin at the bottom of the Depression, I was hired by two partners of Ernst & Ernst, the accounting firm where I spent my career. Turned out they were the first two partners to be fired. That shook me up for quite a while."

I got my first taste of the Barden philosophy of retirement in a group discussion at the Kenilworth (Ill.) Union Church. Seven of us, including the pastor, Dr. Gilbert Bowen, had been talking about the adjustment period—a time that had been difficult for at least three of us.

"The problem with many retiring people," Barden said, "is that they don't have a plan, they don't have a program. I'm fortunate. I think I must be one of the happiest, most contented retired guys in the Northern Hemisphere and I think that's because I *did* have a program. When I was in my late fifties, I decided to retire at sixty-two and I told my partners so. It gave them and me four or five years to think about it."

Barden wasn't aware of it, but his ideas about having a "program" fell on eager ears. My ears, for two. I had approached my own retirement in a pretty half-baked manner and so had most of the other retired people that I knew. Here, I thought, was a man that my readers and I ought to know more about. I made a date to interview him his home office two weeks later.

Hod Barden and his wife now lived in a small, neat house in Kenilworth, directly across the street from the larger house that had been home during his career years. The small house and its small garden turned out to be an integral part of the Barden program. There was room here for a secluded office at the rear, room to exercise the Barden talent for landscaping, room in the basement for the Bardens to paint in watercolors together, a guest room for children or grandchildren. There was no excess room or land, nothing to become a burden later on.

The house, as I would learn that day, had been laid out lovingly and specifically to fit phases one and two of the Barden program. I would hear about phase three later on.

Phase one had been Barden's "cooling-off" period, something he regards as "very valuable."

Although he had retired from his accounting firm, he had not put behind him his zest for the profession. For four years, he had lectured to accounting students at the University of Wisconsin and had worked on projects for the American Institute of Certified Public Accounting. It was hectic, although Barden does not use such overheated words. Besides commuting between Kenilworth and Madison, Wisconsin, he had done "a lot of traveling" for the institute, interviewing business people in different businesses in different parts of the country. He was out of town so much that he often took his wife with him on the trips. Based on the interviews and other research he had done with the help of two university students, he had wound up phase one by writing a book for the institute. "I got a big kick out of all that," he told me. Writing the book ("on strictly technical stuff") had been a lot of fun, "in spite of the fact that the research director and I didn't always agree on the content."

But now it was time for phase two.

"There were still a lot of things I thought I wanted to do for the community and my family," he told me. "During my career, I had had very little time for things other than work." Public accounting had been a "tough game" when he got into it. He had often worked seventy to eighty hours a week, particularly in the peak period from December through April. As he had built up the firm's Indianapolis office, he had also built up a reputation for expertise in cost accounting. He became active in affairs of the American Institute of Certified Public Accounting. And he went on "the speaking circuit." He regards none of that as unusual. "Anyone who's out there punching his way through the jungle is going to neglect his family. I did." He had also, he felt, neglected his responsibility to his community. He wanted, now, to change his goals, shift his emphasis.

Barden's "community" is smaller than the other Chicago suburbs that surround it, small enough for me to offer a feeble joke: "For years, I drove from Wilmette to Winnetka and never once knew I'd passed through Kenilworth," I said. (Barden was kind enough to laugh.)

Small or not, Kenilworth has a history and a historical society, a town hall, a pension fund for its employees, a governing board made up of non-paid residents, controversial taxes, a commuter station, some the area's best-known churches, and Dr. Gilbert Bowen. In 1982, Hod Barden was very much involved with all of them.

Barden had gotten into local government by one of those happenstances that later seem inevitable. A neighbor had asked him to help with the affairs of the Kenilworth Historical Society. "Until around 1973," he said, "the society had been an informal, kaffeeklatsch kind of thing. That year [the same year in which his book came out], we had a chance to get some money from an estate—enough to build a town hall that would hold the police department and the historical society. In the deal, the society gets free rent and maintenance. My neighbor asked me to help with the contract and the financial work—which I did. The next thing I knew, they had elected me treasurer of the village, a job I still hold."

Barden on the treasurer's job: "Well, we board members try very hard to give people the services they want and need at the minimum cost. Our attitude is that if you want to live here, you should be willing to pay that much, at least. In spite of that, we get criticism believe me. Right now, people want us to cut taxes by twenty-five percent in some areas.

"One of my jobs as treasurer—I do the financial results and forecasts the board needs to make its decisions. I've had all sorts of compliments on that from people who've served on the board. But I feel I've done my share now. I think we should get someone else but I want to continue working for the historical society and a few other community things.

"I always have some of the society's things here to work on. I've got something to do almost every day if I want to do it. One thing—there was an older lady here in town who wrote a history of the village and developed the stories of the first sixty houses here. She did a great job of putting it all together except that she didn't think about making it last and it got in pretty bad shape. Well, we decided it ought to be preserved, and I worked on that with a young woman who helped with the typing, helped with the editing, helped me mount everything on acid-free paper. The same older woman also had about 130 pictures of trees and she had stories she wrote about them—a little wild, they needed editing. Well, the next thing I knew, I was studying up on architecture so I could do stories on other houses, too. Right now I'm spending a good deal of my time talking to present owners, trying to find out what I can about previous owners and their histories."

Dr. Bowen had said to me of Hod Barden that he is a man with a "strong philosophical bent." I told Barden so and that was good for a *real* laugh.

"Well, I do have a connection with Gil Bowen that's a little unusual. I listen to his sermons pretty carefully—he's a tremendous preacher—but he's a little too orthodox for me. So I write him a memo once in a while and take a sermon apart. I don't do that every week or every month but I think he looks on me as someone who monitors him and he's right. Then, when my wife and I took a course on the Bible from Gil, I made a five-page, chronological outline of what he'd said—the Bible jumps around a lot in time, you know—and Gil gave me a B+ for that. I'm also a great reader of philosophy and I write about that from time to time. Look—I kept out this recent talk because of a concern that Gil expressed in it: that we are not passing on to the new generations the moral and ethical values we inherited. Gil talks a lot about the fact that many young people today know little about morality except what they see on the tube."

Barden is clearly grateful for his own childhood experience. "I sometimes tell people I've been self-supporting since I was nine years old—except for my room and board up through high school. I had newspaper routes, worked in book stores and Kodak stores—things like that. And I was completely self-supporting in college, mostly by playing for dances. I think I had about fifty dollars more when I got through than when I started. It seems to me that when you come up that route, you have a different perspective on things. I have some appreciation of a lot of things that some of my friends don't have."

"You know what you have here in your office, Hod?" I said. "What you have is an intellectual jungle gym."

"Yeah," he said, laughing, "I guess you could call it that."

Barden on his grandchildren: "Well, we're not like some people who know every cough and sneeze of the grandchildren. But we're pretty proud of the eight of them and pretty interested in what they're doing.

"The one grandchild we're closest to happens to be the oldest. He's had a lot of trouble finding himself. His father and mother are divorced and he was pretty bitter about the family breakup. He quit school and went out West to work on a ranch. Then his stepgrandfather, who by that time was living alone, had a stroke and the boy went all the way to Florida to take care of him for the next fifteen months. I used to write him a lot during that time, trying to encourage him.

"Well, my grandson finally went back home to school at twenty-one or twenty-two and got himself a girlfriend in the bargain. We had a good visit from him for about five days. By that time, he was really interested in business school, so I took him to see my firm's old office and to see the Morgan Stanley office in town. He's interested in art, too, so I took him to the Art Institute and he loved the Remingtons. This kid really did need help and I tried to give him what help I could in the way of advice.

"The main thing we've done for the grandchildren is to establish trusts for their education. I've tried to use those trusts to help the children learn how to be financially responsible. I developed a reporting system for them to use when they were in college. It's very simple. It involves monthly reporting, based on a budget. And it's worked pretty darned good."

"So far," Barden said at last, "you haven't asked me about phase three, my exit plan."

I did a slow take. "Exit plan?" I asked.

"Well, we don't want to get to be burdens to our children or the neighbors—or 'ourselves—so we're looking at the Presbyterian Home over in Evanston.

"What are you going to do over there: become philosopher-in-residence?"

He laughed. Hard this time.

"Well, you can pretty well manage your own life over there. We'd have a town house first. You can always take your meals in the dining room—a lot of people do—but we'd mostly do our own cooking. It's not a hospital, but there are nurses and doctors there every day and you can go into the infirmary when necessary. When the house gets to be too much, if it does, you can move into the apartment building. The real point is, you can be pretty *independent* as long as you want to be. We feel we ought to do that.

"My mother and my mother-in-law both got to be burdens and it would have been better for them and for everybody if they had done some of the planning and work for themselves.

"You have to face up to it somewhere along the line. The more you can do to plan for yourself the better."

Hod Barden seems to have been born a realist.

"I've never been unhappy with my lot in life," he told me,

"because of my philosophy of things. In my old firm, for example, I was never the top man. But I always felt I made a big contribution, particularly in personnel. In our kind of organization, personnel is a tremendous factor. I got pretty good at recognizing the kind of different talents we had and getting them into spots where they and we could make the most of those talents. . . ."

That, I thought, was a good way to describe Hod Barden's retirement so far. He had gotten himself into spots where he could make the most of his talents.

And have a lot of laughs along the way.

LEO SCHOENHOFEN
Retirement on the installment plan

The February before, Mountain Lake had served up seven perfect golfing days in a row. Cloudless. Low seventies. All but windless.

This February, I was lucky. A heavy, steady rain had started on Friday afternoon and now, on Sunday, there were still no signs of a break. Instead of playing golf as we'd planned, Leo Schoenhofen and I were sitting in his living room talking about retirement—his, mine, and other people's.

And I, at last, was asking him the right questions.

Up to now, Schoenhofen had been friendly and encouraging but firm. I was talking to the wrong man, he'd always said. He had nothing interesting to contribute to this book. Why didn't I talk to so and so—there was a guy who really had something to say. . . .

My problem with Schoenhofen was not Schoenhofen. It was me.

I was convinced that he had had painful problems after leading Marcor into the merger with Mobil. He *must* have had. After all, I said to myself, the man merged himself right out of a big, powerful job. A real plum of a job. Maybe the merger was good for Marcor stockholders but it had to have been bad for Schoenhofen.

Not so, he had always said.

But surely he'd had *some* problems. At first anyway? An

emotional letdown? Feeling at loose ends? Waking up every day to the question, "What in heaven's name will I do with myself today?"

"Sure there were problems," he'd always said. "But not those. Life poses two kinds of problems: good problems and bad problems. This was a good problem.

"Retirement was a natural next step for me. I would have been bored just hanging on when Mobil really didn't need me. Besides that, I looked at retirement as an opportunity to do things I could never do before. And it's been great, just great. . . ."

Now, on this rainy Sunday morning, I found the right tack. Not everyone has been as smart, or as lucky, as you, I said. A lot of people are just plain miserable in retirement. A lot of people suffer real tortures as retirement time gets closer. Why is that, do you think?

"Well, for one thing," he said, "many men get so involved in what they're doing, their jobs, that they have no time for or interest in anything else. Then comes mandatory retirement or something else and those men exist in a vacuum.

"You and I both know someone like that. He's been the head guy at that great big company for twenty-three years. Now he has to retire in a couple of months and he's fighting it. One of his associates tells me that getting [him] to face the reality is like pulling teeth. It's the most painful thing he's ever done. It's just too bad. People could and should look to retirement with enthusiasm, not depression. It's an opportunity.

"Look at Tom Brooker [his neighbor at Mountain Lake and his predecessor as chairman of Marcor].

"Brooker has always been terribly interested in whatever he does and he's managed to find a lot of things to do in retirement. For example, he helped found a group of retired executives who donate their time and talent to the Chicago charities that the United Way supports. He got it off the ground, got it organized, recruited me and a lot of other friends to help and to spread the word among retirees.

"He's like that with everything. If he's going to take a trip to Greece or Egypt or some place like that, he gets in touch with archaeologists and museums and he buys eight books on the subject—he makes a big project of everything."

Schoenhofen may have merged himself out of a job but he had not merged himself into a "vacuum."

Far from it.

He was still a director of six blue-chip corporations. In spite of the demands of Marcor business, he had made the time to be a working board member and he had become known as a heavyweight contributor. ("I hate just showing up at meetings and collecting a director's fee.")

This posture had paid off in retirement. Even without the title, the power and the position, he was in demand as a professional director, and people gave him "plenty of opportunity" to contribute. I knew some of the stories about his contributions, at least in outline:

The chief executive of one of his companies had died suddenly and this had forced the board of directors to put the new man in place much sooner that they had expected. In a predictable world, the new chief would have had several more years to prepare for the responsibility. As it was, he asked Schoenhofen and two other directors to help him in areas where he was inexperienced, which led to a collaboration that worked for everyone. (Schoenhofen has a dry, ho-hum way of talking about his successes. But his eyes refused to play the false-modesty game this time. They told me he'd *loved* this experience.)

In a second situation, one of Schoenhofen's fellow directors helped me piece the story together. Schoenhofen came to the board at a crucial time: the company's main business was healthy, but a large recent venture had lost money from the start and continued to take an outsize share of management time. The question before the house was, how do we fix this thing? Schoenhofen suggested that this might not be the right question at all. His analysis argued that the losing end of the business would *never* fit into the company's scheme of things. Shouldn't the management and directors conclude that they had an irretrievable mistake on their hands? His view won the debate and the new venture was sold. However, if there were any ego wounds around, they got a dose of the most powerful possible medicine: soon after the divestiture, the remaining lines of business took off and the price of the company's stock multiplied by six times. Exclamation points.

After having changed little in several generations, a third company made radical changes during Schoenhofen's tenure. He was in on the ground floor during a surprise change in chief executives; lived through other major (and painful) personnel shifts; had voted that the company acquire half a dozen other businesses; had seen the company's sales and profits go up exponentially. Schoenhofen accepts no specific credit for his part in the transformation. Nonetheless, there is a handsome new oil portrait of himself in the living room of his condominium in Lake Forest, Illinois—a thank-you present from this company which requires its directors to retire at sixty-eight. It seems to me symbolic that the painting shows Schoenhofen in his shirt sleeves.

I agreed with Schoenhofen. Retiring to a "vacuum" is a big, big problem for many people—but it isn't the only problem. What other mistakes had he seen people make?

"Well, so many people pull up roots and change everything overnight. They retire and—bingo—they change everything in sight without having any experience. It's too much to deal with all at once, so they can end up not dealing with any of it."

He and Emily had changed a lot of things, I said. And I knew that Emily, at least, had had her problems with moving from the house and the community where they'd lived so long. Moving is tough on women, I said. Every woman tells me that.

Sure it's tough, he admitted. Especially when you move to a place you don't know and surround yourself with strangers. But Mountain Lake wasn't exactly strange for either of them.

"We took places here for ten years before I retired. Several people from home were here and we found the others congenial. We were comfortable with everything about it, we felt perfectly natural about buying this house. One great thing for us—Mountain Lake is low-key socially, not like some of those places on the East Coast. I like a community where people have small dinner parties and you can have a conversation. I hate those great big cocktail bashes people give to pay back all their social obligations at once."

Even on the business side of his life, he had kept "a lot of continuity." His directorships helped keep him connected, of course. But timing was on his side when he needed an office for himself, his files, and his secretary of thirty years. Gaylord Freeman, retired head of the First National Bank of Chicago, invited Schoenhofen to join him and four other retired executives who share a suite of offices in the Loop. He'd known his office mates for years, they were still involved in a variety of things as he was, and "there was always someone around who knew what was going on, someone who was free for lunch."

Golf, too, serves to keep him connected with people who speak his language. When he and Emily are in residence in Lake Forest, he plays at Old Elm, an all-male club whose members speak fluent business as well as fluent golf.

Mountain Lake is forty miles from Orlando, a part of Florida where old attractions and landmarks date back ten years and ancient ones twenty-five. In the context, the community is as much a curiosity as the "mountain" part of its name. Edward Bok, the great editor and publisher of the old Curtis Publishing Company, built one of the first houses here in 1921 and liked it so much that he endowed a carillon tower and bird sanctuary nearby. The mountain rises to 200 feet or so above sea level—not to be despised in a state so flat that it makes the Iowa and Kansas landscapes look positively craggy.

Mountain Lake is not a town or a country club or a public resort. It is, in part, a real estate development, but it is also a $3.5 million business whose property owners are the stockholders. It owns and operates a small, first-class hotel mostly for friends of the owners; a water system; a landscaping service; a cable television facility; 600 acres of citrus trees; and a golf course that has been in the championship class since the days of mashies, cleeks, and spoons.

Perhaps by process of natural selection, Schoenhofen has become chairman of the budget and finance committe here. "It may not sound like much—$3.5 million—but we have every problem you can find in a $3.5 *billion* corporation. It's fascinating. For instance, we were facing a big water shortage until all the rain came along this year." Looking at the downpour he said, "If you can't be smart, be lucky."

Golf, for Leo Schoenhofen, is a pastime, but not an idle one. The opportunity to play golf the year-round played a powerful part in his choice of the two-climate life.

Although he has reason to be proud of his game, Schoenhofen has never told me much about it. As we talked, I knew—not from him—that his current handicap was seven, that his last round at Mountain Lake was a 73, that he was the current champion at Old Elm, that he often played in Seniors' championships—serious if friendly competition. I knew that he often got in four or five rounds a week.

But the most telling measure of his benign addiction was this:

Six months before, pain in one shoulder had sent him to an orthopedic surgeon. It hadn't kept him from being club champion, but the pain did wake him up every hour or so at night. The diagosis was one he didn't want to hear: he had a tear in the rotator cuff—the kind of tear that surgery can repair. *But.* But the recovery period involves six weeks with an airplane sling and another six weeks of physical therapy to rehabilitate the muscles. No golf for three months!

Schoenhofen came to a decision that any committed golfer would understand. He would leave the shoulder alone. At least it seldom hurt when he swung a club—only when he took too deep a divot.

"Another problem with a man's retirement," Schoenhofen said, "is what it can do to his marriage. A lot of women get mad at their husbands when they retire. Retirement for their husbands can mean a lot of sudden losses for them. They lose freedom and privacy and other prerogatives they have learned to love a lot and they resent it.

"Every couple has things to work out, but some of the smartest of them don't seem to be smart enough to see it. It's a shame. A wife has a lot of power to contribute to her husband's success in retirement as well as in his career—if they're compatible. I think marriage is a big ingredient in retirement—it's a very big piece of the whole thing.

"I've been lucky. Emily's always been interested . . . interested in everything. Actually, she's a great motivator for me—she gets me interested in things. For example, she's become an expert on the Bible, an interest she shares with several other women around here. I don't have to amuse her or she me, but if the need or occasion arises, we can count on each other."

I thought that was an understatement. Leo had told me once that he and Emily had grown closer than ever in retirement. Emily said that they are "each other's best friend." They have even been known to hold hands when among close friends.

Gerontologists observe that there are as many differences between age sixty and age eighty as there are between age twenty-five and age forty-five. I had heard that but I failed to think about it until that rainy day at Mountain Lake.

"I'm only a couple of years away from being seventy," Schoenhofen said, "and that's when I'll be going into my second retirement. The remaining boards I'm on all have age limits and I'll be phasing them out of my life one by one."

(A month later, I would hear Gerald Ford talking about his and

Betty's ideas for *their* second retirement. Others had touched on the same concept. The retirement experience, I now see, is not like adolescence, not a one-time only change. Schoenhofen had given me an important new thought.)

"Emily and I are thinking about our second retirement right now, even though it's quite a while away. Without the boards to connect me to Chicago, we'll have less reason to keep the apartment.

"We do want another place, though. Everything we do here sort of comes to a halt in the summer. For three months or so, we'll want to be somewhere else. Northern Wisconsin maybe—I love it up there. Or Pennsylvania, near where we lived when I ran that Container Corp. factory."

As he talked, I thought that where was not his big consideration. The main issues were what new opportunities would he find, what new chances to learn, what new ways to grow. He spoke again of Tom Booker, admiringly. "Intellectually, that guy's as lively at 78 as a thirty-year-old is."

Voilà!

Another of "life's good problems."

HILDA WARD

"I have learned how much a little help can mean to many people."

When Hilda Ward retired in 1969 after thirty-three years as a secretary at Dow Chemical Company, she was hit with an urgent problem:

Her neighborhood grocery stores moved away.

She did not drive.

There was no public transportation that would work for her.

She walked to the nearby office of the Council on Aging where, she knew, the volunteers could and would help. What she didn't know was that this was one of the most significant walks she would ever take.

Looking around her, she observed that the council office needed skills like hers, and offered to help with the clerical and receptionist duties. She took on the job of organizing the filing system. It was satisfying work.

By 1980, failing eyesight was making it difficult for Miss Ward to do her filing and other clerical work. But that problem, too, failed to daunt her.

She simply switched to answering the telephone and to substituting at the reception desk.

"There is no limit to the types of calls and requests the council gets," she said. "We handle everything from questions about Social Security to requests for transportation or meals. Sure there are problems we are *not* equipped to deal with, but we refer our callers to agencies that *can* do the job.

"So many older people need help but want to maintain as much of their independence as possible," she said. "I'm not the only one who couldn't live on her own without the services of the Council on Aging."

Hilda Ward clearly has a knack for turning her problems into opportunities. Recently, she helped found the Visually Impaired Support Group that meets monthly at the council office. Members of the group share ideas and experience on how to live with low vision. In so doing, they draw strength and support from each other.

All of this, Miss Ward said, has been a "wonderful learning experience."

Indeed.

JAMES A. LOVELL, JR.
"Every day of my life now is a bonus"

Apollo XIII. April 1970.

The spacecraft passes the point of no return on its way to the moon, but the astronauts won't have much time to rejoice.

Behind Jim Lovell, Ken Swigert, and Fred Haise, one oxygen tank is empty. The other is leaking, working up to an explosion.

Suddenly, bad news spreads like chicken pox. *B-bang!* (A noise that is *not* on the program.) Signal lights cry "crisis." The spacecraft pitches and rolls. In moments, Lovell will pronounce eight words that will live in millions of memories:

"Yes, Houston, I think we have a problem."

April 1972. The MacDonnell Douglas Company, St. Louis, Missouri.

Jim Lovell is there to help design the cockpit for the space shuttle. This sort of work is not new to him. Thirteen years before, he had been in the same room, helping to design a cockpit—the cockpit of the F-4 Phantom fighter. Suddenly, he gets "a crushing feeling of *déjà vu.*" Thirteen years, he thinks, and all he'd done was to make a 360-degree turn. All he'd been was an "exotic jet jockey."

Yes, Houston. Lovell has a problem.

When Apollo XIII had crippled its way back to Earth, Lovell could count four flights in space, more than anyone up to then, but he had little hope of making another. There were twenty-five qualified astronauts who had yet to fly their first missions. "If I had gone for a fifth," he told me, "I might have been stabbed in my bed."

To be sure, he was a Navy captain with a solid record. Bureau of Personnel would find billets for him and he stood a good chance of serving out his thirty years. But he knew that he was out of the race for admiral. He'd had no combat experience. And there would be no tour at the War College for him. Too late.

From his point of view, there was nothing for it except to retire.

To what? He was only forty-four.

"I did *not* want to trade on the past," he said, "although I could have. I could have been a glad-hander. Or I could have been a door-opener—someone who could get you in to see important people.

"But I didn't want that.

"I wanted people to want me for what I was now, not what I had been."

The past that Lovell wanted to put behind him was the sort they give you trophies for, trophies by the boxful.

Here in his study, I could see the cream of his collection. There were citations, medals, letters of commendation, models of supersonic fighters he had flown as a test pilot. There were pictures of Lovell with Presidents Johnson and Nixon. Letters from Johnson and Nixon. A letter to Marilyn Lovell from Pat Nixon. A handwritten letter of congratulations from Charles Lindbergh. There was the first 1969 cover of *Time;* it was captioned "Men of the Year," and pictured Lovell with Frank Borman and Bill Anders, his mates on Apollo VIII, the first manned craft to orbit the moon. There was a great, handsome brute of a globe—of the moon, not the earth—standing against one wall. On the desk, there was an exact reproduction of a moon rock (no actual samples yet available for astronauts). His "diploma" as an Eagle Scout hung there with all the rest.

Lovell had been puzzled about my wanting this interview. "I'm not retired yet," he said. "Or if I am, I wish someone would tell me. I've never been busier in my life."

I had said I knew that. He wasn't retired of course, not in the traditional sense, but he did represent a large class of people who had been through all the problems of retirement—regardless of age. He was in the same boat with sports stars, opera stars, star entertainers, many politicians. Such people had had fame and success early. They had to confront long futures out of power, or out of the limelight. Or both.

"Don't forget the military," he said. "It's interesting to talk to admirals who have retired in their fifties. They've been very powerful men. They've commanded thousands of people and fleets of ships. They've had chauffeurs and they've had classy quarters on their flagships. They've been king of the hill. Then they retire and it takes a certain kind of mind to readjust. They may get a high-paid job on the staff of some defense manufacturer but they have no authority any longer. It's tough."

The astronauts had a new kind of stardom to deal with.

There were all kinds of exhilarating things: the crush of publicity, the parades up Broadway, the receptions at the White House. John Glenn had even been asked to address a joint session of the Senate and the House of Representatives. Everybody knew you and you were in great demand. You were "authentic American heroes."

Furthermore, you had the feeling that you were on the leading edge of the trip to tomorrow. Every flight was a new experiment. Every flight added to man's understanding. "I would have paid money to be a part of NASA," Lovell said.

There was trauma as well—as Buzz Aldrin wrote in his book, *Return to Earth.* That book told a lot, Lovell thought. It helped you understand why so many prominent people end up "having a lot of emotional problems when it's time to take a back seat."

Lovell himself had had traumas when his time came. For one thing, he likes to fly and had loved piloting the T-38s that went with the job. When he and his peers had been in training, it was NASA policy that they maintain their flying skills. Thus, they were given high-priority access to these jet trainers. If he had to fly from Houston to Los Angeles on NASA business, he had only to make a telephone call and take off. If he had to refuel en route, he simply signed a chit and "never knew what it cost." And he would get to his destination ahead of commercial jets.

That was a "great fringe benefit" for him, one that "even people who have made it in civilian life don't have." That and other lifestyle benefits, things "you can't equate with money," had made up for the relatively low pay.

With all of this pulling and tugging going on in his mind, Lovell made his decisions.

He would retire from NASA and retire from the Navy as well.

He would find a new job in the private sector and start a new life.

"Thinking back," he said to me, "I was braver than I realized. Everything I knew about business I had learned in fourteen weeks at the Harvard Business School's Advanced Management Program. That taught me just enough to make me dangerous."

Lovell and Bill Anders came to their retirement decisions at about the same time and entered into an intense dialogue about their futures. Should it be a large company or a small one? Something to do with aerospace or not? What could they offer a private employer besides the glamor of hiring an astronaut? Lovell, for one, had an engineering degree—but he had no specific field of engineering expertise. On the other hand, they had had intense training in leadership, in dealing with people, in problem-solving.

"It was a thrill for me when, later on, I proved that my people skills and my problem-solving skills *were* transferable to a different field. Not many people believed in the possibility. When I later approached some aerospace companies, they said they'd love to have me but I was 'overqualified' for current openings." Lovell thought the real message was: "Sorry, Lovell. You're *under*qualified for management."

In the end, Anders and Lovell agreed that a small company was the answer, one that needed generalist-type skills, that offered real authority and responsibility, that gave them room to exercise their entrepreneurial instincts.

It was that strategy which led Lovell from space ships and moon shots to a tugboat and peat moss (!) business, then to a small telephone company, eventually to his present job as an executive vice president of Centel Company, a growing factor in business telecommunications.

The Lovell luck had always had a way of serving him better than his best-laid plans. He became an astronaut not because he dreamed of going to the moon but because he was fascinated with the technology of liquid rocket fuel. He wanted to be a rocket engineer like Werner von Braun. This had led him to Annapolis, not because he wanted to be a naval officer but because he didn't have the money for a blue-ribbon engineering school like M.I.T. or Cal Tech. After test pilot training, he had become project officer on the F-4 Phantom because he had been lucky. He was drafted for his *last* choice of assignments as a test pilot—electronics test— but this turned out to give him so much more flying time than "luckier" pilots that he vaulted over eighty-five of his seniors into the Apollo program.

When Lovell got into the telephone business, his timing was lucky as ever. The technology was changing. The structure of the telephone business was changing. And the needs of telephone users were changing.

It fascinated me to hear Lovell talk the talk of the telephone world.

Bell was in a bind. . . . Because it had been good for their rate structure, they had been very slow to depreciate their billions of dollars worth of electromechanical switching equipment. . . . Now there were computerized PBX systems that could do everything but the talking for you and they could save a company really serious money. . . . That gave companies like Centel a chance to grow and grow fast. . . . He "couldn't have found a better career to replace NASA."

It seemed to me that Lovell talked about the phone business as though he'd been born to it and had been in love with it all his adult life. That must be a great feeling, I said.

"Well, it is interesting to get into a business and do well in spite of making a lot of mistakes. I just hope I can continue to do as well.

"I realize what a lot of other people might think: that this is a stodgy job by comparison with my glamorous old one. But if you really get into it, this is a job with many interesting angles and they make it *very* worthwhile to go to work every day.

"And my philosophy has changed, too. I see things differently today. That happens. I remember Frank Borman coming by one day while I was still in training. He had gone to work for Eastern Airlines and he said, 'I can't imagine doing all that training again. I'm into something fascinating and entirely different.' "

Sometime during our two conversations, Lovell spoke of the "withdrawal problem" that he shared with so many other men. Clearly, he'd gone through a lot of heavy introspection to get from his old life to his new one. What, I asked, had he learned from the experience that might help others withdraw and do it with a minimum of pain?

His prescription is short and simple if not surprising. The only hard part is to work up the willingness to take his brand of medicine.

As Lovell sees it, this is the philosophy that worked for him:

1. You don't look back. You go forward.

2. You don't just retire and live in the past. The old values soon erode. People forget what you were. They want to know, "What are you good for now?"

3. You get honest with yourself and realize that what you did before is behind and beyond you now—for reasons of age or change in management or something else.

4. You set new goals.

5. You get your values up to date.

6. If there are any residual benefits from your past achievements, fine. Lovell: "I make an occasional talk about space flight. That gives me some extra income, but I don't try to live on it."

7. Take life one step at a time. Lovell: "My last flight was almost catastrophic. I thought we'd had it. So every day is kind of like a bonus for me."

Jim is not the only Lovell in the big house in Lake Forest who seems to me to have The Right Stuff.

As I drove across town to our first interview, an enormous flash of lightning flared out from the Lovell's direction. The thunder was close—so close that I said aloud, "My God. It hit his house."

It wasn't the house, actually. It was the dead oak on the front lawn.

But the bolt left its calling card. It discombobulated the Lovell televisions, bewitched the telephones, made mischief with the electronic security system. Just for good measure, it spewed oak bark all over the freshly groomed lawn.

While Lovell and I talked for two hours, Marilyn Lovell had to cope with the following:

Random electronic squawks from the telephones.
Telephone calls that mysteriously got through, then got cut off.
Repeated and relentless shrieks from the security system.
Neighbors at the door who wanted to make sure all was well and to swap stories of what happened.
A visit from the security people who wanted to check things out.
Working out a schedule for the repair people.
Reassuring Lovell's secretary who called in alarm.
Making coffee for me.

Through it all, she wore the same big smile with which she'd answered my knock at her door. She smiled even when I made some feeble joke about Apollo XIII revisited.

"Just another quiet evening at the Lovell's," she said.

"But it's my fault. I had to go and pray for rain."

PHILIP H. SCHAFF, JR.
"I run a small business. I am a small business."

The man was sitting in a rocking chair, in his study, footstool handy. Collar open. No tie. Looking forward to an afternoon golf date with his wife.

There the resemblance to the retired-man stereotype ended.

He said: "Retirement is a bad word. A lousy word.

"It just doesn't describe situations like yours and mine. When we leave our main careers behind, that doesn't mean we're retired, not from life. We close one book, that's true, but we open up a second one and we need a new word for that. Our generation is on the cutting edge of a new concept of retirement. We're pioneers, as you say.

"When I stepped out of the chairman's job at Leo Burnett, people would come up to me and say, 'Hey, you're retired now, aren't you?'

"That made me feel very funny—embarrassed is not the word. It made me feel *uncomfortable*—that's it—very uncomfortable.

"Nowadays when people say 'you're retired,' I tell them no, I'm running my own business and that knocks them for a loop. And when I tell that I'm opening an office with my name on the door, that throws them even more.

" 'Why are you doing *that?*' they say."

I did not have to ask Phil Schaff why he was doing that.

At the time he said these things (June 1983), he and I had known each other for thirty-two years, more than half our lives, and I knew it was impossible for Schaff *not* to work. The only question in my mind had been: Work at what?

Working and working hard had always been Schaff's style. For fifty-eight years, flexibility had been nothing but a word in his dictionary.

"Handling flexibility—that's a learned skill," he said. And he had never had time to learn it, although he thought he was making some progress now.

"From when we were born, we were programmed. No one ever said to me, 'Gee—do you want to go to kindergarten or not?' I went and never thought to question it and all through grade school I never questioned it. And my family had plans for me in the summer and that went on right up through college. It never occurred to me to skip college or drop out or anything like that. And then came the war when I graduated from college and my program was laid out for me. You went to war and did your best and hoped to come back and then your program was laid out for you again: you must go to work. I never had the luxury or the flexibility to say, 'Gee, am I supposed to go to work—or can I get a Ph.D. in anthropology or something like that?'

"So I went into business and I didn't have the luxury of catching the 9:19 train and arriving at 10:00 or 10:30. I'd better arrive early and leave late and then I went to night school and I worked on Saturdays, anything to get experience so I could do a better job.

"And I'd also been programmed by my family to do a certain amount with volunteer activities. Then there was marriage. We didn't have the living-together deal then—whether that would have been better or not I don't know. But we were programmed, or at least I was, right up to retirement. Right from the day we left the womb, we were programmed to *work*."

As long as I'd known him, Phil Schaff had had little taste for idle or unstructured conversations. Even when he and I traveled together on business, he always had a written list of the subjects we might want to cover together.

On this June day in 1983, he was prepared as usual. Knowing that I wanted to hear specific things about his work, he had right at hand a copy of a letter he had written to his accounting firm which, he felt, had not been responsive to his needs. This is how the letter begins, minus the too-personal names and numbers:

Dear _____:

Mary and I are in a business with a net worth of $_____ and cash income of $_____ a year. This is no trust fund operation but a vibrant business consisting of many parts and many actions each day.

It requires management information, management control, comparative information, three-year forecasts, cash flow forecasts etc., etc., as well as income tax returns and trust and estate work.

This business, for example, has interests in at least _____ different oil wells with bills and checks every month; at least _____ different limited partnerships, perhaps _____ different stocks and bonds ["I just decided to list all this damn stuff"]. Covered stock options. At least five different bank accounts and five different bank loans and bank loan interest of $_____ last year.

This business has commercial real estate interests ranging from Hilo in Hawaii to the Silicon Valley in California to Chicago to the Museum Tower in New York to Southern California.

The oil is in several states.

Other interests include a mine in Arizona, quarries in Georgia, a food-freezing business in Florida, and an outdoor advertising business in Chicago.

Even though I abhor lawsuits, I am involved one way or another in three.

At the moment, my list of charitable contributions, going back five years, covers _____ pages.

When I leave Leo Burnett Company completely at the end of this year, there is a question whether to form Phil Schaff Company or Phil Schaff Company Incorporated or just operate as an individual. . . .

What the letter did not say was that Schaff is bored by passive investing. What gets his adrenaline going is to invest in small companies which need—and want—his active participation as a director and consultant.

"I don't want to just invest money," he said. "That isn't any fun. What I really like is having some things where I put in some money and where I'm so drawn into it that it requires my time and my talent. The people have to be compatible—but it plugs you right back into life in a very meaningful way."

To make his point, Schaff told me about his involvement in one small company. He had been an important investor and director in the firm for two or three years when the operating statements began to turn sour and the directors dug into the situation.

"One thing you learn about these small companies is that they require a lot of care and feeding. You have to pay attention," he said, "or they can go right smack off the rails."

He had gone to a regular board meeting and "there was blood all over the floor. The thing was *hemorrhaging*. I took a look at the statement and we were losing money so fast that if we hadn't done something, we would have been broke—dead—in ten months.

"Well, several of us at the table directed the management to come up with a plan to reduce costs and we adopted the technique that you and I have used before. Instead of having our next board meeting several months from now, we asked to have it next *week*. We did have a meeting the next week and we said OK, now that you've got this underbrush out of the way, get out some more underbrush. And we took a look at the projections and said that by such and such a date, the income must equal the outgo. We may have stepped in just in time.

"In a case like that, you're dealing not only with money, you're dealing with values of all kinds. I find in a situation like that that I'm very comfortable because of the experience I've had.

"In such situations, I find I'm sitting on the edge of my chair, I'm tuned into everything that everyone is saying and it's a very interesting, fascinating experience. You can only handle so many of these at one time and right now—within the spirit of my own flexibility and freedom—I have as much on my plate as I can manage."

The obvious question for Schaff was *why?*

Why did he work so hard for money? He had plenty. Why didn't he put it into tax-free bonds and let some trust company manage it? Why didn't he just go out and enjoy what he'd worked so hard so long to get?

Not to live any better, he said. He and Mary Schaff already had everything they needed or wanted. They had no interest in yachts or Rolls Royces or big suites in hotels. They had been to both Egypt and China the year before and they already had three residences that suited them. To be sure, he does occasionally fly to Europe on the Concorde, but otherwise tourist class is good enough.

Then why?

"In the first place it's a game and I *love* the game. It keeps me involved with life and people in a very vital way. If you're in business, you're making something or you're creating a service and you gotta use your brains to figure out how that product or service can be better than the competition, have some edge going for it. You're dealing with the management, you're dealing with all the human problems of a business.

"It is a game but it's a game you play for keeps, as opposed to playing backgammon for pin money.

"But, if I don't need the money to live on, what's there to do with it except take it out and look at it from time to time and have fun with it, have fun in the process of earning it?

"Well, I do have an interest in giving the money away and I would really like to target in on a few of what I call 'leveraged' situations. One leveraged situation on which I may be overboard but which I'm 100 percent sold on is Princeton University.

"By leveraged, I mean leveraged for the good of the human race. I think that for every dollar I put into Princeton, I will get untold dollars back in terms of human good. You are betting on the concept of uncommon individuals and important ideas."

He had just demonstrated his conviction by giving a large sum to the cause.

"I felt really good about giving that money. You know the old saw about giving till it hurts. Well, I think the next level is giving until it feels good. That's a level beyond giving till it hurts. I don't want my name on a building or carved in stone or anything like that. It gives me great pleasure to know that that money is going to be marching through the corridors of time in the form of outstanding individuals who will either create important ideas themselves or manage important ideas. Princeton will turn out poets, writers, composers, scientists, inventors, great lawyers with that money. . . ."

Schaff's feeling for Princeton has deep roots.

As a young alumnus, he made his full share of screening visits to prospective students in the Chicago area. As a trustee, he had worked hard at a variety of committee assignments. (I particularly remember the sticky issue of whether or not to keep an ROTC unit on campus). After his retirement, he had taken on the task of raising money from the class of '42 for its fortieth reunion gift to the university and had been duly gratified when his classmates' response had broken all records, ancient or modern. Most recently, he had accepted election to the class presidency, a job that offers another excellent outlet for excess energy. During his term, he would be planning and organizing a two-day seminar for his classmates. This event would be held in Washington and he had won agreement that the focus would be on—retirement.

"Another thing you can do with money (besides investing in the advancement of society and playing the participative-investor game) is give it to your kids. And that's what your and my friend, Marty Snitzer, calls a high-class problem.

"I think you can give your kids too much money too soon. You can cause them to slack off and take it easy and just wait till you die and pick up a bundle." He had seen too many parents do that to their children, he said, and he thought it was a serious breach of responsibility.

Phil and Mary Schaff had tried to discharge their responsibility by setting up two trusts for their two sons and three daughters.

"We call the first trust 'the learning money,' " he said.

Schaff had told each child that, at twenty-one, he could do

whatever he wanted with his learning money. He, Schaff, would not veto any choices although he would give advice if asked. The one thing they had to realize was that when the money was all spent that was the end. "That money would be gone. G-O-N-E—gone."

By the time we had this conversation, all five children were working and each had had his experiences with his money.

The first child, a daughter, had been divorced and had "knocked around" from one rented apartment to another. Finally, with her salary high enough to make her independent, she had spent all her learning money on a condominium.

The second child, a son, was a foreign currency trader for a large firm. He also decided to buy an apartment and drew down about 20 percent of his money to help with the purchase. Then he changed his mind and wanted to put the money back in the trust. "We wouldn't let him," Schaff said. "So I think he bought government bonds with it. And he learned something."

The third child, a daughter, is a fashion designer, trying to get her own business off the ground. By 1983, she had withdrawn all but 10 percent of her money and Schaff was concerned. With her permission, he and the children's trustee took a look at her records and suggested that she concentrate on selling some of her products rather than on side issues. A week later, she reported that she'd made a substantial sale of one item and reckoned that she should make some more of those. "So the pressure's really on her," Schaff said. "*Learning* money!"

The fourth child, a daughter, is a stockbroker. She, too, wanted an apartment but chose to buy it only after sweating out the numbers, including the tax impact. Giving up her backlog had been tough for her, something that obviously pleased Schaff.

The fifth child, a son, works for an advertising agency and, in 1983, wasn't yet making quite enough money to survive on—in spite of living in a one-room apartment and buying second-hand clothes. He had reluctantly tapped his learning money twice in order to make ends meet but was working hard to get to the break-even point. "He really doesn't want to fritter away that money." Schaff said.

The second, larger, trust for the Schaff children is their "inheritance." The Schaff's wanted them to know how much they could expect and wanted them not to count on having any more when their parents died. "I suppose they will get more," Schaff said, "because I don't intend to die broke. But they know they can't count on that."

As in many other areas of his life, Schaff had had a written goal for himself as a parent: "To help each child, girls and boys alike, to become strong, independent *individuals*."

The night before our conversation, Schaff had stayed up until 1:30 A.M., writing a preface for a book he's thinking of doing. He wanted to try it out on me.

As he read the results of his work aloud, it seemed to me that what he had in mind was a sort of intellectual autobiography. His ideas, many of which I had heard from him before, ranged from the duties of a citizen as he sees them, to business philosophies, to the responsibilities of parents, to retirement.

One idea in particular caught my ear that day. His proposed chapter heading was "The $500,000 Senator." He was exercised by what he regards as the insanity in this country of paying public officials and policymakers far less than what outstanding people can get in private business. He felt that only by making public executives as well-paid as those in the private sector can we hope to get the best talent to train for and to seek public service as a career. I agreed. And I wished him well.

By the end of 1983, Phil Schaff, his secretary, and their IBM Personal Computer were preparing to set up shop in a new office building on Michigan Avenue in Chicago.

Phil Schaff Enterprises was alive and well and just getting into high gear. And having a lot of fun in the process.

ROSCOE NASH
The head-hurting problems of scientific pig-raising.

I was very grumpy on the day I met Nash.

My wife and I had been promised that the seat between us would be empty on the four-hour flight. At the last minute, a smallish, grey-haired fellow begged our pardon and wedged himself between us.

He wasn't grumpy. He was obviously delighted to have made this flight at all.

To kill the time, I buried myself in my crossword puzzle book until, an hour later, my wife called across our neighbor to me. She had been talking to him, asking him questions, drawing him out (she has always been better than I at making the best of a situation). "Howard," she said, "tell Mr. Nash about your computer. . . ."

Nash had been a partner in a firm that specialized in securities law. Now eighty, he had long since retired, although his old associates still provided him with a desk, a telephone, and secretarial service.

But he didn't want to talk about the law.

His mind was on the true passion of his life: the hog farm in Iowa that he had inherited from his family.

It had been tough to hang onto the farm. The Depression had lasted a long time. And hog-raising was chancy at best. Always had been. Probably always would be.

His problem right now, he told me, was that the profit-equation kept getting more and more complicated. A hog-feeder could not just buy a bunch of piglets, feed them willy-nilly, and hope for the best. He had to contend with uncontrollable energy and labor costs, with the politics of price supports, with the caprices of weather, and an escalating list of other variables. To make a profit today—and to continue in business—an operator had to stay on top of a mountain of paperwork and do it in "real" time. He understood that I had a computer. Did I think a computer could help him?

Nash was talking to a self-taught amateur of home computing and a know-nothing of hogs. But, as he described his need, I saw that an Apple II computer like mine and three or four of the popular computer programs probably *could* help.

He was already gathering the facts, I pointed out. By entering his data into a computer, he could determine which kinds of pigs gained the most weight on the least feed. And he could get insights into optimum market-timing.

Yes! he told me. Yes, he could see that it would work. Yes, he thought he could learn to run an Apple just as I had. He could type and he was used to numbers. He was "pretty good" at working machines. He beamed at me.

As we talked, I said to myself, "I have just witnessed the birth of a true believer."

At the very least, the flight had seemed a lot shorter than four hours . . . .

ARTHUR M. WOOD

"You might say I took the easy way out. . . ."

It was the kind of day on which anyone might ask, "What are these two fellows doing here?"

Less than a month before, Chicago had suffered a new all-time low-temperature record (–27° F.). Now, in February, half-frozen slush was everywhere and a miasma of molten salt-dirt-water hung over the expressways, fighting a winning battle with windshield washers and wipers.

It was a great day to be retired and be elsewhere, playing golf and soaking up the sun.

Yet here we were, Arthur Wood and I, sitting in his big office on the 51st floor of the world's tallest building, admitting to each other that a working style of retirement was what we both needed to be happy for very long. For his part, Wood loves books, golf, fishing, and gardening . . . *but.*

"A full-time diet of those and I would go stir-happy," he said.

At the time we talked, it had been four years since Wood had retired as head man of Sears but he had been "extremely busy" all that time. "It's probably not a typical schedule for retired people," he said. "And some people might ask, 'Does this fellow want to work forever? Doesn't he have a plan for his retirement? Why doesn't he go up to the north woods for the summer or to Arizona for the winter—try something new?' You might say I took the easy way out by going on working."

I told him that I wouldn't say that. Much as I myself loved golf and much as I loved painting and reading, it was still the work of problem-solving that got me up, out, and going in the mornings. The question, I thought, was not *what* you did in retirement but how you *felt* about it.

Wood still had a role to play at the company when he retired. The Savings and Profit-Sharing Fund of Sears employees has been, for more than half a century, a big chunk of the employees' nest eggs in retirement. As chairman of the fund, Wood could speak for both company and employees in Congress. He could provide company experience and guidance to the fund staff. And, since his name and face were familiar to most of the firm's 250,000 employees, he was a source of confidence to them. It had been an important position, although it was not a full-time job, for "the last five or six former chairmen of Sears." He had also, like his predecessors, continued on the Sears board of directors and as a member of several board committees. "I don't intervene in any way in the operation of the business, but my successor does seek my reaction to major personnel changes," he said.

In addition, he had joined the boards of three big Chicago-based companies. This provided him with a year-round schedule, with the opportunity to keep informed of changes in the laws and regulations affecting employee benefits, with exposure to interesting and different kinds of businesses.

It seemed to me, however, that it was two other assignments that had given him his greatest gratification these past four years.

When he had retired from the top job at Sears, John J. McCloy had asked him to join a new oversight committee, a group whose job was to help the American Institute of Certified Public Accountants design for itself a system of self-regulation. "I debated with myself whether to commit the necessary time to do this," he said. "But I had been talking for years about our 'half-free' enterprise system and about the problem this country has with too much governmental regulation and so I did it. It's been very interesting. It opened up another field about which I didn't know much, gave me an opportunity to keep learning.

"You know that's very important. Learning keeps you young and it sure helps you avoid the problem of 'what am I going to do today.'"

Of all the items on Wood's smorgasbord of jobs, it was my guess that the one to give him his greatest pleasure was the chairmanship of the Art Institute of Chicago.

Wood took over the job at a troublesome time. The museum had recently lost to thievery three paintings of Paul Cézanne and had gotten unwelcome headlines all over the world. It was in the thick of a search for a new professional director. It would have to find large new sources of revenue if it was to continue as one of the country's great centers of art.

The pressure on the institution to change and to renew itself on a dozen levels was intense.

Wood knew all this, knew that the job would take a lot of time away from his family ("the briefcase came home with me five nights a week"), but he had been a trustee of the museum for twenty-five years and had "a deep interest in and affection for the institution." So, he might have said, did his wife, Pauline. She was a granddaughter of the Mrs. Potter Palmer, who had been a power in the institute's affairs, had been the first American to collect French Impressionists on a large scale, and had left many of those masterpieces to the museum when she died. (Behind Wood's desk in the Sears Tower is a Monet, one of his famous "Haystack" series and one of Mrs. Palmer's prizes.)

Wood seemed to feel good about his contributions as chairman. "We accomplished a few things," he said. "We are moving forward and we have great expectations for continued growth and excellence. That's been a big reward for me, the progress—and progress has to be a great motivation for anybody. It sure meant a lot more to me than getting my golf handicap down by two strokes—something I probably couldn't have accomplished anyway." For a former captain of the Princeton golf team, that, I thought, was a large statement.

Now, on this February day in 1982, he was beginning to get into a new phase in his retirement. In less than a year, he would be stepping out of his Sears jobs if all went according to schedule. The corporate directorships would follow in time.

"I am sensing a desire to be less scheduled," he said. "I have been having to make meetings and take my briefcase home for quite a few years since I got out of Harvard Law School. I sense, too, that my staying power is somewhat diminished. I do think that one should slow things down as he gets older and I am just about at that spot. I turned down another term at the Art Institute because I didn't want to continue the daily and weekly commitments of time and the problem-solving load. This will, however, give me the time to do some other things I want to do over there."

We were running out of time. Wood had a meeting at the Art Institute that he was eager to make. The conversation took a philosophical turn.

"I don't know what medical professionals and psychologists would say about a working retirement," he said. "But I think a busy schedule does good things for your health and your mental activity. I think that if you have a schedule and keep busy and have obligations—and if you continue to take an interest in what goes on in the country and the world—it probably does prevent deterioration of the mind and body.

"I do realize, however, that I've been in a special position as a former head of Sears. I have a wide circle of business friends, I've been involved broadly in civic affairs for a long time. That brought me a lot of opportunities when I retired. What about people who don't have such special positions? There have to be different retirement prospects for such people."

I said that, in my view, we all have the same prospect when we retire. We all face an enormous question. The question is: What's important now? We know what *was* important to us: the job, whatever the job was. But we—all of us—have to come to terms with the here and now. Every single one of us, no matter who or what he's been, has to come up with a new hierarchy of values and a new set of priorities. Looked at that way, no one has a "special position" when he retires and no one has an easy way out.

"I think you've got it, Howard. You're right," he said. "As long as you're happy and I'm happy, who's to ask us 'why didn't you do such and such.' "

Listening to the tape of our conversation long afterwards, I realized why the two of us had sounded so cheerful in spite of the weather and our respective schedules.

Both of us had been about to leave for sunny places and could look forward to enough golf to suit any addict.

Thus, I thought, we were demonstrating another of the rewards of retirement.

Flexibility.

As Arthur Wood had said, "It's great to be able to work over the weekend if you want to and then go fishing for the next three days."

CLARENCE SPENCER

Mister President of the Santa Claus Girls.

Santa Claus Girls goes back more than seventy-five years in Grand Rapids County, Michigan. Its self-generated mission: to wrap donated gifts for delivery to children who might not otherwise get any Christmas presents at all. In a recent year, 200 volunteers did up packages for 9,826 children in 4,635 families.

Admirable. And perfectly straightforward, except for one thing:

In 1983, the president of the group was an honorary female, Clarence "Cy" Spencer, seventy-three-year-old retired accountant.

Spencer's wife, Hester, had gotten him into all this a year earlier. Barbara Waite, then president, was searching "desperately" for a qualified person to serve as deputy. Enter Hester Spencer.

"Why not Cy?" she asked.

Waite presumably swallowed hard once or twice, mindful of the precedent she would be setting. But, she said, "it's difficult to find people who are willing to devote two months of full-time work at the busiest time of the year."

Spencer was qualified by more than willingness. As a former board member of the Senior Neighbors social service group and as incumbent secretary of the Standard Annuitants Club of Western Michigan, he was a veteran organizer and administrator.

Cy Spencer was in.

Next step: Number 1 "girl."

ROBERT (RAB) ISHAM

"It isn't the sun, the exercise, or the scenery. . . ."

When Rab Isham retired, he literally did not know he'd done so. His only idea had been to sell his little manufacturing company at the right time and at a good profit. After taking some time off, he would find another small company to buy, to run, to build up, and to sell. It had been fun the first time. It would be fun to do it again.

"As things turned out, though, I had gotten too spoiled," he said.

"I had gotten spoiled by having a terrific product to sell, by working with an outstanding dealer organization, by having a nifty manufacturing setup, by the short commute from home to the plant.

"Once I started looking at other little companies that were on the market, I couldn't find anything that came close to what I had had. It took me nearly three years to see that I never would."

Isham had been disappointed in a way. But not bitterly. By then, life in retirement had come to have its charms. He had a comfortable small office five minutes from home. He was doing OK at managing his investments. He and his wife were spending more and more of the winters in Santa Barbara, California. And then there was the Isham approach to golf. . . .

There are a lot of reasons to play golf in retirement and hundreds of thousands of people do. There are the scenery, the exercise, the sunshine and fresh air, the companionship. There is what Ben Hogan once called "the perpetual illusion of lower scores"—the magic that keeps a million golfers coming back. Then there are the people who collect golf courses as other people collect stamps or bird-sightings; Isham knew a man who had played more than 600 courses in his life.

Isham understood those reasons.

For him, however, what turned him on about golf was something very different.

Competition.

"I *love* the competition," he told me.

Isham had been an excellent golfer, even in his teens, and had been a low-handicap player all his working life. But competitive golf? "I was lucky if I did well in the club championship," he said.

It was only after he had sold his company that he started trying to qualify himself to play in senior tournaments.

He committed himself to work at it. Hard. Systematically. He even built a practice sand trap in his own back yard.

"For five years," he said, "I played over 200 rounds a year and practiced on fifty or so other days.

"Even though I've tapered off some, I still practice every day for a month before I play in a tournament. I give myself definite assignments. I hit from fifty to 100 shots with the driver, fifty to 100 with the five-iron, practice chipping and putting the same way."

Why does a serious golfer have to practice so hard? Why isn't regular play enough?

"Well," he said, "I know at least one thing about myself. The more I *think* about my swing and my strokes, the worse I play. I have to practice with the goal of getting a certain *feeling* for each shot. The feeling comes from repetition. It's like learning the multiplication table by rote. I try to build the memory of that feeling into my muscles—so that when I get on the golf course itself, they do the right thing *without* my thinking.

"I do it, too, for reasons of confidence. So darn much of golf is confidence—of taking a positive mental attitude. When I step up to the ball on the golf course, I say to myself, 'You *can* do it! You've hit this shot 500 times the past week and you can *do* it.' And putting works the same way. It may sound weird—but it works for me."

The "Isham system" had given its owner a lot of pleasure by the time we talked in 1982.

The year before, he had won two invitational tournaments of The United States Seniors' Golf Association, each with a different partner. (He lent me a copy of the current association yearbook. There had been ten such tournaments that year. His was the only face to appear twice among the winners.)

"That was a big year for me," he said.

But his biggest year—"my Walter Mitty year"—had come when he played for the association on its international team against Canada and England.

"There were nine of us on that team," he said. "Six of my teammates had played against England on U.S. Walker Cup teams. Some had been U.S. Amateur champions. They were guys like Billy Joe Patton, Ed Tutwiler, Dale Morey, and Bill Campbell. That was *really* the big leagues for me. Those were men I had never played with before or even known."

The chance to play with golfers like that gave Isham a second motivation to practice hard. As long as he could play to a handicap of six or seven, he would be paired with the Billy Joes of the Seniors world. . . .

Isham's name appeared in a third prominent place in the

yearbook. He was currently serving as chairman of the Midwest Invitational Tournament, a three-day event played on as many different golf courses.

"It's not a particularly onerous job," he said, "except for the two months before the Midwest tournament itself. It's a big one and there are a lot of arrangements to be made as the time gets close.

"But the job does keep me involved all year-round. The other chairmen are all congenial people, we all love competitive golf and we learn from each other—how to deal with problems and so on. It's fun."

"Fun" did not seem to me—a man with a *twenty*-seven handicap—a strong enough word.

"Heaven," maybe?

PAUL C. HARPER, JR.
"Halfway over the bridge"

October. Sun bright. Air bright. Foliage brilliant. Everything supercharged to the point of frivolity, I thought.

Except the theme of the conversation.

"I immediately felt anxious, reluctant to proceed," Paul Harper was saying. "I was reluctant to the point that I had an operational blockage. It was almost impossible for me to get on with it.

"Little by little I began to sort out what it was I was afraid of. One thing—I had known many men who left positions of authority for retirement and had just come apart. They seemed to lose interest in life, to dry up, to develop physical or psychological symptoms or both—symptoms I didn't want any part of. Another thing—I had a fear that I would lose my identity, my sense of self."

Two years before, Harper and his key associates had started planning how to transfer his power at Needham, Harper & Steers to younger men.

Now, he and I were commencing a two-day conversation about retirement: his, mine, and other people's. He had promised to talk about his problems and plans. I had promised to tell what I had learned from my own experience and from gathering material for this book.

We had started the process in the car. On the way from the

Harpers' apartment in New York to their weekend place in Lyme, Connecticut, he filled in some of the gaps in my knowledge of him and his career.

After Yale and the Marine Corps, he had come back to Chicago and found a job at the advertising agency Needham, Louis & Brorby. To the extent that he thought about his future in those days, he rated himself a long shot—"25 to 1"—to succeed Maurice Needham. His talents and training pointed him in the direction of creative work, he believed. Not toward management. Indeed, rising to the top had forced him to learn skills that he sees as unnatural to him and the work had often seemed overwhelming.

I was aware that this was Harper's view. But, if I had known him only from news stories of the agency during his time at center stage, I would not have guessed that he had such doubts. On the contrary.

At the time he became chief executive officer, N, L & B was a medium-size and long-established firm, clubby and intimate. It was the advertising agency for S. C. Johnson & Son, State Farm Insurance, and a short list of other blue-chip clients. Its competitors respected its work and were grateful that it had not been aggressive in pursuit of new business.

Harper changed all that. His first big move was to acquire a New York agency with a similar profile, Doherty, Clifford & Steers, and to put a new name, Needham, Harper & Steers, on both doors. Not long after, the New York office began to lose business and to put the whole enterprise in peril, precipitating another major change. Harper moved himself, his wife Cooie, and their six children to Fifth Avenue in the Nineties, moved his office to Fifth Avenue in the Forties, made a turnaround his first priority. That and stability came slowly, but they came. And so did such rewards as the Xerox account.

From his New York base, Harper led the new agency to a major position in West Coast advertising, to the winning of the McDonald's account ("You deserve a break today"), and a long list of other prize accounts. He laid out the strategy that was to make the agency a power in markets around the world (the N, H & S name is now on doors in Auckland, Düsseldorf, Hamburg, Hong Kong, London, Melbourne, Montreal, Munich, Singapore, Sydney, Toronto, and Wellington, as well as New York, Chicago, Los Angeles, Washington, Dayton, and San Francisco). He himself did much of the work of colonizing.

In the years after Harper took charge, the agency had gone public, had seen the stock market stubbornly undervalue its present and future, had gone private again. In spite of its award-winning creative work, it had—only months before we talked—lost McDonald's. Harper and his associates had then rebutted with a spectacular new business drive and had more than replaced the lost revenue.

Not a bad career for a 25–1 shot, I thought as we drove up the turnpike. To round it off, he had been honored by his peers in the industry and would soon do a one-year tour as chairman of the American Association of Advertising Agencies. Meanwhile, he had taken himself beyond the point of no return within the agency. While he still held two of the three handles of power, he had delegated the day-to-day authority over operations. There would not be (as at CBS and other companies) an embarrassment of crown princes, each of whom would have his short time in the sun, while the sun king himself clung hard to the mantle.

The Harpers' modern house crowns all that's left of an ancient mountain. Except for a new driveway and two primitive paths, the slopes are thick with second-growth trees, bull brambles, and fences that are shedding their substance, stone by stone. The land no longer can support dairy cows at a profit.

The view is not in the same price class as the one from their apartment, but it stretches farther. The valley in the foreground still supports one farm; its silver silos thrust up a mile away. In the middle ground, there marches a long row of worn-down hills, afire for now with foliage. Through a gap, we see the mouth of Long Island Sound. The tip of Long Island itself is visible but out of focus on the horizon. Everywhere are yellow, russet, a dozen shades of gold.

The scene seems to have been composed by a painter—which was what Harper had decided to be when full-time retirement came.

Now, with my tape machine running, Harper was analyzing the losses he expected to have to deal with in his new life—his "support system," for one.

There were his secretary; the members of the N, H & S Board; his associates; his clients; other people in advertising. "That adds up to support of enormous psychic proportions. What happens when all those ego props are removed, one by one? That's a big part of my fear of withdrawal.

"And what happens when I go from a highly transactional life with dozens of people in it to a life that is reflective and solitary?

"Solitary is the word. Painting is such a *solitary* occupation."

As he had tried to deal with his "operational blockage" and the concerns that had caused it, he had come to a watershed decision. "I had thought I had a good concept for my retirement," he said, "but thinking about it was clearly not going to be enough." The fears were not going away on their own and he sought help from a psychiatrist.

"This just isn't an intellectual exercise," he told me. "I have to make a real emotional shift, a seismic one. I *have* to . . . ."

Here my tape registers a long pause followed by a belly laugh.

He was laughing at himself. "I just said 'I *have* to' again. I've been issuing orders to myself for forty-five years. I don't *have* to do a damn thing. My doctor says that issuing orders to myself won't work anymore because doing that isn't relevant anymore. I'm going to need some discipline just to get through my daily living, but I don't need a whole new bunch of 'oughts' and deadlines and tight organization.

"Would you believe it—if we go to Burgundy, I have to look at every Romanesque church—every last one of them—and make notes?" We laughed. We are much alike.

Harper's doctor had been helping him to understand his dilemma.

On the one hand, his concerns about retiring were real and natural. It would have been unnatural to hand over his position, power, and perquisites without a second thought.

On the other hand, the force and extent of his desire to paint were equally real.

During his career, he had focused all his time, energy, and effort on the tasks at hand. He had had to lead, to plan, to organize, to deal with the numbers. The stage for that had been set by cues from his parents and by his family responsibilities.

"But," he said, "events left many things in me unexpressed." Taken together, these things "*added up to almost another person.*

"Now I realize I have a strong drive to develop the *rest* of myself."

The "rest of himself" had never been altogether silent, in spite of what his career had demanded of him.

For as long as I could remember, he had taken first-rate photographs which had a strong, painterly feeling. On the second evening of our visit, he showed us the remarkable images he had collected a few weeks before while he and Cooie Harper were on a picture-taking safari in East Africa.

To go with the photographs, he had written a sort of journal. Reading it later, I said to myself that it sounded like a painter writing:

> It is hard to describe the vibrations that a lion's roar can send through the night. It leaves everything in doubt. . . .
>
> David's old gunbearer had once been bitten in the thumb by a black mamba. Knowing he had only two choices, he took his panga and chopped the poisoned thumb off. . . .
>
> Central Kenya is high and dry, but it is right on the equator. It is cool at night, but by noon the sun can poach your brains. . . .
>
> Crocodiles will attack anything with meat on it and, once having satisfied their hunger, will sleep for two or three days. The trouble is you never know what digestive phase they are in. . . .
>
> The golden-crowned crane looks as though it had been designed by a Paris couturier. . . .
>
> The bou-bou sings duets with its mate—together they sound like a bell chime. When several pairs of bou-bous sing at the same time, they sound like a carillon in a cathedral. . . .
>
> At the height of the season, one million flamingos feed in this lake at the same time. [Even now] it was rimmed with bobbing pink shapes and the air was laced with flights of incoming birds. . . .
>
> It is easy to become fond of the lion and the cheetah when seen from the safety of the truck. . . .

Harper, like me, had painted off and on for years. However, when he became fully aware of the pull of painting, he set out with determination to prepare himself.

In spite of the limitations on his time, he became a trustee of the Brooklyn Art Museum, of the Rhode Island School of Design, and of the Lyme Academy of Art—"a small but valid art school"— which asks him often for advice on how to grow.

He found a painting coach from whom he took lessons weekly. He cultivated teacher-pupil relationships with two other art professionals. He sought through them to get a "sense of triangulation" on his path and progress.

He himself turned professional. When the Rhode Island School of Design offered him a place in a show, he accepted—even though it meant having to produce a number of new pieces under pressure of a deadline. That in itself was good for him, he saw, but there was more: he had the pleasure of selling several paintings. (Anyone who has ever crossed the line between amateur and professional knows what the sound of the cash register did to his adrenal glands.)

Still another subject in his cram curriculum was art history ("I'm short on that") and he began to visit museums and galleries on schedule rather than on impulse.

"Last week," he said, "I had to go to Washington on business. I decided that I would spend half a day seeing the Braque retrospective at the National Gallery. It was a once-in-a-lifetime opportunity to look at a large exhibition of work by a painter I greatly admire." This was good for him in more than one way, he thought. "It was wonderful to go without regarding it as a self-indulgence, almost a sin. It was a legitimate part of my preparation for the future and I was proud of myself. Three years ago, my conscience and the work ethic would never have let me do it."

What impressed me most was the contrast between his studio and mine. My tools are stuffed into a small, dark, old-fashioned back-hall room. His are laid out in a large, all-white space, separate from the house and designed for the purpose. There is a huge skylight, aimed due north and backed up by a great wash of fluorescent lighting. There is a counter that runs the length of one wall; there are drawers beneath, a sweep of Formica on top, and the wall above is corkboard. The room said to him and all comers, "I'm ready for business."

Harper had recently been experimenting with half-abstract, highly simplified impressions of his African experience. Eight or ten studies were pinned to the cork. One stood out. There were a bare few lines, a hint of two or three planes, a feeling of light everywhere, and no place to hide. One's eye could keep reaching out to infinity.

It was almost time for the drive to LaGuardia and the plane for Chicago.

I was thinking that my friend had demonstrated intelligence, courage, and willingness to work at getting ready for retirement. None of those nouns had applied to me or to most of the retired people I knew. I told Harper this.

"Well, I've probably projected myself to you as someone who's largely solved his retirement problem," he said. "That's not so. I'm perhaps halfway across the bridge to that." He was still concerned about isolation, still unsure that his "unused resources are there and that it's not too late to develop them."

I understood. But I doubted that he put the full value on his knowledge of himself and of his need to change habits and attitudes. "I need to be constructively reflective," he told me. "I have the ability. I just don't do it. I need to do that, to meditate, to spend more time integrating myself with my world and the events in it.

"Now's the time for me to redefine myself for myself and to set new priorities. I will say I'm finding the process increasingly fascinating. I'm responding to old experiences in new ways, enjoying new experiences.

"I'm making progress—but I'm only part way there."

I reserved the last word on his progress for myself.

When I got home, I wrote to him: "My compliments on the latest expression of your painting, writing, and photographic talents. Don't blame me if you find yourself flying around the country, wearing yourself out, signing autograph books, and smiling at ineffable bores. Fame is a bitch of a mistress."

EDGAR H. LOTSPEICH
"Yes, you can fight City Hall"

Mid-February.

A long way away from Walloon Lake and Petoskey, Michigan.

Removed by a temperature difference of 100 degrees.

Ed Lotspeich and I are sitting on the balcony of his rented condominium at Sanibel Island, Florida, looking at "the best view here." Sun hot. Gulf water blue. Breeze gentle. From this aerie, it takes little imagination to play Captain On The Bridge. The sea is that close.

We ignore these semi-tropical seductions. The events Lotspeich (LOT-speech) is describing have mostly occurred around his retirement home up north. . . .

The last time I had seen my friend and client of many years, his retirement day was right at hand. As I then saw things—I was still working—his plans for retirement were bizarre. He *had* no plans, he told me. For a career Procter & Gamble man to say that he had no plans and mean it was startling. System, planning, and testing had been at the very heart of his business experience. Surely Ed Lotspeich was capable of something more than a no-strategy strategy for his retirement.

He was.

What I didn't understand was that Grace Lotspeich had a health problem. A year earlier, she had had both hip joints replaced. As her surgeon had put it, the "insult" to her body was as great as though she'd "been hit by a truck." Even as Lotspeich was carrying out his five-year decision to retire at sixty, he and his wife were still up in the air about retiring to Walloon Lake. They wanted to. His educator-parents had built a cottage there in 1929 and he'd always loved it. Both he and Grace had dreamt of living there full time. Both like to fish, to ski. There were plenty of other things to do. But now . . . .

In the situation, Lotspeich had done the only thing open to him. Until they resolved the where-to-live question, he would avoid any long-term commitments. Meanwhile, he had faith in his resourcefulness. He was sure he would find engrossing things to do, wherever they lived.

He was right.

"As I look back on my seven years of retirement," he said, "a lot of exciting things have happened to me, things I could never have anticipated or planned for. Why shouldn't just as many exciting things happen in the next seven years?"

One thing Lotspeich had not anticipated was an eight-day illness that had once put him in Northern Michigan Hospitals in Petoskey. He had been impressed, very, with the staff and with his treatment. If the opportunity ever presented itself, he would like, he decided, to work for the hospital.

Once the Lotspeiches were in permanent residence, he told a trustee-friend how he felt about the institution and found himself, *zap*, raising money. With his woman co-chairman (she did not mind "co-chairman" as much as he minded "co-chairperson"), he raised $200,000 among the residents of Walloon Lake.

(What do you do with such a fellow? You make him a trustee, of course, and elect him chairman of the development committee.)

This, however, was preliminary to the—so far—main event in

Lotspeich's involvement with Northern Michigan Hospitals.

By 1983, NMH was a major hospital by any set of standards. Its rural setting was a fooler. Its physical facilities and medical staff qualified it to offer open heart surgery, renal dialysis, neonatal care, neurological surgery, many other kinds of sophisticated treatment. It had attracted a group of crack specialists from Detroit and other urban medical centers. It served as a referral center for upwards of twenty smaller hospitals in a ten-county area.

Enter a snake into this "Eden": A fat document entitled "Medicare Prospective Pricing. . . ."

As in many other hospitals today, over 50 percent of NMH patients come under Medicare. The federal government had become a full partner in NMH service to its community. "To that extent, we are socialized, like it or not," Lotspeich said.

For NMH, Medicare Prospective Pricing, as written, would have threatened "its very survival" as a first-class hospital. The problem lay in proposed new definitions of "urban" and "rural" and in new and more stringent criteria for referral centers.

Example: A hypothetical patient has a choice. He can go to nearby NMH or to a distant, urban hospital. In either, he receives exactly the same treatment. Same services. Same quality of service.

But there the similarity ends.

Under the proposed new pricing, NMH would be reimbursed $2,400 for its care of that patient. The urban hospital would get $3,600. To be sure, this is perfectly logical—*if* the Medicare assumption is correct—*if* costs in a city are indeed 50 percent higher than those in a "rural setting."

In the case of NMH, the assumption is not correct. Its costs are, in fact, within 11 percent of the costs in Detroit, within 5 percent of the costs in the growing Grand Rapids-Kalamazoo area.

If the ruling could not be modified, NMH stood to lose most of its top medical specialists. It could no longer provide a wide variety of state-of-the-art treatments on a variety of major illnesses.

Now, enter Lotspeich.

In the crisis, he is elected chairman of the government relations committee.

"We had never had such a committee before," he said. In fact, our government relations were intolerable. The belief was that 'you can't fight city hall.' Well, I just don't buy that. I've had too much experience that says you *can* fight city hall when you have a good case."

Although Lotspeich had been in advertising and brand management at Procter & Gamble, he was a Washington familiar. "The company does not delegate government relations," he said. "Every officer of the company has to play quarterback on all dealings affecting his end of the business. In my case, I was the quarterback in Federal Trade Commission matters. I can't tell you how many hours I spent—far too many hours—on FTC business. I had some very exciting times.

"So I had been in what might be called big-league operations. But none of them had been bigger-league than a meeting I attended on November 22, 1983. . . ."

In this "bigger-league" session, there were three people representing NMH: President Jim Raney, a top medical staffer, and Ed Lotspeich.

To represent the government: "The woman who runs the whole Health Care Financing Administration and who reports directly to the secretary," Senator Carl Levin of Michigan, Congressman Robert Davis of the NMH district, delegates from the offices of Congressman Guy vander Jagt and of the governor of Michigan.

By meeting time, the congressmen's files were stuffed with letters from the Petoskey area. There had been few recent issues that had stirred up so much heat. The hospital had encouraged the letter campaign—but only that. "The voters took it right away from us," Lotspeich said. "The support was overwhelming."

To bring light as well as heat to the subject, the hospital's financial officers had, within forty-eight hours, put together a tight, compelling presentation: numbers, relevant comparisons, and much other data. It went well.

"I later sent a message to the board," Lotspeich said. "I told them that I had attended a lot of Washington meetings but I had never seen one better or more effectively handled. The congressman is optimistic and so am I. But if we lose this battle, we'll simply start the campaign all over again." The cause, he felt, deserved no less.

All of this had led to a first for him—an appearance on the evening television news.

(Months later, I would get the news: NMH had *not* lost. It had been reclassified as an "urban referral center.")

Another surprise event had led Lotspeich into a different kind of fight with "city hall."

He heard a story one day, a story that made him all eyes, ears, and question marks. The newest thing at Walloon Lake, he heard, would be something called "funnel developments." One developer had already started work.

Someone had hit on a—to him—attractive marketing idea. He would buy ordinary, undeveloped lake-front lots and create private "parks." The parks would have piers, slips, swimming facilities, and other recreational equipment. Membership in the parks would be limited to owners of small lots up and away from the lake itself. At modest cost, the small-lot owners would have access to water sports on a virtually unlimited basis. It looked as though there was lots of money to be made.

While Lotspeich "expects and welcomes development" on his old and beloved lake, "funnel developments" sounded more like piracy than progress. "Twenty of those and the lake would be a zoo," he told me.

Although he had never been involved with the Walloon Lake Association, he knew that these happenings would concern its officers and he asked them what was cooking. They too were alarmed but pessimistic. They felt that "you can't fight city hall."

(Enter Lotspeich again. Lights. Camera. Action.)

Suddenly, Lotspeich found himself on the board of the association and at the head of committee with a mission to "do something."

Acting on a strong hunch that funnel development was inherently illegal, Lotspeich retained an attorney, a specialist in Michigan real estate law. Jackpot!

In the opinion of the lawyer-specialist, funnel development would lead to a violation of all homeowners' riparian rights. Under Michigan statutes, he said, riparian rights include intangible interests in the health and well-being of the entire lake.

Encouraged, the Walloon Lake Association sued the developer who was already underway. Lotspeich acted as point man. Committee members provided great help and support. "It was fascinating and it was a hell of a lot of work for six months," Lotspeich said. "But we won big. The other party decided not to go to court."

Furthermore, the association won a court order that became a pattern. Three of the five townships that abut the lake had adopted it. It did not restrict use of the land but did restrict use of the lake proper—the first time anyone had used zoning laws to regulate the use of the water. A fourth township was to consider adoption of the pattern within a few days. Lotspeich believed that this emerging precedent would be important to all the rest of Michigan and to other states as well.

"Could I have anticipated and planned for that sort of excitement when I retired?" he asked me. "I felt as happy about that court order as I had ever felt about my business successes."

Reader, it is yellow flag time. You now believe that the Lotspeich retirement story is all a matter of white hats and black hats and of wars between them—understandable, but wrong. Listen:

> I think I got through the adjustment period pretty well when I retired. If that's true, I owe much of it to my education and my parents. My mother founded the Lotspeich School in Cincinnati. My father was a professor of English at the University of Cincinnati. Father was a staunch believer in [studying] literature and history and the other liberal arts because of the kind of *person* it made you. I have never taken a "practical" course in my life. Not a business course. Not even an economics course. I majored in English literature and French and almost in philosophy.
>
> Today, one of my chores—I am a member of the schools committee of the Princeton Club of Michigan. In this capacity, I maintain contact with a half dozen high schools in our part of Michigan and I try to find star youngsters who might be interested in going to my old college. If they apply, I interview them and I help them with their applications. As I do this, I find myself continually preaching to them about the value of a liberal arts education; and if they talk about the "market value" of a particular course, I try to tell them that that isn't the reason you get educated. I say it doesn't matter how many business courses you've taken—if you can't think clearly, if you don't have a sense of history, if you can't write a letter, if you can't organize yourself—what good is it if you took a business course?

In Edgar Lotspeich's view, studying the liberal arts would be "the best possible medicine for adjustment to retirement. I make a point of rereading a few of Shakespeare's plays every year, not only because I love them as drama but because of the wonderful things he says." In the year just past, he had reread *King Lear*, *Hamlet*, *Othello*—"I prefer the tragedies because that's where the philosophy is."

Lotspeich still belonged to the Literary Club of Cincinnati, had twice made the 1,000-mile round trip by car in order to deliver a paper to the members.

His more recent paper—7,000 words—addresses the history of a bridge. Here are the opening paragraphs. (Do you, too, hear echoes of "you *can* fight city hall"?)

> It is easy to understand why many people believed that a bridge across the Straits of Mackinac could not be built. How can you bridge four miles of blue water in the Upper Great Lakes? The water is too deep—in some spots nearly 300 feet. The winds are too strong. It is not unusual for the wind at the Straits to gust up to seventy miles an hour. No bridge could survive those savage Mackinac storms. Furthermore, no bridge could survive the pressure of Mackinac ice. At the Straits, the water is known to freeze solid five or six feet down. Wintry blasts coming down from Lake Superior or across 100 miles of open Lake Michigan pile ice and snow in windrows forty feet high. The ice is constantly moving and cracking and heaving because of wind, water currents, and temperature changes. When the ice starts to break up in the spring, an April storm can drive massive ice floes through the straits with the force of a battering ram. Those people who talk about building such a bridge are dreamers!

"The fun of working on [such] a paper is the research," the author said. "It's the reading and interviewing you have to do. For my next paper, I plan to restudy the Renaissance and the Reformation. . . ."

Up to now, Ed Lotspeich had told me a lot about himself that I hadn't known. But he had not surprised me. His activism in retirement, his talent for organization and for getting things done, his intellectual pursuits—all seemed logical outgrowths of the business abilities I had observed for thirty years.

What I was not prepared to hear about was his membership in the Society for the Preservation and Encouragement of Barber Shop Quartet Singing in America.

"Well, I have a lot of musical background," he said. "As a child and young man, I played both the piano and the clarinet. I sang in church choirs for many years. Still do.

"But I have learned a lot about making music with my mouth from barber shop—how to breathe and how to open my mouth. That training can give anyone a fine voice. It's simply the most disciplined kind of music I've ever been in."

Ed Lotspeich would not be Ed Lotspeich if he could see only one side of things in his retirement.

"I don't want to paint too rosy a picture," he said. "When people ask me about my retirement, I say I like it fine but I don't always like it as well as working.

"For one thing, I miss the people, the contacts. I miss my peers at Procter & Gamble and sitting at lunch with them. I miss the wisdom, the stimulation, the gentlemanly behavior. You can count your blessings that you worked with [principled] people like that. It's great therapy against cynicism.

"No, I don't want to sound as though retirement were perfection. There are things you have to watch out for. I have to guard, consciously, against living in the past. And I have to guard against nit-picking—getting into little fights that don't matter, writing letters to the editor, that kind of thing.. If I were still working, I wouldn't have time for that.

"And I used to have another big worry—it really bothered me: alcohol." He'd seen a lot of people retire and get into the bottle too much. He had never had a problem with it himself but he worried that it *could* happen. He had talked to his doctor about it and his doctor said, "You only have one problem with alcohol—you worry too much about it." And he'd gone right on worrying. Then he'd met a minister by chance and had developed a special respect for him. One day, Lotspeich laid out his worry for the minister who said, "Well, if you're so worried about it, why not abstain altogether? Then you won't have anything to worry about." Lotspeich grinned at me. It was such an obvious idea. He knew that. But it had taken that particular man to say it at that particular time. "Do you know, I haven't had a drink since that day—two years—and that man was right. I haven't worried about it. Haven't *had* to worry about it. Curious story, isn't it?"

While we were together, Lotspeich made sure to give me a tour of his pleasure places. The spot where he likes to fish. The Ding Darling Wildlife Sanctuary. The great seafood restaurant. The beach at the foot of his apartment, "still one of the great shelling beaches in the world." I particularly liked that beach. The city fathers allow it to maintain itself naturally. I liked seeing the skeletons of sting rays and other fish, liked seeing the birds and other carnivores cleaning up, liked seeing the story that was laid out there for the seeing, the story of death begetting life. I said to Lotspeich that I could see why he liked taking his winter vacations here.

"Yes," he said. "Life's easy and relaxed and I love it. But I can see that I need more to do."

I decided I wouldn't worry about that.

Already my friend had found a church choir in which to sing.

And he had brought along his new electronic typewriter. . . .

GEORGE P.
*A determination
to be self-sufficient*

When I met George P., I was not yet thinking about this book, so his last name did not stick in my mind.

But his story did.

P. was seventy-three. He had been completely retired from his Wall Street law firm for three years, had been a widower for five.

Unlike other older lawyers I had known, P. never went near his old office, although he was welcome. He felt the firm was in good hands. And he had definite ideas about retirement, his own at least.

Immediately after leaving the law behind, he began pursuing his talent for painting and, when I met him, had already had his first one-man show. Furthermore, he was working on pieces for his second.

He had also begun working down a long list of books he had always wanted to read, books which had to play second fiddle to his career.

And he wanted to make a significant contribution of his time to the battle against alcohol and drug abuse. His wife had been an alcoholic and his daughter was recovering from the disease.

But George's main ambition was to be completely independent, to maintain self-sufficiency for as long as possible.

It was not a piddling job. For one thing, he had gardens at both his homes, one on Long Island and the other in Florida. When he told me that he did all the gardening himself, I did not doubt that he meant exactly that. He did all the weeding, all the planting, all the cultivating, mowing, pruning—the whole shot.

Although he admitted to being in "some" demand as an extra man at dinner parties, he himself did the marketing, the preparation, the cooking, the cleaning up, and the putting-away for seventeen or eighteen meals a week.

Furthermore, he housekept his homes himself: the vacuuming, the dusting, the beds, the bathrooms, everything. And he took his laundry to the laundromat. I keep wishing I had asked him about his ironing—an art that baffles me.

I had no doubt that P. could afford all the help it would take to "free" him from his chores. But I did not think it was a question of money.

The issue, I was sure, was another kind of freedom.

Which of us Americans is going to quarrel with that?

ARTHUR C. NIELSEN, JR.
"I'd like to fill some voids in my life."

December 28. Has snowed. Is snowing.

Today, 35 mph will be reckless, 55 suicidal.

I have to leave my house far earlier than I would on a dry day, but I do not grump. I can put the hour-and-a-half to excellent use.

As I inch along in a controlled skid and defend myself from macho truck drivers, I can try to picture Art Nielsen's frame of mind: How would I feel if I were he? I'll listen better if I do that.

Nielsen, I knew, was a one-speed man: flat out. People don't get busier than he. And this was not a case of work for work's sake. When he had joined his father in the A. C. Nielsen Company, the business offered just three market research services and did $4 million a year. Today's comparable figures were 125 and $700 million. And Arthur Jr. had been chief architect of the growth.

He would say to me later, "I thought a way for me to make a name in the company was to start something new. I had seen people with small companies do very well by maintaining the status quo. For a while. But when technological changes came along, they were stuck. They didn't have the money to do new things. You have to put a lot of bread out on the waters [if you want to survive]."

His had to have been a wonderful game. Creative. Intellectually challenging. Loaded with psychic compensation.

Now—suddenly, surprisingly—he was coming up on sixty-five and retirement. He himself had set the sixty-five-and-out policy for the company. Soon, very soon, he would feel obliged to step off the fast track, to find other ways to satisfy his drive.

Would I spot withdrawal symptoms as we talked?

Would I find him fudging on his decision? Hinting at staying on a little longer—"just to be sure" that all would be well? Policy or no, he could do so.

Nothing like that: I found him relaxed and comfortable, ready and willing to look at the future of the company with me.

"I've never had much concern," he said. "I spent a lot of time in the U.S. Army—four-and-a-half years. I saw a lot of changes then. Men coming and going, in and out of organizations. Organizations have a great life of their own, a strength that goes beyond any one man. Nobody's indispensable. Leadership is important, of course, and I knew it would be better to pick the right person than to make a poor choice. Oftentimes, people *don't* have the qualifications that their predecessors hope they have and the organizations suffer. But you make the best choice you can. You have to. How many good ideas does one person have? Sooner or later you run out of ideas and you may not know it yourself. People do tend to stay on too long if they can. . . ."

Granted. But what about his own new life? What would he do with all that energy, mental as well as physical?

Well, conditions were not going to change all at once. For one thing, he would continue on the board of the company for a while and chair some committees. "I'll extricate myself gradually—if that's the word." He wanted to give the new group what help he could "but I think they will want and need it less and less."

He would also continue on the boards of several other corporations, "something I enjoy very much."

And there were some personal things he wanted to do. He felt he'd missed out on a lot.

"I want to start filling some voids in my life—such as friends," he said. "As I got more and more involved with the company, I found it harder and harder to keep up my friendships. And to make new ones. I've met a lot of wonderful men in business but I've had very little time to cultivate friendships with them. I think you've got to put a lot into a friendship if you want to make it amount to something. I remember a book by one of the Plinys, I don't remember which. It said that if you have twenty friends in a lifetime you are indeed fortunate. I didn't believe that when I read it in college but I do now."

And he wanted to spend more time with his wife. "I don't think Patty and I have ever had more than two weeks to ourselves— we've always built our vacations around business trips. It would be fun to go somewhere and stay for a while. Our daughter lives in Florence, you remember—I'd love to take a villa there, up in the hills. . . ."

Furthermore, he had an idea for a book. "I've taken a camera with me to all fifty of the countries I've visited on business," he said. "I think I could put together a sort of photojournal of a businessman, something that would show what he saw and where he went and what interested him. At least it would get me out of Patty's way for a while."

"What about tennis?" I asked. I knew that tennis for him was more than a pastime. He had played it with fervor all his life. His father and he were once a champion doubles team in the father-son class. They had organized and built one of the first indoor tennis clubs in the world.

He grinned. "Well, I have a dream about that, too. All my life I have had trouble with one particular shot on my backhand. I would love to go to Harry Hopman's camp down in Florida—you remember Hopman, the old coach of the Australian Davis Cup Team. I'd like to show him my problem and see if he can fix it."

That wish-list of Nielsen's reminded me of my own. I had had just such ideas of what to do in retirement.

But I knew that Art Nielsen's psyche would never let him rest there any more than mine had me. On a sudden hunch, I showed him the section in this book entitled, "Your own boss. At last."

"Well, I sure see your point," he said. "One word in there really got me. the word 'important.' I've got three or four ideas I've always wanted to develop. I've never had the time before."

Aha, I said to myself. "For instance?"

"Well," he said, "in my early career, I got a chance to go into five different countries as part of a productivity team. Back when the Marshall Plan was trying to raise the standards of living after World War II. I went into that as a great believer in the free enterprise system and democratic institutions."

He had gotten a shock. "My ideas were *not* welcomed with open arms as I thought they ought to be and that bothered me. It seemed so *obvious*. But the more I studied the systems, the more I realized that each country had its own problems, that every economic system was different and came out of certain traditions and needs." Maybe, he said to himself, he was not as right as he'd thought.

"I think people in this country—and I include myself—make a mistake when we think there is only one best system. There are a lot of good things about communism and socialism. There are a lot of terrible things in capitalism. I think of China. I've been to China four times and I think they have a lot we could borrow from—how to help people at the low end of the scale, for example. They really know how to get the people at the bottom organized for their own good. I conclude that countries ought to borrow the good things from all these systems and try to construct better ones.

"Frankly, I've been afraid to speak out on issues like that, issues I think are important. If I went around making speeches to that effect, people might say 'what kind of a nut is running the Nielsen Company?'

"Now that I'll have a little more time, I think I'll make a few talks about things like this that interest me."

What else?

"Well, I have a whole big question about our organizations today. So many companies and other organizations aren't as effective as they could be because they don't know how to mobilize to get things done. Market research companies are one example. Most of them—like George Gallup's company—are very good at research but they don't get very large. There are principles of organization that are not getting followed and that holds companies back."

"For example?" I asked.

Well, he thought, a lot of people ignore the principle of focused responsibility. In any operation, large or small, you need someone who can say yes or no instead of maybe. The buck has to stop somewhere. He thought of the Winnetka schools.

"A few years back, I was working for our high school. They

weren't doing very well. The building wasn't getting painted. The plant was running down. They didn't have enough money for the teachers. A lot of things."

Nielsen had asked the superintendent what was wrong and the answer was that they were not getting enough money from the state.

Aha. Next time Nielsen saw Richard Ogilvie, then the governor of Illinois, he asked him why he wasn't giving the Winnetka schools enough money.

That was easy, Ogilvie said. Illinois wasn't getting enough money from Washington.

The buck never stopped.

"That's the problem when no one is responsible," Nielsen said. "I think that's one reason that governments at all levels are not working very well right now."

Would he like to make some talks on that subject, too? Yes. What else?

A question that had been nagging at him for a long time: "How much money must society provide to a person if it is to be a just society?"

It was a philosophical question he'd asked himself, so Nielsen had done the logical thing. He had gone to a philosopher, Mortimer Adler. Adler had just written a book on six of the great ideas, among them the idea of justice. To be just, what should society provide a man? Nielsen asked. Well, Adler had said, a man at minimum needs the money to shelter himself, to feed and clothe himself and his family, to educate his children and himself. Yes, Nielsen had said, but how much more should any one man have than the minimum? Five times the minimum? Ten times? More than that—so that we don't stifle incentive? "Well, Adler didn't have an answer for that," Nielsen said, "and I guess I didn't get him interested. Too bad." The issue is so *basic*. To politics. To economics. To the human spirit itself.

Some intellectual agenda, I said to myself. He's got enough ideas to keep three men busy in retirement. But Nielsen had yet another, and this time I heard the professional researcher speaking.

"We've *got* to find a better way to get intelligence data." A lot of history, he said, has been as it's been because governments did not have very good data. "Think back through your lifetime and think about the mistakes." Hitler thought his armies invincible. Japan attacked Pearl Harbor because it preposterously underestimated the will and the military potential of the United States. France had been convinced that its army was the best in the world and had allowed it to fall generations behind the times. The United States had its ghastly misadventure in Viet Nam for lack of good intelligence.

"How do you get better intelligence information? Critical question."

"Well, yes," I said. "But wouldn't you agree that a lot of those situations occur because somebody who's Mr. Big wants to hear things that support his emotional bias?"

"Sure, that can be true of big decisions. I grant you that. But every day governments make mistakes. For instance, the United States decides they're going to discipline the Russians by not shipping them any wheat. Of course that didn't do a damn bit of good and it did hurt the U.S. farmers. We decide not to ship them any pipe-laying equipment to finish a gas line so they just get it from somebody else. There are big, big mistakes and there are little mistakes—a ton of mistakes. If businesses were run the way governments are, you'd be canning the chief executive officer of corporations right and left.

"I think it has to have something to do with the bad intelligence they collect. They don't understand the strengths and weaknesses and the motivations of other countries.

"Here we have the Middle Eastern problem where we thought we'd lean on the Israelis and get them to pull out and when they did, the Syrians would pull out of Lebanon. Well, we get the Israelis to pull back alright but—whoops, wait a minute!—the Syrians aren't pulling out and we have to tell the Israelis, 'Hey, don't pull out—get back in there.' Somebody made a mistake, huh?

"I proceed on the assumption—and perhaps this comes out of my training in marketing research—that if two equally intelligent people get the same data and the data's right, they come to the same conclusion. I've always thought that if the data's right and you present it accurately, the decision's easy.

"The problem is that the data aren't good. So how do you get better data? That's my premise here. Generally speaking, the people who make these decisions are not dumb, they've got good brains. . . ."

We were running out of time.

Another subject, this one a lot less global, came to my mind.

I wondered aloud how much time the Nielsens had spent, gathering intelligence on each others' agendas for retirement.

I told him about my innocence of my own wife's ideas, told him something of what I'd learned from listening to other women, told him about the Bradfords and their lack of communication in advance of Leland's retirement. I suggested that some good, down-to-earth discussion *before* Art's retirement might save the Nielsens a lot of pain later.

In retrospect, I think he'd have been justified in telling me to mind my own business. More than justified.

But he didn't get mad. He thanked me.

"I appreciate your alerting me to this subject," he said. "I'd have just muddled into it otherwise. I think you've helped me a lot."

I'd like to think so.

ANDREW HOLZSCHUH
EDWARD FIEDLER

Helping people go into business and to stay in business.

By 1984, the "clients" of Messrs. Holzschuh and Fiedler had included antique stores, restaurants, nonprofit workshops for handicapped people, a word processing service, machine shops, a chiropractor, a dog kennel.

The members of this oddly assorted group had three things in common: they qualified as small businesses. They had applied for advice and counsel to the Small Business Administration. They drew as consultants two Midland, Michigan men who had retired from Dow Chemical Company and had volunteered to work with SCORE, the Service Corps of Retired Executives.

SCORE's role in the SBA scheme of things is strictly advisory. Whether clients are thinking about starting a business or want help with a going concern, "*we* don't make the decisions," said Holzschuh, who had been involved with SCORE for eleven years. By leading people through a good, hard look at reality, "we hope to help lower the risks and cut down on the failures."

In this work, success is measured as much by what didn't happen as by what did. When a SCORE counselor takes a would-be entrepreneur through the real-world advantages and disadvantages of starting a business, the chances are only 50-50 that he will decide to go ahead. Starting a successful business has always been hard. Better to know that *before* taking the plunge. . . .

According to Fiedler, a seven-year man, SCORE's advice is not all of the make-or-break variety; not all clients are having problems with their businesses. "Sometimes they just need to discuss a concern with someone," he said. "It can be lonely being a small business person and it helps to have an outsider tell you that you're going in the right direction."

For Holzschuh and Fiedler, SCORE provides a nice balance to their retired lives. They like using their professional skills, like dealing with a clientele that varies all the way from "skillful and successful to naive and inexperienced." It is challenging stuff. "But," Holzschuh said, "it doesn't tie me down too much." The two men work an average of twenty-five hours a month and attend a monthly meeting in Detroit as well as a two-day seminar once a year.

What's the greatest reward?

"It's satisfying," Fiedler said, "to see a client go from the 'red' to the 'black.' "

THE REVEREND MONSIGNOR VINCENT COOKE

"Unselfishness is nondenominational"

When Vincent Cooke retired, at sixty-six, he moved from one exotic neighborhood to another.

From his long-time home and office at the epicenter of Skid Row in Chicago, Cooke migrated to the Coachella Valley in

California, where three of the thoroughfares are named Bob Hope, Frank Sinatra, and Fred Waring, and where Rolls Royce owners keep Jaguars as second cars.

For his first forty-two years as a priest, Cooke had worked in orphanages and other facilities of the Catholic Charities of Chicago. For the last twenty-three of those years, he had been "head honcho", supervising 2,000 employees and a $30 million budget, ministering to a wider and wider spectrum of needs. His "parishioners" were alcoholics and other drug addicts. They were homeless men, homeless children, homeless refugees from everywhere. They were disturbed children, abused children, blind children, deaf children. They were helpless old people, foreign people, pregnant-and-unmarried women, survivors of suicides, estranged couples. They numbered in the tens of thousands.

If every neighborhood has a common denominator and if, on Skid Row, the common denominator is trouble, in the Coachella Valley, it is golf.

This is a natural desert, to be sure. In World War II, it served as a rehearsal hall for George Patton: it was here that he and his troops toughened themselves for war with Rommel.

It is now, however, a desert with an electrifying difference: water. In abundance.

Beneath the mountain-ringed flatland is a mammoth underground lake, relic of another eon's inland sea. Today it irrigates forty golf courses and ten thousand perfect lawns; feeds hundreds of artificial lakelets, brooklets, geysers, waterfalls. Having superseded the once-mandatory palm tree, water stands today as the premier material of the local exterior decorators.

With supplies of water and sunshine guaranteed, the stretch from Palm Springs to La Quinta is the answer to the addict's dream of weatherproof golf.

It was golf—his "retirement addiction"—that brought Monsignor Cooke here.

But golf was not his first thought when he landed in 1972.

"When I got off the plane," he wrote friends, "I suddenly knew how my mother and father felt when they emigrated from Ireland to the United States. I had never until then understood their feelings of loneliness, uncertainty, wonder, and fear. . . .

"Where would I live? Could I learn to cook and keep house? Who will do my laundry? Can I make my way around a supermarket? How long can I afford to live here before I move into The Little Sisters of the Poor?"

Cooke had no role models to help him. Among priests, he was one of the first ever to retire at "normal" retirement age and to benefit from a church pension plan. Until his day, priests often served their parishes until age seventy-five and, when they did retire, would live out their lives in the rectory, helping out as they could. He had had no need to deal with the nuts and bolts of daily life. Priests like him drew tiny salaries but they received house-keeping, cooking, laundry, and other services along with the territory.

In the midst of a place that has been second home to ex-presidents, Hollywood royalty, and intercontinental celebrities, as well as to thousands of the merely rich, Cooke found a room in a motel, ate "beanery" meals for six months, spent evenings "going over and over my financial situation and wallowing in self-pity."

When in time he traded those chilly comforts for a room with a kitchen, he began a "comedy of errors as cook-housekeeper." A reader of his annual reports to friends can reconstruct the scene. Here is part of what he wrote in 1975:

"Housework is twice as strenuous as jogging or calisthenics [he had lost thirty-five pounds after retiring]. . . . 350 degrees for thirty-five minutes solves ninety percent of cooking problems but cleaning an oven is harder than fast or abstinence. . . . Boil-in-the-bag meals are faster, thriftier with fuel, and smoke-free. . . . The electric dishwasher is a greater invention than the automobile self-starter. . . . "Fluff and Fold" is the most efficient and cheapest laundry service. . . . Freeze-dried coffee is much less expensive than perked—for a single person. . . . To prevent ripoffs in the supermarket: divide prices by ounces. . . . The greatest blessing of all is neighbors who invite you to dinner."

When Cooke retired, he shared a concept with most of the rest of the world: that the proper role of the retired person is to go away somewhere and take it easy. "That's a big problem we have," he told me. "We figure we've always worked for other people and now other people are supposed to work for us." However, by the time he had reduced daily housework and daily golf to a routine, he was becoming more and more restless. He recalled that restlessness had also plagued his father after retirement. "Dad said that when he wasn't getting in Mother's hair, he was clipping the hedge and finally cut it so much that 'it was lower than the lawn.' At that point he started up a bar and grill in a store-front building he owned."

Cooke and I met on the golf course at Del Safari Country Club in Palm Desert. He and his golf cart (inscribed, like a yacht, with his nickname: Ye Olde Monk) were landmarks. If my wife and I teed off at 9:00, we might meet him where the first and sixth fairways touch each other; he was among the earliest of the early-morning faithful. That first year, I assumed that he was on vacation as we were. Retired priests were as unfamiliar a phenomenon to me as they had been to him.

The following year, we rented the house next door to his and, in the course of neighborly chitchat, I learned his true status and asked for an interview.

Cooke's rented condominium was much like ours. To the west, through his living room window-wall, he could look past his small swimming pool and garden toward the players on the first fairway and toward the snow-topped mountains twenty miles away. The furniture, too, was like ours. His walls, however, were alive with photographs: Father. Mother. Brothers, sister. Priests-friends. Friend-friends. Himself with Pope Paul VI in Ireland. His breakfast table served as altar; the geometrically laid-out paraphernalia included an antique, intricately worked silver chalice, his ordination gift from his parents.

He owed these comforts, Cooke told me, in part to a modest inheritance from his father, in part to his own retirement benefits, in part to a generous landlord who kept his rent below the market.

He owed his *joie de vivre*, however, to the priestly work to which he'd returned on a part-time basis. (Among other things, he was serving two churches as assistant pastor.) He told me that taking it easy had only seduced him into further self-pity.

We were in the middle of Lent as we talked and he was saying Mass and delivering homilies seven days a week. "It's a joy," he said. "I get home at night and wonder what I'm going to say the next evening and I get the readings out and sit there looking for my next idea." He seemed to me as gung ho as a rookie curate, perhaps because he had only eighteen months of pastoral work in all his years in Chicago.

Furthermore, he said, his messages from the pulpit had led him into "the most remarkable experience of my life."

"Someone who said he liked my 'matter-of-fact' way of talking came up one day and said he needed a priest for a marriage encounter program over in Riverside, sixty miles away. I said I'd take a crack at it. And it *was* remarkable.

"You know, I was being perfectly objective when I went over there to look at it. I wasn't applying it to myself at all. I was just over there studying it. Well, here were three couples with families that had been through the program. And their whole pitch was—this is the way we felt before marriage encounter and this is the way we feel now. It's based on feelings, you know. The whole thing's based on feelings.

"These people weren't getting paid. They had given up the weekend, you know, and they did that about every two months. And the message was, here are three couples and if those couples can do it, you can do it.

"When I got into it, each "old" couple would have five new couples under their wings and I would have to make fifteen talks—I had to be in on all of them, you know. And I used to say in my first talk, 'You're not here to listen to me. You're here to listen to people who are in the trenches. I'm just here to tell you that the Church and God approve of everything they're saying to you—in case anybody's got doubts about that.

"You know, Mormons, Baptists, everybody under the sun came to this thing. It was really a great experience but finally, physically, it got too tough for me. Forty-four hours! Five hours' sleep Friday. Everyone with marriage problems or spiritual problems would want to see Father. Saturday night I might get six or seven hours. But I got a greater kick out of seeing the changes in those people's lives than I ever—than anything I'd ever had in my life.

"I was worried about letting 'em go home at noon Sunday . . . afraid half of 'em were going to get killed in an automobile accident . . . they might just as well be on LSD, they were that high. So *loving!* I didn't know how long it was going to last but it was really something."

Although Cooke's housekeeping, golf, and churches provide his day-to-day structure now, he has gotten involved once more in an old cause of his—the rehabilitation of alcoholics.

"You know there's room for one thing in your book—the role of alcoholism among older people. Just this year, I've had three people from right around here. One of my girls was one of the first people to go through the program at the Betty Ford Center over there at Eisenhower Hospital and the *difference* in that life . . .! I went to a young people's party at her house the other night—it's spring break for the college kids—and she was the happiest person there.

"And Alcoholics Anonymous. You talk about the spiritual end of retirement—if a guy would join the AA and go to the meetings—you know—as often as he wanted to. . . . An AA meeting is the greatest spiritual family that exists today. It's a group of people trying to help each other and having a hell of a lot of fun doing it.

"You know, there's an awfully cute meeting over at the Indian Wells city hall. . . . Why is it cute? Because it's got all the big shots in the desert. You've gotta be the chairman of the board to get in there, I think.

"But that's one of the sad things about older people, I think. Out here you go to any of these clubs and these old guys get crocked every night. Have you run into it? I tell you, you go down to La Jolla to those retirement houses they put up there and every building has three or four cocktail parties every night.

"Thank God, they've got some good people out here working on rehabilitation. Including Jim West. Have you met Jim? If you slice your drive off the tenth tee, it'll wind up in Jim West's yard. You know, he was a top surgeon in Chicago, one of the first to do kidney transplants, but he'd always been interested in alcoholism. He set up a detoxification center for us on Skid Row, he handled most of the groups of priests who contracted alcoholism, he was at it day and night. I could talk about him by the hour. . . . If I had to nominate a layman for sainthood, he'd be the one. And he's here now. He came out and studied for the California psychiatric license and now he's working on alcoholism full time.

"You know, there are a couple of things about booze that happen when you get older. Your ability to absorb it goes down, that's one. But the other is self-pity. A guy loses his wife, for example, and he takes out his grief on the bottle. . . .

"But there *are* great people working on it around here. You know the woman I was talking about? Well, I was asked to help with her—it's called intervention. We got her husband and her kids in and plotted how to confront her with her problem. There was no screaming. It was all 'we love you, Mom, but when you did this and you did that. . . .'

"Well, once you do some of that, people get to thinking you're an expert and they call you up. . . . I had a two-hour phone call from Chicago the other day. But . . . Doc West. That's what I tell 'em. 'Go over and see Doc, don't talk to me. I don't have all the answers.' "

Prior to our conversation, I had read eight of the monsignor's annual reports and it had struck me that the theme of humility ran through all of them. "I gather," I said, "that you regard humility as one of the cardinal virtues."

"That's why I play golf," he said. (Funny man.)

"The key word . . . you know, as you go through life, you try to figure it all out—and for me, I've got it down to one key word. *Unselfishness.* The perfect example of an unselfish being is God. He gives us everything, we kick Him around, he forgives us. Unselfishness! You know, in that speech I gave on my fiftieth anniversary as a priest, I said I had confessed to God that I'd been selfish—not that I had sinned but that I had been selfish.

"If every time you do something, you say to yourself, 'Now, is that selfish?' It brings you serenity and happiness and everything else in the world.

"I think that humility and unselfishness means that you're above—you're not still striving to get recognition. You don't have to have it, you can get along without recognition. Self-pity—that's a big one—the first thing you've got to get over when you retire is self-pity. . . ."

I told Cooke that I had a theory about self-pity in retirement: that many of us, including me, have defined ourselves and drawn our self-esteem almost entirely from our jobs, particularly in the last years. When the job's gone, we mourn the loss of ourselves, the selves we were. What did he think?

"You can be *more* important after you *leave* the you that was," he said. "The only way you're going to get satisfaction in retirement the way you did in your job is *helping somebody else!* I say that from the pulpit—there are a lot of older people out here, you know. I say, 'Anytime you're sitting in your house feeling sorry for yourself, think about your neighbors—this lady just lost a son, this one just lost her husband—go over and see them. Go over and *see* them! Think of the other guy all your life! Especially in retirement.

"I say to my parishioners that I know unselfish is what God wants me to be. 'You can't really claim to be a Christian unless you are helping others,' I tell 'em. But religious faith has nothing to do with it. Unselfishness is nondenominational."

In spite of our mutual devotion to golf, we had not talked about it during our conversation. However, Cooke had often shared his wisdom and experiences with the readers of his annual reports. In his year-end letter for 1982, he wrote the following.

1. January 27, 1982, the fifth day of the seventy-seventh year of my life, shot third hole-in-one!

2. January 1, 1972, set a target of 18 holes per day. As of November 17, 1982, have played 73,098 holes or an average of 18 holes a day for 11 years and 43 days.

3. Suggestions for aged golfers: look decrepit and talk plaintively on the first tee. Make the lip mightier than the stick. Buy a putter with an extra-long shaft and a midget grip. Excellent for gimmes.

4. Why golf at all? Preventive medicine against wheelchair status. Greatest source of patience, tolerance, and general character building, with humility at the top of the list. 27 holes a sure cure for insomnia.

Cooke can be said to put his money where his convictions are. After playing golf at Quigley Seminary for decades, he wanted younger priests to have access to the same pleasure he'd had. He has donated a substantial part of his income to that cause every year since his retirement.

The last time we saw Monsignor Cooke in 1983, he was standing in the door of his garage, hosing down the concrete, the monsignoral britches rolled right up to his knees. He had just come in from golf, he said, and was about to get dressed to say Mass and deliver his homily for the day.

"First, though, I've got to do this," he said. "Today I'm in need of some help with my humility."

X
PERSONAL
POSTSCRIPT

ME, MY RETIREMENT.
THIS BOOK.
A SELF-EVIDENT MORAL.

When I was very young, I wanted to write novels.

I also yearned to run like Glenn Cunningham, to bat like Jimmy Foxx, to play tennis like Henri Cochet. To be another Lone Eagle.

But my chief heroes at ten were James Willard Schultz; Ralph Henry Barbour; Charles Dickens (!); and the creators of Alexander Botts, Scattergood Baines, Tugboat Annie, and Judge Ephraim Tutt.

My hero-worship burned hottest when, in my teens, I discovered Hemingway, Fitzgerald, Huxley (Aldous, not Thomas), and Wolfe (Thomas, not Tom). Theirs was the life for me, I thought.

Oh to be rich and celebrated!

Ah, the *freedom* of it all!

But. I was a child of the Depression. I'd had first-hand knowledge of hard times. As a practical matter, I could not wait for the mail to begin bringing me checks rather than rejection slips. Furthermore, I wanted to marry.

249

And I yearned for a car, an apartment, clothes, a solid place in society.

Like so many other would-be novelists of my day, young men with a yen for middle-classhood, I turned (it wasn't easy in those days) to the writing of advertising. At least I was using my talent, I told myself. When things got easier at the office, I would again try fiction.

Things never got easier, only harder.

The problem was that I got better and better at my business. I earned bigger and bigger chunks of responsibility and, along with them, the privilege of working as many hours as it took. Several years, I had to be ordered to take vacations.

And I loved it. I liked the writing part very much but I *loved* the selling. And the excitement. And the position. And the power of decision. It was a hell of an adventuresome way to make a living. I stopped thinking about writing novels.

Then I retired.

And became a card-carrying citizen of Past-Tense Land. I who had always been an is was now a was.

I kept waiting for the phone to ring. "Soon," I said to myself, "those guys at the office are going to get into a pickle and they'll have to call. I'd better stay close to home."

They didn't call.

Most times when my phone rang, it was someone who wanted to sell me stocks, bonds, annuities. Often the man said, "I saw the news ['Shank Retires'] in the paper and thought I could 'help' you."

Two people did call on business—of a sort. They wanted me to resign as a trustee. They didn't put it that way, they apologized for breaking in on my retirement, they hemmed and hawed. But the message was clear: they wanted people on their boards who were still working and still had clout. I resigned.

When we went to parties, I flunked the dinner table test. Repeatedly:

Dinner Partner: And what do you do, Howard?

Howard: I'm retired.

Dinner Partner: Retired! You're too young. What are you *doing?*

Me: Oh, reading. Working on my tennis. Painting some . . . .

Dinner Partner: Painting? Rooms or furniture?

Me: Canvases. On an easel. You see, I . . .

Dinner Partner: That's nice. But *you* can't retire! You're too *young*.

I may have been too young to retire but I was past the point of interesting *her*. Soon, I knew, she would turn to the man on her other side. Maybe *he* would say something worth hearing.

I had to churn around for two years and go down a bunch of blind alleys before I saw the opportunity that was sitting there right in my own lap:

I was my own boss.

I could parcel out my time to suit myself.

I no longer had to think of money first.

I had a first-rate place to write.

I had a subject—retirement—that I'd learned something about.

I had the talent.

And I knew a lot about the disciplines of writing.

Ecclesiastes says, "To everything there is a season, and a time to every purpose under heaven."

One day my season came.

I hadn't been thinking of any of the above. Suddenly—completely out of context—this thought took over:

"Why don't you write a book about retirement?"

"Why don't you write a book about retirement?"

That moment was one of the four great turning points in my life.

Now I knew what I was going to *do* with the years that were left to me.

Now I knew who and what I was going to *be*.

Until the day I started to do this book, I was like someone eating nothing but caviar and dessert. As a steady diet, that cloyed. What I needed was meat and potatoes.

I needed something to push my mind hard.

I needed a goal, a purpose, a passion.

I needed a centerpiece for my daily, weekly, and yearly schedules.

I needed problems that I could carry around in my head and work on wherever I was.

I needed to go back to real work.

For almost three years now, my retirement has been entirely different.

I am an ex-advertising man just as I am an ex-baby. Today—the day that counts—I am a professional author, looking forward to full-time work on my next book (about creativity). I live again in the present tense.

I have met and talked retirement with literally hundreds of people, ranging from ex-laborers to an ex-president. Fascinating!

I no longer flunk the dinner party test.

I was invited to be principal speaker at a seminar on retirement, organized by members of the Princeton class of '42. The response was heady.

Two organizations have elected me a trustee.

Busy as I am, I have discovered that the more I do, the more I *can* do.

What is your retirement opportunity going to be?

I hope you'll be able to spell it out *before* you retire.

That will put you in compliance with the first law of successful retirement (which is, by chance, the same as the first law of wing-walking):

> Never leave hold of what you've got
> until you've got hold of something else.

Let me know how it all turns out.